The Art of War

The Art of War

Sun-tzu

(Sun-zi)

TRANSLATED WITH AN

INTRODUCTION AND COMMENTARY

BY

John Minford

VIKING

VIKING
Published by the Penguin Group
Penguin Putnam Inc., 375 Hudson Street, New York, New York 10014, U.S.A.
Penguin Books Ltd, 80 Strand, London WC2R 0RL, England
Penguin Books Australia Ltd, 250 Camberwell Road, Camberwell, Victoria 3124, Australia
Penguin Books Canada Ltd, 10 Alcorn Avenue, Toronto, Ontario, Canada M4V 3B2
Penguin Books India (P) Ltd, 11 Community Centre, Panchsheel Park,
New Delhi–110 017, India
Penguin Books (N.Z.) Ltd, Cnr Rosedale and Airborne Roads, Albany, Auckland,
New Zealand
Penguin Books (South Africa) (Pty) Ltd, 24 Sturdee Avenue, Rosebank,
Johannesburg 2196, South Africa

Penguin Books Ltd, Registered Offices: Harmondsworth, Middlesex, England

First published in 2002 by Viking Penguin, a member of Penguin Putnam Inc.

1   3   5   7   9   10   8   6   4   2

Translation, introduction and commentary copyright © John Minford, 2002
All rights reserved

A portion of this work first appeared in *The New England Review*.

LIBRARY OF CONGRESS CATALOGING-IN-PUBLICATION DATA
Sunzi, 6th cent. B.C.
[Sunzi bing fa. English]
Art of war / Sun-tzu (Sun-zi) ; translated with an introduction and commentary by
John Minford.
p.   cm.
ISBN 0-670-03156-9
1. Military art and science. I. Minford, John. II. Title.
U101 .S93213 2002
355.02—dc21   2002069192

This book is printed on acid-free paper. ∞

Printed in the United States of America
Set in Guardi and Fairfield Light
Designed by Nancy Resnick

In memory of my father,
Leslie Minford

Acknowledgments

I would like to thank a number of friends who have kindly helped me with materials and in other ways. H. C. Li, of the Hong Kong Polytechnic University Library, generously presented me with several invaluable modern editions of *The Art of War*, and introduced me to the work of Li Ling. Agnes Chan and Tong Man went to great lengths to find various articles for me in Hong Kong, while Red Chan overcame considerable obstacles to send me a photocopy of Father Amiot's translation from the Cambridge University Library. Günter Wohlfart and Steve Balogh shared stimulating thoughts on philosophy and a host of other topics. Ivan Turner provided technical expertise on a universal scale. David Hawkes kindly read the proofs. Caroline White, at Viking Penguin in New York, commissioned the translation in the first place and has been a most sympathetic and encouraging editor. Above all, heartfelt thanks to Rachel May for continuing to keep an eye on my errant idioms and for persisting in her dogged attempts to teach me the Art of Pruning.

Contents

x   Contents

Introduction

The Way of War is a Way of Deception.
—Master Sun, Chapter 1

Master Sun's short treatise *The Art of War* is both inspirational and worrying. It is beautiful and chilling. It encapsulates a part of the irreducible essence of Chinese culture and has been familiar to literate Chinese down the ages. For that reason alone, it is an extraordinarily important book and one that should be read by anyone dealing with either China or Japan. During the Second World War, E. Machell-Cox produced a version for the Royal Air Force. "Master Sun," he wrote, "is fundamental and, read with insight, lays bare the mental mechanism of our enemy. Study him, and study him again. Do not be misled by his simplicity."[1] Today, with China playing a more and more integral role in the world, Master Sun has become prescribed reading for global entrepreneurs. "Ultimate excellence lies not in winning every battle but in defeating the enemy without ever fighting" (Chapter 3). Or, in the words of Gordon Gekko, the corporate raider in Oliver Stone's brilliant exposé of late-twentieth-century American capitalism, *Wall Street*, "I bet on sure things. Sun Tzu: 'Every battle is won before it is fought.' Think about it."

But *The Art of War* offers more than an insight into Chinese ways of doing things (including business). Like its venerable predecessor *The Book of Changes*, it lends itself to infinite applications. It has been used as a springboard for an American self-help book about interpersonal relationships.[2] It could no doubt also serve as the basis for a book on tennis, cooking, or defensive driving. The strategic advice it offers concerns much more than the conduct of war. It is an ancient book of proverbial wisdom, a book of life.

Cunning Plans, Popular Culture

The Empty City

The novel *The Romance of the Three Kingdoms,* written sometime in the four-
teenth or fifteenth century, has been described as a vernacular expansion of
Master Sun's ideas, a novelistic "folk manual of waging war, a description of
the classical strategic and tactical solutions which were a part of the ancient
theory of war, a popular lecture on classical theory [of warfare]."[3] In a scene
from Chapter 38, the most famous of all China's strategic wizards, Zhuge
Liang (181–234), the "Sleeping Dragon," finally meets Liu Bei (161–223),
pretender to the throne of the crumbling Han dynasty. This is Liu's third
visit to the recluse's hermitage, his two previous visits having proved fruitless. The Dragon is at home, and Liu meets him face-to-face, a striking figure in his silken headscarf and Taoist-style robe lined with cranesdown,
emanating the "buoyant air of a spiritual transcendent."[4] Liu eventually
succeeds in recruiting the hermit's services, and the Dragon, "though having never left his thatched cottage," proceeds to "demonstrate his fore-
knowledge of the balance of power." He goes on to mastermind Liu's
military campaign with extraordinary cunning. One of the most famous of
the Dragon's many strategic victories occurs some twenty years later, in the
year A.D. 228, five years after the death of Liu Bei himself. Chapter 95 of the
novel finds Zhuge cornered in the city of Xicheng (West City), with a paltry
force of five thousand, against one hundred and fifty thousand troops of
the northern state of Wei, led by the redoubtable marshal Sima Yi:

> The Sleeping Dragon dispatched half of his troops to transfer the
> grain and fodder from the city to where the main body of his forces
> was encamped, which left him with a mere 2,500 soldiers in the city.
> [The astute seventeenth-century commentator Mao Zong'gang ob-
> serves at this point: *Twenty-five hundred against one hundred and fifty
> thousand? Let's see how Master Sleeping Dragon manages to get out of this
> one!*] His officers were aghast at the state of affairs. Sleeping Dragon
> mounted the battlements to view the situation for himself, and sure
> enough he could make out the two columns of the huge Wei army,
> raising an enormous twin cloud of dust into the sky as they con-
> verged on the city. He now gave orders to conceal all military flags
> and pennants [Mao: *Strange! Weird!*], and announced that all the sol-

diers were to stay within their billets. Any discovered wandering around or making a din were to be instantly decapitated. *[Decidedly weird!]* He ordered the four gates of the city to be thrown open, and at each gate posted twenty soldiers in civilian attire, with instructions to go about casually sprinkling the ground and sweeping the streets. *[Weirder and weirder! Where twenty-five hundred could not withstand one hundred and fifty thousand, twenty can! Highly ingenious!]* "When the enemy arrives," ordered Zhuge Liang, "no one is to make a move. Leave everything to me. I have a plan." *[I wonder what Sleeping Dragon has up his sleeve?]*

The Master then donned his Taoist robe lined with finest cranesdown, and his silken headscarf, and made his way up to the watchtower above the main gate, accompanied by two page-boys and carrying his lute. There he lit incense and sat calmly playing an air on his lute. *[Weird! Ingenious! Just like the olden days in his hermitage! Doubtless the air he was playing on the silken strings of his lute was going to annihilate the enem. . . .]*

The scouts of Marshal Sima Yi, the enemy commander-in-chief, had meanwhile arrived before the city, and seeing this strange state of affairs, did not venture within the walls but hurried back to report to their general. Sima laughed, and found it hard to believe what they were telling him. *[So do I, to this very day!]* He ordered his troops to halt their advance, and galloped ahead to a vantage point from which he could observe matters for himself. Sure enough, he espied Sleeping Dragon seated up above the gateway, a smile on his face as he played his lute, surrounded by clouds of incense. To his left stood one page-boy, holding a ceremonial sword; to his right another page-boy, with a fly-whisk, emblem of the Taoist priest-magician. Within and without the gate, twenty-odd townsfolk could be seen casually cleaning the street. There was not another soul in sight.

Marshal Sima was filled with misgivings. *[So am I, to this very day! It must have been a most extraordinary sight!]* He returned to his army, and ordered his men to turn around and head north into the hills. His son protested: "Surely Sleeping Dragon is doing this precisely because he has no troops. Why are you retreating, Father?" *[Smarter than his father . . .]* "I know Sleeping Dragon," replied the Marshal. "He has always been a man of great caution. He never takes risks. I am sure that this throwing open of the gates is simply a ruse. He has definitely set an ambush for us. If we go in, we walk straight into his trap. You are too young to understand. No, we must retreat with all speed."

So both columns of the Wei army turned around and retreated. Zhuge, seeing them go, laughed and clapped his hands. His officers were astonished, and begged their commander for an explication. *[No doubt Sleeping Dragon had chanted some sort of "Spell for a Retreat" as he played his lute. . . .]* "The Marshal has always known me for a cautious man," Zhuge began. "He knows I never take risks. He was bound to suspect an ambush. That is why he decided to retreat. *[He knew that his enemy was familiar with his character; and therefore he acted out of character. . . . Brilliant! Genius!]* I wasn't gambling. I simply had no other option. . . ."

His officers were dumbfounded at their commander's inscrutable genius.[5]

Two of the early commentators on Master Sun's *Art of War* tell a briefer version of this same story (which is probably apocryphal—historically speaking, Marshal Sima Yi seems to have been somewhere else at the time). Their comments come immediately after the Master's statement in Chapter 6: "If I do not wish to engage, I can hold my ground with nothing more than a line drawn around it. The enemy cannot engage me in combat; I distract him in a different direction." Certainly Zhuge Liang the wizard had little more than a line between himself and the massive Wei army. The "Ruse of the Empty City," as it came to be known, was graphically retold by many a medieval storyteller and went on to become a subject for opera and for popular woodblock prints (*nianhua*—in some of these the Dragon completes the picture of relaxation by having a cup of wine before him).[6] It forms the thirty-second of *The Thirty-six Stratagems* (a popular condensation of traditional Chinese strategic wisdom, of obscure origin), where it is presented as a clever psychological strategy for use in desperate circumstances. It is also used to illustrate the forty-third of *The Hundred Unusual Strategies* (another popular compilation, probably from the Song dynasty).[7] Here the "unusual strategy" being advocated is the subtle use of illusion, of deception or bluff, against a numerically superior enemy, what Joseph Needham calls "obtaining the desired effect through a discreet use of appearances, thereby avoiding an actual battle."[8] Both of these late popular works were based largely on Master Sun's much older treatise. Zhuge Liang, the Sleeping Dragon, is himself (improbably) credited with a short work on the Art of War,[9] while Cao Cao, Zhuge's adversary in his early campaigns (he is already dead by the time of the Empty City), is the prime commentator on Master Sun's *Art of War*.[10] Both Cao Cao and the Sleeping Dragon are household names in China, emblems of military skill and strategic cunning, while Master Sun's *Art of War* and *The Three*

Kingdoms have continued to fascinate the Chinese popular imagination into the twenty-first century.[11] Both the treatise and the novel exercised a considerable influence on Chairman Mao, and in its recent lavish television serialization, *The Three Kingdoms* captured a huge audience in China, Hong Kong, and Taiwan. Cartoon-strip versions of *The Art of War* enjoy large sales throughout the Chinese-speaking world, while the number of Web sites (in Chinese, Japanese, and English) devoted to Master Sun continues to grow.[12]

From Proverbial to Popular Culture

The most Skillful Warrior is never warlike; the most Skillful Warrior is never angered; the most skilled at defeating the enemy never strives (*The Way and Its Power,* Chapter 68).

The Skillful Strategist defeats the enemy without doing battle (*The Art of War,* Chapter 3).

In war it is best to attack minds, not cities; psychological warfare is better than fighting with weapons [Mao Zong'gang: *These words are not to be found in* The Art of War. *They are the summit of the Art, superior even to the teachings of Master Sun and Master Wu.*] (*The Romance of the Three Kingdoms,* Chapter 87).

"Know the enemy, know yourself, and victory is never in doubt, not in a hundred battles." We must not underestimate the wisdom of this saying of Master Sun, the great military thinker of ancient China (Mao Zedong, *Selected Works,* vol. 1, p. 187).

In ancient times there was a man called Han Xin [d. 196 B.C.], one of Liu Bang's [247–195 B.C.] senior generals [stories of Han Xin's military exploits recur throughout the commentaries on *The Art of War*]. Why was he so successful as a general? Even as a young man, Han Xin was an exceptional person. As a youth, he liked to practice martial arts, and one day he was walking down the street, carrying his sword, when a local ruffian blocked his way with his hands on his hips. "What are you carrying that sword for? Have you got the guts to kill someone? If you have, cut off my head." He stuck out his head. Han Xin thought to himself, "Why should I cut off this man's head?" The ruffian saw that Han Xin was not going to kill him, and said, "If you haven't got the guts, then crawl between my legs." So

Han Xin crawled between his two legs. [This story is ultimately based on the biography of Han Xin in the *Records of the Grand Historian*.] The way he accepted this humiliation showed that Han Xin had a heart of great forbearance. And yet he was just an ordinary person. As practitioners [of Falun Gong], we should be much better than he. Our goal is to rise above and beyond the level of ordinary people and to strive toward high levels (Li Hongzhi, founder of the proscribed Falun Gong movement, from Lecture Nine on his Web site).[13]

Ways of thinking such as these, psychological strategies in warfare and conflict such as the Ruse of the Empty City, belong to a field of human activity that concerns us all immediately. They are far from the ivory tower of pure philosophy. It is hardly surprising that they should have spread so far and so wide within Chinese popular culture. That quintessentially Chinese domain known as the martial arts, for example, is based on ideas of this kind. The sixth of Master Yang Chengfu's (1862–1935) Ten Precepts in *Taiji Shadow Boxing*, as recorded by his disciple Chen Weiming, reads, "Use thought, not force. Your body should be utterly relaxed; no physical exertion is necessary."[14] Chen Weiming himself, when describing the *taiji* practice of *tuishou* ("push hands"), wrote, "When you attack, it is like a bullet penetrating neatly *(gancui)*, without recourse to force. . . . This is real *taiji*. If you use force, you may move your adversary, but it will not be *gancui*. If he tries to use force to control or push you, it will be like a man catching the wind or chasing shadows."[15] In Shaolin kungfu, we encounter the same ideas: "The tactics and strategies used by a Shaolin disciple during combat are an intelligent application of principles generalized by some of the best warriors in the past. Some of these principles include:

> Signal to the east, strike to the west;
> Avoid an opponent's strong points, strike the weak ones;
> Trick an opponent into advancing without success,
> Then strike decisively with just one blow;
> If an opponent is strong, enter from the side;
> If he is weak, enter from the front;
> Use minimum force
> To neutralize maximum strength.[16]

And if we search further back into the past, we find similar ideas and stories throughout the Taoist classics and in *The Book of Changes*. When we approach *The Art of War*, when we deal with its ideas and their reception, we are dealing with a concatenation of ancient text and medieval event; of treatise, history, and novel; of commentary and legend; of theory and practice. We are dealing with a book whose ramifications extend through the vernacular entertainment culture of China's Middle Ages to the contemporary popular medium of Chinese State Television.

Master Sun's *Art of War* is one of China's key proverbial texts. Its seminal ideas have permeated Chinese culture, as Arthurian legends and ideals have permeated European culture. And yet, if we turn to this short text itself, we are confronted with an author about whom virtually nothing is known and a book that (in the words of one contemporary Chinese scholar) "presents the reader with greater difficulties than almost any other work of comparable antiquity."[17]

Let us begin with the "Sage" himself, Master Sun.

Master Sun and His Times

The Harem Sergeant-Major

Most of the little we "know" about Master Sun is contained in his biography from the *Records of the Grand Historian* by Sima Qian (ca. 145–ca. 85 B.C.), historian and master storyteller:

> Master Sun Wu was from the state of Qi. On account of his treatise on the Art of War he obtained an audience with He Lü, the king of Wu [reigned 514–496 B.C.].
> "I have carefully studied the Thirteen Chapters of your treatise," said the king. "Would it be possible for you to give me a small demonstration of the drilling of troops?"[18]
> "Certainly I can," replied Master Sun.
> "Can this demonstration be performed with women?"
> "It can."[19]
> The king authorized him to proceed. One hundred and eighty of His Majesty's most beautiful concubines were summoned from the inner apartments of the palace, and Master Sun divided them into two companies, putting one of the king's favorites in command of each company. All of the women warriors were given a halberd to hold. Master Sun now addressed them.
> "Can you tell your front from your back, your left hand from your right hand?"[20]

"We can," replied the women.

"When I give the order 'Eyes front!' you are to look forward," said Master Sun. "When I command 'Eyes left!' you are to look to the left. 'Eyes right!' look to the right; 'Eyes rear!' look to the back. Is that understood?"

"Yes!" replied the women.

With these rules established, Master Sun had the executioner's ax set up [to show that he meant business], went through the commands again, and explained them several times.[21] Then he beat on the drum and gave the order to face to the right. The women all burst out laughing.

"If my orders were unclear," said Master Sun, "and not properly understood, then I, as your general, am to blame."

So he went through the commands once more, explaining them in detail. This time he beat out the order to face left. Once again, the ladies of the harem burst out laughing.[22]

"While my orders were unclear, and not properly understood, I, as your general, was to blame. But now, since my orders were clear, and since you understood them properly, the fault lies with your commanding officers."

And he gave the order for the concubines placed in command of each company to be decapitated.

The king was watching all of this from his terrace. He was appalled by this order to behead the two concubines he loved most in all his harem and dispatched one of his aides with the following command:

"His Majesty has already witnessed sufficient evidence of your ability as a general. Without these two concubines, His Majesty would lose his appetite. He therefore desires that the order for execution be rescinded."

"Please inform His Majesty," replied Master Sun, "that as his personally appointed general, I have total authority in this matter. I am unable to obey certain of His Majesty's commands."

And so he proceeded to have the two concubine-commanders beheaded, as an example to the rest.[23] The two concubines next in rank were now installed as the new company commanders. Once again Master Sun beat the drum. This time the ladies faced left, faced right, marched forward, marched backward, knelt, rose to their feet, all in the strictest conformity to Master Sun's commands, and all in total silence. Afterward he submitted the following report to the king:

"Your Majesty's troops have now been correctly drilled, and Your

Majesty may inspect them. They will perform Your Majesty's every bidding. They will go through fire and flood for Your Majesty's sake."

"You may take a rest," said the king, "and return to your quarters. I have no desire to inspect my troops."

"I see Your Majesty is only interested in words," was Master Sun's reply. "You have no desire to put them into practice."

With this, King He Lü knew Master Sun to be a capable commander, and took him into his service as a general.[24] To the west, he conquered the state of Chu, entering the city of Ying. To the north, he struck fear into the states of Qi and Jin and became renowned among the feudal lords. And Master Sun shared in the king's might.[25]

The moral of this story sits a little uneasily with the main drift of *The Art of War* of Master Sun as we have it today. The Jesuit Father Amiot (Master Sun's first Western translator) struggles to point a parallel between the two: "From this incident, as they tell it, and as I have told it in their fashion, be it true or imaginary, one can conclude that severity is the basis of the general's authority."[26] But the Master as we know him from the book has many other more interesting things to say about being a general and is certainly a great deal more subtle on the subject of discipline: "Discipline troops before they are loyal, and they will be refractory and hard to put to good use. Let loyal troops go undisciplined, and they will be altogether useless. Command them with civility, rally them with martial discipline, and you will win their confidence. Consistent and effective orders inspire obedience; inconsistent and ineffective orders provoke disobedience. When orders are consistent and effective, general and troops enjoy mutual trust" (Chapter 9).

The whole incident with Master Sun and the ladies of the harem is almost certainly apocryphal.[27] The eminent Song-dynasty scholar Ye Shi (1151–1223) considered it "utterly preposterous and incredible."[28] But the astonishing fact is that, apart from this one incident and a couple of brief references elsewhere in the *Records,* we know very little else about Sun Wu (the name Wu means "warrior"). If he was indeed an adviser to King He Lü (who is definitely a historical person), then he would have been a contemporary of Confucius (551–479 B.C.). And yet he is not mentioned once in *The Zuo Commentary,* the principal source for the history of the period. Despite this fact, by the Han dynasty (206 B.C.–A.D. 220), everyone knew of Master Sun the strategist, and his name had become inseparable from his treatise on the Art of War.

We know a little more about another strategist of the Sun family, a certain Sun Bin, whose biography follows Sun Wu's in the *Records*. In it we are told that Sun Bin lived some one hundred years after the death of Sun Wu.[29] Modern scholarship puts his dates at around 380–316 B.C., making him a rough contemporary of the second major Confucian philosopher Mencius (371–289 B.C.). The name Bin means "amputated at the knee," and "Cripple" Sun had been mutilated in this way (and branded) by his erstwhile fellow student of military strategy, Pang Juan, when the two of them were advising the king of the northern state of Wei. The biography tells in some detail the story of the famous battle of Maling (341 B.C.), at which Sun Bin (by now working for the rival state of Qi) had his revenge on Pang Juan.[30]

The Warring States and the Hundred Schools

The period in which both of these members of the Sun family are believed to have lived—the late Spring and Autumn, Warring States period, from the sixth century to the late third century B.C.—was one of enormous turmoil in the Chinese world.[31] The central authority of the feudal Zhou regime had long disintegrated, and a varying number of states were engaged in per-petual struggle for predominance. It was, as the contemporary historian William Jenner puts it, "a world of absolute insecurity, in which any state might be attacked by a combination of any of the others. Faced with ab-solute threats, states had to be able to mobilize all their human and material resources for total war."[32] Among these material resources were the newly introduced crossbow (fifth to fourth century B.C.) and the deployment of professional cavalry (somewhat later). This struggle for hegemony came to an end only in 221 B.C., when the despotic northwestern state of Qin suc-ceeded in reuniting the Chinese under a single (though short-lived) dynasty once more, establishing "a new kind of state power with a degree of direct control over the whole population that is hard to parallel in any major state elsewhere in the world before the eighteenth century."[33] In the meantime, these centuries were a period of extreme violence and incessant warfare, with hundreds of thousands of foot soldiers sent to their deaths on a regu-lar basis. As a modern commentator has remarked, "It is extremely unlikely that many generals died in bed."[34]

Rival states contended for the best available advice, both strategic and ideological. The king of the eastern coastal state of Wu, He Lü (reigned 514–496 B.C.), who so ill-advisedly allowed Master Sun to play at soldiers with his harem (if we believe the Grand Historian), was himself engaged in a life-and-death struggle with his neighbors and needed all the advice he could get. (His son Fu Chai would see their state of Wu conquered and an-nexed by the southerners of Yue in 473 B.C.)

Confucius, born in the state of Lu, to the north of Wu, traveled from state to state, preaching an ethical doctrine of benevolence, righteousness, and ritual, of civilized conventions of decency, of the power of moral example, in the hope of saving Chinese society from chaos, without having to resort to the wiles of the military strategists such as Master Sun, or the heavy-handed imposition of draconian laws later practiced by the state of Qin. Confucius "was witnessing the collapse of civilisation—he saw his world sinking into violence and barbarity."[35] Unlike Master Sun, Confucius never "shared in the king's might." He was just one of the many wandering scholars of his time, whose propositions made this and the subsequent two centuries one of the golden ages of Chinese thought, a period of intense debate and exploration of fundamental philosophical issues. The "hundred schools" of philosophy bloomed, each with its own recipe for success, its rules for the conduct of personal and public life. Many of the great "sages" of Chinese culture emerged during this period: Confucius (Master Kong), Laozi (or Lao-tzu; Master Lao), Master Sun, Master Mo, Mencius (Master Meng), Master Zhuang, the Master known as Lord Shang, and Master Hanfei. It was the thinking of these last two that prevailed when the state of Qin briefly succeeded in imposing its ruthless brand of totalitarianism on the whole of China in 221 B.C. During the subsequent Han dynasty the milder creed of Confucianism was adopted as the official state ideology (and remained so until it was supplanted by Marxism in the twentieth century), but there was always a strong undercurrent of authoritarianism in Chinese public life, just as there was always a strong undercurrent of Taoist thinking in personal life.

Master Sun's thinking, as reflected in *The Art of War,* represents a point of view at fundamental variance with the stance of the Confucians (Confucius himself, Master Meng [Mencius], and Master Xun [ca. 298–238 B.C.]). For the Confucian gentleman, war was evil, but if it had to happen, the main issue was an ethical one, whether or not the cause was a worthy one, and whether or not the ruler had the moral support of his people. In the fifteenth chapter of *The Book of Master Xun,* the Master listens to a general of the state of Chu expounding some of the accepted tenets of Master Sun's strategic thinking: "What is important in War is [the dynamic of] the situation, and [the seizing of] advantage, cunning and swiftness of maneuver. The Skillful Warrior moves suddenly and secretly. No one knows where he will appear. [Master] Sun and [Master] Wu followed this method and had no enemies. Why is it necessary to have the moral support of the people?" Master Xun replies, "You are wrong. I am talking of the troops of the Benevolent Man, of the purpose of the True King. You prize [such things as] plotting, scheming, the use of situation and advantage, sudden attacks and maneuvers, deception. These are the methods of the lesser rulers. The troops of the Benevolent Man cannot be fought with deception. . . ."[36]

By contrast, the Taoists (Master Lao, Master Zhuang) were primarily interested in attuning the human microcosm and its energies with the larger harmonies of the universe. For them, all war and violence were "contrary to the Tao. And whatever is contrary to the Tao will soon perish" (*The Way and Its Power*, Chapter 30). Master Sun shared (some would claim, abused) many of the Taoists' basic notions, as did the so-called Legalists (Lord Shang, Master Hanfei), better described as Chinese Fascists, who derived from certain Taoist points of departure a chilling justification for their Orwellian state. The tenth chapter of *The Book of Lord Shang*, "Methods of War," is built on a series of quotations from Master Sun. It is a lineage that should not be forgotten as we read this book.

But we have already started to do what every reader tends to do: treat Master Sun and his book as one and the same thing. Perhaps it would be best to forget the harem sergeant-major altogether for the moment.

The Art of War: A Book of Life

Bamboo Strips

Until quite recently, there was considerable scholarly skepticism about the little military treatise known as Master Sun's *Art of War*. There were some who doubted its authenticity altogether, and suggestions were made that it had been heavily rewritten or even altogether concocted many centuries after the supposed existence of Master Sun himself.[37] Then, in the 1970s, copies of the text on bamboo and wooden strips were unearthed in two widely separated archaeological sites (Shandong and Qinghai), both dating to the Former Han dynasty, one to a period as early as the second century B.C.[38] Interestingly, perhaps surprisingly, the texts deciphered from these strips turned out to be very close to the accepted traditional text in thirteen chapters.[39] With this discovery the book began to command a renewed scholarly respect. As a popular work, of course, it had never ceased to exert influence and fascination. It was one of the books that helped both Communist leader Mao Zedong and the Nationalist Generalissimo Chiang Kai-shek (and the Japanese commanders in World War II) formulate their strategic thinking. But finally it became legitimate to look at it (along with two other puzzlingly short texts, the Confucian *Analects* and the Taoist *The*

Way and Its Power) as a genuine product of that early phase of Chinese conceptual thought, when the Chinese were "beginning to learn and develop the techniques of writing continuous prose in which philosophical and political propositions are advanced and defended through the use of an increasingly sophisticated literary style and logical structure."[40] It may have had little or nothing to do with a historical person called Master Sun, if such a person existed. Instead, it probably evolved over time, from the recorded teachings of some "unknown Warring States strategist,"[41] only settling into an accepted text after many years.[42] The final text is probably best described as the collective "product of a long process of sedimentation of strategic reflexions, which eventually crystallized into the form of a manual."[43]

Handbooks for the Yellow Emperor

What sort of book is it? Well, it is not really a book at all, in our modern sense of the word. "Ancient Chinese thinkers did not write books," the distinguished sinologist, poet, and philosopher Angus Graham once wrote. "They jotted down sayings, verses, stories, thoughts and by the third century B.C. composed essays, on bamboo strips which were tied together in sheets and rolled up in scrolls."[44] *The Art of War* is such a roll (or series of rolls) of bamboo strips, a collection of more-or-less organized military and miscellaneous sayings and maxims, written in an epigrammatic prose style, using elements of free rhyme. It may even have incorporated early soldiers' rhymes, similar to our own:

> Oh, the Grand Old Duke of York,
> He had ten thousand men;
> He marched them up to the top of the hill,
> And he marched them down again.[45]

Just as *The Book of Changes* must have had among its many layers old sayings similar to our "Red sky at night, shepherd's delight," *The Art of War* almost certainly incorporated a number of proverbial sayings. Take, for example, this passage from Chapter 4: "To lift autumn fur is no strength; to see sun and moon is no perception; to hear thunder is no quickness of hearing." Or this, from Chapter 5: "With an understanding of weakness and strength, an army can strike like a millstone cast at an egg." Or this, from the same chapter: "By their nature, on level ground logs and boulders stay still; on steep ground they move; square, they halt; round, they roll." Or this, from Chapter 6: "Water shuns the high and hastens to the low. War shuns the strong and attacks the weak." Take the saying in the commentary on Chapter 12: "Unless you enter the tiger's lair, you cannot seize the tiger's cubs," which means much the same as our "Nothing ventured, nothing gained."

Master Sun seems to have been very partial to a simple form of repetitive parallelism. This, together with his use of near rhyme, highlights his sense, brings out the emphases and connections of the text.[46] It also gives the book a style and a force of its own. The literary style of *The Art of War* has had many admirers. The early critic Liu Xie (ca. 465–ca. 520) made a point of saying that Master Sun, although he was a military man, had a fine command of language (literally, "his writing was as beautiful as pearls and jade").[47] Again and again critics and commentators have praised the terseness and elegance of the writing, its combination of brevity and profundity.[48]

In terms of both form and content, the book belongs to a genre peculiar to Chinese culture: the written version of a set of guidelines for success and well-being, a handbook for some aspect of life. Such handbooks have existed since earliest times in a variety of domains: medicine, sexuality, self-cultivation, martial arts, *fengshui* (the geomantic art of locating dwellings), alchemy, art, calligraphy, cooking, Go strategy, politics, war. The most ancient claimed authority from some legend of revelation, usually involving an encounter between the mythical ancestor of the Chinese people, the Yellow Emperor, and a female medium. The *Classic of Geomancy,* for example, was ascribed to the Yellow Emperor.[49] The sex handbook *Wonderful Disquisition of the Plain Girl* was cast (as were nearly all such books) in the form of a dialogue between the Yellow Emperor and a woman knowledgeable in the ways of the bedchamber.[50] According to legend, this same Yellow Emperor, after being defeated in battle nine times and having spent three uncomfortable nights in the fog on the slopes of Mount Tai, encountered a woman with a human head and the body of a bird, who introduced herself as the Dark Girl (or the Plain or White Girl, depending on the version). When she asked him what he was seeking, he replied, "The Art of Victory." So she gave him a treatise on the Art of War.[51] In actual fact, handbooks (in all the various domains) were often compiled by such-and-such a Disciple (or Disciples) of such-and-such a Master, some charismatic figure around whom they had once gathered. This may well have been how books such as the *Analects of Confucius,* the powerful Taoist classic *The Way and Its Power* (several short passages from which I quote in my commentary), and Master Sun's *Art of War* came into being.

Shi: Shared Energy

The common ground shared by *The Art of War* and other handbooks on a wide range of different topics can be seen in their common use of one key term: *shi,* "position" or "situational energy." This is the word used for the title of Master Sun's Chapter 5, "Potential Energy," where I have explained it as "the inherent power or dynamic of a situation or moment in time," a latent potential to be subtly exploited to its full by the Skillful Warrior. It is also a key term in Chinese geomancy, *fengshui,* referring to the energy or power of the earth *(dishi)* at a particular location.[52] In the arts of painting and calligraphy, *shi* is the structural energy or life-giving movement sought for in a brushstroke or in a landscape composition. "If there is *shi* in a painting of a forest, then despite all manner of irregularities and twists and turns, the forest will be perfectly poised and alive. . . ."[53] In the art of letters, *shi* comes to mean a writer's literary style, spirit, tendency, bent, manner.[54] In the delicate art of playing the *qin* or Chinese lute (musical instrument par excellence of the cultivated Chinese gentleman), each carefully poised hand position is a *shi* (e.g., "the right hand position known as Flying Dragon Grasping the Clouds").[55] In the Art of Love (the sex handbooks) *shi* is the term used for a sexual "position" or "posture." Chapter 2 of the *Wonderful Disquisition of the Plain Girl,* for example, is entitled "The Nine Positions [or *Shi*]" and includes "Flying Dragon," "Striding Tiger," etc. In the martial arts, *shi* is used as the opening or closure in a sequence that could include moves such as "Crouching Tiger" and "Hidden Dragon" (whence the title of Ang Lee's film).

The shared use of this one term in such diverse domains points to a way of thinking that permeates them all. It comes from the observation and contemplation of the forces at work in the environment, from the attunement of the microcosmic self to the energies of the macrocosm, that is very much part of the Chinese perennial philosophy. It is at the heart of the Taoist attitude to nature and life, which teaches that rather than struggle blindly against obstacles, we should understand the true dynamic of the situation in which we find ourselves and act accordingly, in harmony with it. We find this thinking already in the great classic, *The Book of Changes,* which towers behind the Confucian *Analects,* the Taoist *The Way and Its Power,* and Master Sun's *Art of War.* "The *Changes* provides us with the means to know when and how a situation has come about and to follow it up to where we are now. This process is defined as 'going with the flow' (*shun,* literally compliance)."[56] The entire premise of the *Changes* (as of *The Art of War*) is that it is possible to see into potential changes before they occur, to grasp the subtle configurations of Yin and Yang and thus attune oneself to the energy at work in the world around us. "The Master [Confucius] said, 'To know the pivots [the springs of opportunity] is divine indeed. . . . The pivots are the first, imperceptible beginning of movement, the first trace of good or bad fortune that shows itself. The superior man perceives the pivot and immediately acts. He does not wait even for a day."[57] The similarity with Master Sun is striking.

A recent formulation of *shi* comes from the art historian John Hay: "The world [as conceived in traditional Chinese aesthetics] is inscribed in energy rather than explained by geometry. Man is implicated from the beginning in this inter-activity. . . . To be fixed is to be temporary, to move in and out is to endure. . . . The commonest term for these changeful and changing configurations of energy is *shi*."[58] The multifaceted essayist Lin Yutang put it in a more old-fashioned way in 1938, having first given his own multiple definition of *shi*: "gesture, posture, social position, battle formation, that which gives advantage of position in any struggle. This notion," he continued, "is extremely important and is connected with every form of dynamic beauty, as against mere beauty of static balance. Thus a rock may have a 'rock posture,' an outstretching branch has its own branch posture (which may be good or bad, elegant or ordinary); and there are 'stroke posture,' 'character [ideogram] posture,' and 'brush posture' in writing and painting, 'posture of a hill,' 'posture of a cloud,' etc. . . . A situation is conceived as static, while a *shi* denotes that which the situation is going to become, or 'the way it looks': one speaks of the *shi* of wind, rain, flood, or battle, as the way the wind, rain, flood, or battle looks for the future, whether increasing or decreasing in force, stopping soon or continuing indefinitely, gaining or losing, in what direction, with what force, etc."[59]

Other key terms in Master Sun's worldview connect with this idea of "potential energy" of the situation: the permutations of Yin and Yang; the cycle of the Five Elements and the Four Seasons; the process of *bian* or "change" (the constantly changing environment within which the strategist has to function); variations in strategy between *qi* and *zheng* (the indirect and the direct), flexible improvisation and reaction to the particular *shi* of the moment; *xing* or the "outward and visible dispositions" of a given military situation, including such things as the disposition of troops and the laying in of provisions; the understanding of *xu* and *shi,* empty and full, weakness and strength, and the exploitation of our enemy's weakness; the concept of *yin* or "conformity with," of "going along with" the enemy's situation (e.g., adopting the line of least resistance, using the enemy's food and fodder rather than sending home for more supplies). Much of this can be summed up in the general statement that "supreme military skill lies in deriving victory from the changing circumstances of the enemy" (Chapter 6). It is a philosophy of maximum effect through minimum expenditure of energy. It is the effortless gliding movement of the *taiji* practitioner, the soft but irresistible force of a brushstroke from a master calligrapher. These are reflected in the effortless victory of Master Sun's Skillful Warrior, his Wise General or Strategist, his Warrior Adept. "Ultimate excellence lies not in winning every battle but in defeating the enemy without ever fighting" (Chapter 3).

The Way of Cunning and Deceit, the Tao of Power and Expediency

It is the business of the general to be still and inscrutable, to be upright and impartial. He must be able to keep his own troops in ignorance, to deceive their eyes and their ears (Master Sun, Chapter 11).

At his best, Master Sun's Warrior Adept can be inspirational: his enlightened general cultivates a "holistic response to the human predicament," and *The Art of War* communicates "a transforming personal encounter with ultimate reality, which can and does inform every aspect of life, from the practices of the monk to the martial arts."[60] It is the same perennial Chinese wisdom that the Japanese geisha in Arthur Golden's novel puts in such simple words: "We human beings are only a part of something very much larger. . . . We must use whatever methods we can to understand the movement of the universe around us and time our actions so that we are not fighting the currents, but moving with them."[61] The Ultimate Warrior fights his battles off the battlefield. Herein lies the particular genius of Master Sun, who succeeded in expounding "the importance of mischief, cleverness and common sense in human conflict—as opposed to brute force."[62] It is a message that contrasts strikingly with the nature of war as widely perceived in the world. Master Sun would surely have smiled "at the American exaltation of firepower, which too easily makes a means into an end in itself . . . As he makes plain, violence is only one part of warfare and not even the preferred part. The aim of war is to subdue an opponent, in fine, to change his attitude and induce his compliance. The most economical means is the best: to get him—through deception, surprise, and his own ill-conceived pursuit of infeasible goals—to realize his own inferiority, so that he surrenders or at least retreats without your having to fight him. . . ."[63] Arthur Golden's sumo wrestler puts it more simply: "I never seek to defeat the man I am fighting. I seek to defeat his confidence. A man troubled by doubt cannot focus on the course to victory."[64]

But we should beware of the stereotype of the Chinese sage, which we have observed even in the twentieth century, the smiling, inscrutable image of some aging (and yet strangely ageless), avuncular (but not necessarily benevolent) Chinese statesman: Mao Zedong, Zhou Enlai, Deng Xiaoping. . . .[65] Very early in Chinese history, the Taoist sage's message of effortless harmony with nature and of the "power" emanating from this harmony was hijacked by the Legalists (Chinese Fascists), who exploited the "absolute understanding" of the Taoists as an ideological basis for "absolute power," for the "omnipotent ruler of the ideal Legalist state." Burton Watson has put this very well: "The Taoist sage withdraws from the world to a mysterious and transcendental realm. The Legalist ruler likewise withdraws, deliberately shunning contacts with his subordinates that might breed familiarity, dwelling deep within his palace, concealing his true motives and desires, and surrounding himself with an aura of mystery and inscrutability. Like the head of a great modern corporation he sits, far removed from his countless employees, at his desk in the innermost office and quietly initials things."[66]

Taoist teachings on the Art of Love (which at their best offer many startlingly modern insights) were also distorted and used in a relentless quest for sexual power, a form of "sexual black magic." Under cover of elaborate sexual-alchemical techniques, the practitioners of these arts promoted a form of sexual vampirism, which reduced women to objects for the enhancement of male potency and "long life" (*caibu*, taking the other's essence to boost one's own).[67] Even that great admirer of Taoism and Chinese notions on sexuality, the Dutch scholar-diplomat Robert van Gulik, denounced this practice: "The Taoist teachings relating to this subject . . . bear a vicious character. They have nothing to do with love, not even with the satisfying of carnal desire or with sexual pleasure. These teachings . . . [are] aimed at acquiring supernatural power at the expense of the sexual partner." For readers of Master Sun, the interesting thing here is that the sex handbooks written for this purpose (dialogues for the most part between the ubiquitous Yellow Emperor and the Plain or Dark Girl) were all couched in the language of the military treatise and used the old (i.e., Master Sun's) strategic ideas about victory, to the extent that Chinese readers might have had difficulty knowing whether they were, in fact, reading a sex manual or a treatise on the Art of War. Van Gulik summarizes the shared ideas as follows: "First, one must spare one's own force while utilizing that of the opponent; and second, one must begin by yielding to the enemy in order to catch him unawares thereafter" ("All's fair in love and war" takes on a new meaning here). The late-Ming treatise *The True Classic of the Complete Union* begins, "A superior general will while engaging the enemy first concentrate on drawing out his opponent, as if sucking and inhaling his strength. He will adopt a completely detached attitude, resembling a man who closes his eyes in utter indifference." The commentator remarks, "Superior general refers to the Taoist Adept. To engage means to engage in the sexual act. The enemy is the woman."[68] Or as van Gulik explains, "The man should defeat the enemy in the sexual battle by keeping himself under complete control so as not to emit semen while exciting the woman till she reaches orgasm and sheds her Yin essence which is then aborbed by the man." This is the Art of Victory on the sexual battlefield.

Victory on Master Sun's or the Plain Girl's battlefield requires considerable cunning, in addition to large doses of self-restraint and meditation. And as we read *The Art of War,* we find that its subtle message of nonviolence in the resolution of conflict goes hand in hand with a calculated and cynical exploitation of one's fellow human beings. It is, after all, in the very first chapter that we encounter the shocking statement: "The Way of War is a Way of Deception." In the film *Wall Street,* it is this passage that Gordon Gekko's young acolyte, Bud Fox, quotes back at the tycoon, once he has done his reading of Master Sun and absorbed the principles of Gekko's Art of Corporate War. The Warrior Adept is often advised to be callous and vicious (as was the Taoist Adept on that other battlefield of the inner apartments). Master Sun's advocacy of deception as the cornerstone of strategy, his abandonment of values in favor of expediency, the disturbing implications of his cult of the cunning, the wily, and the inscrutable must be seen for what they are. In the eighteenth century Father Amiot did not hesitate to challenge them: "It is not necessary to say here that I disapprove of all the author has to say on this occasion about the use of artifice and ruse. . . . Most of the maxims in this section are reprehensible, as contrary to honesty and other virtues held in esteem by the Chinese themselves."[69] James Murdoch, the historian of Japan (where Master Sun's teachings have been widely studied since at least the eighth century), complained that "Sonshi" (the Japanese reading of Master Sun's name) expounded "the dirtiest form of statecraft with unspeakable depths of duplicity. . . ." Murdoch deplored, for instance, "the naked and full-bodied depravity of the old Chinese lore on espionage."[70] In a more recent and deeply provocative study of the nature of violence in early Chinese society, Mark Edward Lewis argues that "the stratagems and deceits by which the military philosophers promised to reduce violence wreaked even greater damage on the fabric of human society than any physical brutality [by stimulating hatred and dishonesty]."[71] For this "damage to the fabric of society" in our own time, we have only to look at the corrosive effect of the Cultural Revolution, its "distortions and deceptions, its confusion of good and bad, true and false, the frame-ups and endless injustices."[72]

For the most part the Chinese themselves have regarded and still regard Master Sun as a "treasure of their national heritage." The early Confucians (as we have seen with Master Xun) had little time for his way of thinking. And the Song-dynasty Neo-Confucian philosopher, Zhu Xi, while admiring the pithy style of his writing, complained that his treatise encouraged "a ruler's bent towards unrelenting warfare and reckless militarism."[73] But otherwise there has been astonishingly little in the way of an indigenous critique of Master Sun's philosophy of expediency and survival, his advocacy of a subtle (even if successful) manipulation of one's fellow men.

This can best be understood as part of what the modern essayist Bo Yang calls the "soy paste vat" of Chinese culture, the Confucian stifling of creativity and the failure to "develop such habits as self-criticism, introspection and self-improvement."[74] Bo Yang sees it as part of the "national character."[75] Since the beginning of the twentieth century, the modern Chinese have been engaged in an agonized quest to unravel the problematic nature of their own culture. With recurring fury and frustration, they have come face-to-face with the darkness of their "Great Wall; that wall of ancient bricks which is constantly being reinforced. . . . The Great Wall of China: a wonder and a curse!"[76] Master Sun was surely one of that wall's original architects. As He Xin, a prominent neoconservative intellectual of the 1990s, gloomily laments the bankruptcy of contemporary Chinese society and culture, we can almost hear him trying to exorcise the specter of Master Sun, even if He Xin himself is too much a part of the "deep structure" to be able to identify the Master as one of the culprits: "The religion of the Chinese today is cheating, deceit, blackmail and theft, eating, drinking, whoring, gambling and smoking. We make laws in order to break them; our rules and regulations are a sham. Our tactics consist in carrying out policy; our strategy is to get people to fall into the traps they have set for others. We think any honest, humble gentleman a fool and regard any good person who works hard and demands little in return as an idiot. Crooks are our sages; thieves and swindlers are our supermen. . . . There are no greater cynics than the Chinese people. We refuse to take on any responsibility that won't profit ourselves and show no respect for any values that transcend the utilitarian."[77] The man who presided over half a century of this social degradation was Master Sun's most notorious twentieth-century disciple, Mao Zedong. As Liu Xiaobo, one of the brightest of the young intellectuals in the Tiananmen movement, puts it: "Seen solely within the context of Chinese history, Mao Zedong was undoubtedly the most successful individual of all. Nobody understood the Chinese better; no one was more skillful at factional politics within the autocratic structure; no one was more cruel and merciless; none more chameleonlike."[78]

But by far the best twentieth-century representative of Master Sun's way of thinking is a little-known writer called Li Zongwu, whose cynical booklet *Science of the Thick and Black* has been an underground bible of survival ever since it first appeared in the 1920s, the early years of the republic. Li openly claims an affinity with Master Sun ("Master Sun and I are one and the same person"), and many of his ideas are elaborated in terms of the characters in *The Romance of the Three Kingdoms*.[79] The "Third Level of Attainment" of Li's *Science*, for example, could have come straight from Master Sun: "Level 3. To have skin that is thick yet *formless* and a heart that is black yet *colourless*; this is the ultimate level of attainment. Then no one will have any idea of how thick and black you are. This is not easily achieved, and one finds the best examples among the sages of the past."[80]

The Art of Reading *The Art of War*

The Art of War should be read, as the Ming-dynasty scholar Liu Yin wrote, not reverentially but "in a lively manner, like pearls rattling around in a dish, with no prescribed order." It should be read not glibly or flippantly but "practically, in an applied manner, from the very beginning. What is the point in simply reciting the text?" The balance for each reader (soldier, trader, corporate manager, marriage partner, tennis player, cook, driver) lies somewhere between the extraordinary wisdom embedded in its pages and its less attractive or acceptable implications. Each reader must negotiate this fascinating but treacherous terrain ("Entangling terrain, like a net, in which one can easily become entangled"—Chapter 10, text with commentary). Each reader must be flexible in response to the book's sometimes startling statements ("infinitely flexible and mobile, infinitely resourceful"—commentary on Chapter 5). Each reader must relate creatively and reflectively to the enormous potential energy of this book, so as to know not just the enemy but also self, so as to decode the book's message of survival and victory and emerge the stronger for it, without succumbing to its insidious cult of deceit and expediency. As another Ming-dynasty thinker urged, "Emerge from the mud untainted; understand cunning, but do not use it."[81] Or as Liu Yin advised, "In reading about the Art of War, you must understand Change; if you only know what is regular, what is unchanging, and do not know Change, you will be like the man who dropped his sword in the water and tried to find it again by making a mark on the side of his boat—wasting your time."[82]

NOTES

1. Quoted by Richard Deacon, *The Chinese Secret Service* (London: Grafton Books, 1989), p. 15.
2. Dr. Connell Cowan and Gail Parent, *The Art of War for Lovers* (New York: Pocket Books, 1998).
3. Joseph Needham and Robin D. S. Yates, with Krzysztof Gawlikowski, Edward McEwen, and Wang Ling, *Science and Civilisation in China*, vol. 5, part VI: *Military Technology* (Cambridge: Cambridge University Press, 1994), pp. 80–81.
4. Moss Roberts, trans., *Three Kingdoms: A Historical Novel* (Berkeley: University of California Press, 1991), p. 291.
5. My own translation. See Luo Guanzhong (with commentary by Mao Zong'gang), *Sanguo yanyi* (Shanghai: Guji, 1989), pp. 1241–42.
6. See several fine *nianhua* on this theme, from Suzhou, Fujian, and Shandong, in the two-volume collection *Xichu nianhua* (Taipei: Yingwen Hansheng, 1990).
7. See *Sanshiliuji xinbian* (Peking: Zhanshi, 1981), pp. 96–100, and Ralph Sawyer, trans., *Unorthodox Strategies for the Everyday Warrior* (Boulder, Colo.: Westview Press, 1996), pp. 126–27.
8. Needham (1994), p. 71.
9. See Thomas Cleary's *Mastering the Art of War* (Boston: Shambhala, 1989), which includes a version of the work *The Way of the General*. Lionel Giles dismisses the attribution out of hand in his *Sun Tzu on the Art of War* (London: Luzac, 1910), p. lii.
10. He was held by some scholars to have extensively rewritten the text himself—until archaeological discoveries completely destroyed this hypothesis.
11. See, for example, the various conversations on the subject of Master Sun between the Manchu emperor Kangxi and the young rogue Trinket in the Third Book of Louis Cha's picaresque martial arts novel of the early 1970s, *The Deer and Cauldron* (Hong Kong: Oxford University Press, 2002).
12. See the Strategy and Leadership series published in Singapore, translated from the work of the Mainland cartoonist Wang Xuanming. See also *Sunzi Speaks: The Art of War* (New York: Doubleday, 1994), by the Taiwanese cartoonist Tsai Chih Chung, translated by Brian Bruya. Of greatly inferior quality are the six volumes translated from the series originally published by Zhejiang People's Art Press, but even these are an interesting example of Master Sun as popular culture. Among the many Web sites worth visiting are "Sonshi.com," "artofwar.com," and "zhongwen.com/bingfa.htm."
13. Available online at "falundafa.org." My translation is slightly adapted.
14. Yang Chengfu, *Yangshi Taijiquan* (Hong Kong: Taiping, 1968), p. 5.
15. Donn F. Draeger and Robert W. Smith, *Comprehensive Asian Fighting Arts* (Tokyo: Kodansha, 1969), p. 38.
16. Wong Kiew Kit, *The Art of Shaolin Kungfu* (Rockport, Mass.: Element Books, 1996), p. 151.
17. D. C. Lau, "Some Notes on the Sun-tzu," *Bulletin of the School of Oriental and African Studies* (1965:28:2), p. 321.
18. Father Jean-Joseph-Marie Amiot (1718–93), in his French paraphrase of this biography (preface to his translation of Master Sun, *Les Treize Articles sur l'Art Militaire, ouvrage composé en Chi-*

nois par Sun-tse [Paris: Chez Nyon, 1782], p. 49), adds a nice eighteenth-century flourish at this point: "The king, who was beginning to find his normal range of court amusements rather lackluster, took advantage of this opportunity to discover a novel form of amusement." One cannot help imagining Versailles. But given that Amiot was himself working with the aid of an eighteenth-century Manchu version of the original Chinese, we should also superimpose on King He Lü's palace features of the Emperor Qianlong's superb hunting lodge at Jehol.

19. Amiot: "Master Sun, aware that the king was endeavoring to make him appear ridiculous, maintained a show of dignity and gave the impression that he was greatly honored to have been vouchsafed not only a view of the inmates of His Majesty's harem but also the chance to direct them in person."

20. Amiot: "Listen to me attentively, and obey every one of my orders. This is the first and the most important of all the rules of warfare. Be sure never to break it."

21. In Amiot's paraphrase, one beat signifies front, two beats rear, three beats left, four beats right.

22. Amiot: "After a few moments of intense effort to stifle their urge to laugh, they burst into uncontrollable fits of laughter."

23. Amiot: " 'They have disobeyed me,' said Master Sun. 'They must die.' And so saying he drew his sword and with the same sangfroid he had demonstrated throughout, proceeded to cut off their heads."

24. Amiot: "The king was stricken with the most intense grief. 'I have lost,' he cried, heaving a heartfelt sigh, 'that which I loved the most in this world. . . . Let this stranger return to his own land. I wish nothing more of him, or of his services. . . . Oh, barbarian, what have you done? How can I live from this day forth?' But, inconsolable as the king was, the passage of time caused him to forget his grief . . . and he sent once more for Master Sun, to advise him in his campaign against the state of Chu."

25. My translation. See *Records of the Grand Historian*, Chapter 65. I have followed Takigawa Kametaro, *Shiki kaichu kosho* (Tokyo: Kenkyujo, 1934; Taiwan reprint, Zhongxin shuju, 1976), p. 843.

26. Amiot concludes, "This maxim, which may not be valid for the Nations of Europe, is an excellent one for the Asiatics, among whom honor is by no means always the first motive."

27. Among the bamboo strips excavated at Yinqueshan (Silver Sparrow Mountain) in 1972 were fragments of a similar version of this story. The fact that this bamboo-strip version also refers to the thirteen chapters of Master Sun's treatise suggests that it, too, was of considerably later origin than the "core text." See Roger Ames, *Sun-tzu: The Art of Warfare* (New York: Ballantine, 1993), pp. 190–96.

28. See Lionel Giles, pp. xxi–xxii, quoting from the *Wenxian tongkao* of Ma Duanlin (1254–1325).

29. Takigawa, p. 844.

30. This story is referred to many times by Master Sun's commentators. See, for example, Chapter 5, where Zhang Yu and Du Mu paraphrase the *Records*.

31. For the dates of these and the other main periods and dynasties in Chinese history, and for a brief chronology of some events in early history that have a bearing on this book, see the Chronologies.

32. W. J. F. Jenner, *The Tyranny of History* (London: Penguin, 1994), p. 20.

33. Ibid.

34. Samuel B. Griffith, *Sun Tzu: The Art of War* (Oxford: Clarendon Press, 1963), p. 21. Roger Ames refers several times, in his translations of Master Sun and Sun Bin, to the "killing fields" of this period. It is hardly an exaggeration.

35. Simon Leys, trans., *The Analects of Confucius* (New York: Norton, 1997), Introduction, p. xxiii.

36. My translation. See *Xunzi xinzhu* (Peking: Zhonghua, 1979), pp. 230–31.

37. For example, the Tang-dynasty commentator Du Mu (803–52) suspected the earlier commentator Cao Cao (155–220) of having substantially rewritten the text, thereby reducing it to the thirteen chapters as we know them.

38. For an excellent account of these finds, see the Introductions and Appendices to Ames (1993) and Lau and Ames (1996).

39. Needham (1994), pp. 18–19: "Archaeological finds of the seventies settled many earlier doubts, confirmed the authenticity of the text known to us, and tended to reaffirm the reliability of the traditional version."

40. Robin D. S. Yates, "New Light on Ancient Chinese Military Texts," *T'oung Pao* LXXIV (1988), p. 219.

41. Griffith, p. 12.

42. Niu Guoping and Wang Fucheng, *Sunzi shiyi fu yundu* (Lanzhou: Gansu Renmin, 1991), p. 164.

43. Jean Lévi, *Sun Tzu, L'art de la Guerre* (Paris: Hachette, 2000), p. 16. My translation.

44. A. C. Graham, *Chuang Tzu: The Inner Chapters* (London: Allen and Unwin, 1981), p. 27.

45. See Iona and Peter Opie, *The Oxford Dictionary of Nursery Rhymes* (Oxford: Clarendon Press, 1951), pp. 442–43. Thanks to Rachel May for this enlightening, and enlivening, observation.

46. Niu and Wang, p. 164. They compare the style with that of *The Way and Its Power* and other philosophical texts such as *The Book of Master Xun* and *The Book of Master Guan*. See also Guo Huaruo (1984), p. 29.

47. *The Literary Mind and the Carving of Dragons*, Chapter 49.

48. See the comments by Ouyang Xiu (1007–72) and Zheng Hou (fl. 1135), quoted and translated by Giles, pp. xxxix, xliii.

49. De Groot, J. J. M., *The Religious System of China*, vol. 3, book 1 (Leiden, Netherlands: Brill, 1897), p. 996.

50. See the translation by André Lévy, *Le Sublime Discours de la Fille Candide* (Arles: Picquier, 2000).

51. Compare Mark Edward Lewis, *Sanctioned Violence in Early China* (Albany: State University of New York Press, 1990), p. 99. The legend he is quoting is from the tenth-century compendium *Taiping Yulan*. See also Anne Birrell, *Chinese Mythology* (Baltimore: Johns Hopkins Press, 1993), p. 137. Birrell dates the original source of the story to the fourth to fifth centuries A.D.

52. See Stephan Feuchtwang, *An Anthropological Analysis of Chinese Geomancy* (Laos: Vithagna, 1974), p. 112.

53. Remark attributed to Zhan Zuo (fl. 1603–29), quoted by George Rowley, *Principles of Chinese Painting* (Princeton: Princeton University Press, 1947), p. 38. Compare Pierre Ryckmans, *Les Propos sur la Peinture de Shitao* (Brussels: Institut Belge des Hautes Études Chinoises, 1970), p. 26.

54. See Chapter 30 of *The Literary Mind and the Carving of Dragons*, "Establishing a Style."

55. Robert van Gulik, *The Lore of the Chinese Lute* (Tokyo: Sophia University, 1940), p. 115.

56. Richard Lynn, trans., *The Classic of Changes* (New York: Columbia University Press, 1994), p. 125, note 7.

57. "The Great Commentary," in the Richard Wilhelm/Cary F. Baynes version, *The I Ching or Book of Changes* (Princeton: Princeton University Press, third revised ed., 1967), p. 342.

58. John Hay, "Boundaries and Surfaces of Self and Desire," in *Boundaries in China* (London: Reaktion Press, 1994), pp. 144–45.

59. Lin Yutang, *The Importance of Living* (London: Heinemann, 1938), pp. 426–47.

60. Robert Wilkinson, Introduction to *Sun Tzu: The Art of War* (Ware, England: Wordsworth Classics, 1998), p. 13.

61. Arthur Golden, *Memoirs of a Geisha* (London: Vintage, 1992), p. 127.

62. Sterling Seagrave, *Lords of the Rim* (London: Corgi Books, 1996), p. 45.

63. John K. Fairbank, "Introduction: Varieties of the Chinese Military Experience," in Kierman and Fairbank, eds., *Chinese Ways in Warfare* (Cambridge, Mass.: Harvard University Press, 1974), p. 11.

64. *Memoirs of a Geisha*, p. 324.

65. For Zhou Enlai as political survivor, see Simon Leys, "The Path of an Empty Boat: Zhou Enlai," in *The Burning Forest* (New York: Holt, Rinehart and Winston, 1986), pp. 152–58. For Deng Xiaoping as mastermind of a decade of purges *well after* the Cultural Revolution, see Barmé and Minford, eds., *Seeds of Fire* (New York: Hill & Wang, 1988), pp. 343–53.

66. Burton Watson, trans., *Han Fei Tzu: Basic Writings* (New York: Columbia University Press, 1964), Introduction, p. 10.

67. André Lévy translates this as "absorption roborative" (p. 77). He, too, describes it as a process of sexual vampirism, whereby "one partner sucks up the energy of the other partner, in order to strengthen his own."

68. Robert van Gulik, *Erotic Colour Prints of the Ming Period with an Essay on Chinese Sex Life from the Han to the Ch'ing Dynasty* (Tokyo: Privately published, 1951), pp. 69, 112–13.

69. Amiot, pp. 104, 159.

70. James Murdoch, *A History of Japan* (London: Routledge, 1949), pp. 630–31. Quoted by Griffith, p. 172.

71. Lewis, *Sanctioned Violence,* p. 135.

72. Ba Jin, "A Cultrev Museum," in Barmé and Minford, p. 382.

73. Giles, p. xliii.

74. Bo Yang, trans. Don Cohn and Jing Qing, *The Ugly Chinaman and the Crisis of Chinese Culture* (Sydney: Allen and Unwin, 1992), p. 54.

75. See Arthur H. Smith's *Chinese Characteristics* (2nd edition, London: Kegan Paul, 1894), with its self-explanatory chapter titles: "The Disregard for Accuracy," "The Talent for Indirection," "The Absence of Sincerity." Interestingly, Smith's work (based as it was on his years of residence as a missionary, with a good command of Chinese and a familiarity with Chinese popular and proverbial literature) has recently received renewed attention among Chinese readers (and has even been translated into Chinese). This is part of the attempted process of "self-reflection" that has included works such as Bo Yang's "The Ugly Chinaman" and Sun Lung-kee's *The Deep Structure of Chinese Culture*. For these, see *Seeds of Fire* and Barmé and Jaivin, eds., *New Ghosts, Old Dreams* (New York: Times Books, 1992).

76. Lu Xun, "Chang cheng," in *Huagaiji* (quoted in *Seeds of Fire,* p. 1).

77. He Xin, "Gudu yu tiaozhan—wode fendou yu sikao," *Zixue zazhi,* 1988:10, p. 39 (quoted in *New Ghosts, Old Dreams,* p. 254).

78. "Hunshi mowang Mao Zedong," in *Jiefang yuebao,* 1988:11, p. 31 (quoted in *New Ghosts, Old Dreams,* p. xxvi).

79. Li Zongwu, *Houheixue Daquan* (Hong Kong: Xuewen, n.d.), pp. 40–41.

80. Quoted in *New Ghosts, Old Dreams,* p. 449. My italics.

81. The fourth saying in the late-Ming collection *Vegetable Roots,* attributed to Hong Zicheng of the Wanli period (1573–1620). See *Caigentan* (Taipei: Zhiliang, 1987), p. 4.

82. Liu Yin, "How to Read the Military Classics," in Liu Yin, ed., *Wujing qishu zhijie* (Changsha: Yueli, 1992), p. 7.

A Note on the Text

Text, Translation, and Commentary

In general I have followed the conventionally accepted text used in the much-reprinted *Shiyijia zhu Sunzi,* although occasionally I adopt emendations proposed by other scholars, or readings from the Bamboo Strips. Since this is a translation for the nonspecialist, I have not given textual details in my commentary, except where it seemed essential to an understanding of the text itself.

The first part of this new translation presents the core text, Master Sun's Thirteen Chapters, unadorned. This is followed in the second part by the same material together with a running commentary, mostly taken from the traditional Chinese commentators. This double format is the one adopted by the most recent (and best) French translator, Jean Lévi. It enables the reader to form first impressions based on an unimpeded view of the early epigrammatic text and then to refine those impressions with the help of more detailed explanatory material. Unlike Lévi, I have divided my translation into short lines, to preserve something of the formal quality of the original. I have also distinguished the text from its commentary as graphically as possible. When traditional Chinese readers read their annotated Master Sun, the words of the classic text are in much larger characters and stand out very clearly from the sea of commentary surrounding them. You always know whether you are reading text or commentary.

There is an accepted canon of eleven standard commentators on Master Sun, beginning with Cao Cao and including five commentators from the Tang dynasty and four from the Song dynasty.[1] Their commentaries take up about twenty times as much space as the pithy original text. They often narrate lengthy episodes from history (usually they are adapting from one of the standard Chinese histories) to illustrate one of Master Sun's points, and I have used a number of these episodes. Liu Yin advised readers to "understand and commit to memory the deeds of great commanders, how some were victorious through certain means and others met defeat through others. This is worthwhile." In addition to retelling these stories, the commentators paraphrase and expand on Master Sun's often bald and puzzling statements. Sometimes one commentator will pick up from where the last one left off: "Yes, I agree with So-and-so but would like to qualify his remark with the following observation. . . ." Occasionally I have run together comments like this, from two or three commentators, thus: "Li Quan/Du You/Zhang Yu." The sheer bulk of commentary is daunting, so I have tried to pick comments that I found helpful, with some guidance from modern editors and translators. Some Master Sun scholars will undoubtedly feel that I have not always selected the best items. Some readers may wonder why I have included so much. My sole aim has been to help readers understand what has been said. I am convinced that the Chinese habit of reading a classic text (in all the genres—philosophy, history, poetry, fiction) together with its commentary serves the Western reader, who often needs a context and a subtext for an epigrammatic text. Keeping this in mind, I have from time to time added passages from other early classics (such as *The Way and Its Power* or *The Book of Changes*) and from *The Romance of the Three Kingdoms.*

I have also quoted (sometimes with slight modification) a number of passages from the commentary by Lionel Giles, whose 1910 translation has stood the test of time admirably.[2] In addition to his considerable Chinese learning, Giles brings to bear a broad knowledge of Western history: he quotes Herodotus, Thucydides, and Livy, not to mention Baden-Powell, and refers to the military exploits of Hannibal, Caesar, Turenne, Napoleon, Wellington, and "Stonewall" Jackson in much the way that the Chinese commentators quote their own histories and refer to the deeds of their own great generals. His translation and commentary are also informed by a lively interest in matters military (it is dedicated to his soldier brother, Captain Valentine Giles). Sometimes in his own commentary Giles neatly summarizes the collective drift of the Chinese commentators. Often he expands them, translating directly from the annals and histories. A good example of this is in Chapter 11, where Master Sun talks of the need to "nourish your men and cherish your troops." Giles refers to Chen Hao's comment and then goes directly to Chen's source, the Grand Historian Sima Qian, telling the full story of the Qin general Wang Jian and effectively doubling the commentator's text.[3] Lionel certainly inherited his father, Herbert's, knack for telling a story. Occasionally I have adopted his version of a comment almost unchanged, in which case it is headed thus: "Du Mu/Giles." Giles has, in a sense, joined the ranks of the traditional eleven commentators. He is the twelfth man. Other translators whose versions I have consulted include Roger Ames, Brigadier General Samuel Griffith, and Jean Lévi.

I have myself from time to time added reflections on war by other writers, both European and non-European, to broaden the vision a little. In five or six places I have added an extended note of my own, where I felt that certain key terms used by Master Sun needed a bit of explaining.

Note on Pronunciation

In this book, Chinese names and place names are in general spelled according to the Chinese system known as Hanyu Pinyin, or Pinyin for short, which is now internationally accepted. (Occasional exceptions to this rule include well-established geographical names such as the Yangtze River, and the cities of Peking, Nanking, and Canton.) The following short list may help readers with some of the more difficult sounds used in the Pinyin system:

c = *ts*
q = *ch*
x = *sh*
z = *dz*
zh = *j*

I should explain at the outset, for those perplexed both by Chinese ways of naming and by this modern way of spelling Chinese words, that Master Sun, Sun Tzu, Sunzi, and Sun Wu are one and the same person. *Tzu* is the old "Wade-Giles" way of writing the Chinese syllable that becomes *zi* in the Pinyin system. The word *zi* was added after a surname in ancient times to signify "Master." Thus, Meng Tzu (Wade-Giles) or Mengzi was Master Meng (latinized by the early Jesuits as Mencius); Lao Tzu or Laozi was Master Lao (the legendary sage to whom the Taoist classic *The Way and Its Power* is attributed). In general I refer to these gentlemen as Master So-and-so. Incidentally, the vowels in Sun Tzu (or Sunzi) do not sound like the vowels in "unto" (however Michael Douglas may pronounce them in *Wall Street*). The Chinese name Sun is *not* pronounced like the Standard English word "sun." The vowel sounds more like the "oo" in book, or the "u" in full. And *Tzu* or *zi* is pronounced like the buzzing "dze" in adze, the tool. As for Sun Wu: Wu was his name.

The following very rough equivalents may also be of help to readers.

Bang = *Bung*
Bo = *Boar* (wild pig)
Cai = *Ts'eye* ("It's eye," without the first vowel)
Cang = *Ts'arng*
Chen = *Churn*
Cheng = *Churng*
Chong = *Choong* (as in "book")
Chuan = *Chwan*
Dang = *Darng* or *Dung* (as in cow "dung")
Dong = *Doong* (as in "book")
Feng = *Ferng*
Gui = *Gway*
Guo = *Gwore*
Jia = *Jeeyar*
Jiang = *Jeeyung*
Kong = *Koong* (as in "book")
Li = *Lee*
Long = *Loong* (as in "book")
Lü = *Lew* (as in the French "*tu*")
Mo = *More*
Qi = *Chee*
Qian = *Chee-yenne*
Qing = *Ching*
Rong = *Roong* (as in "book")
Shi = *Shhh*

Si = *Szzz*
Song = *Soong* (as in "book")
Shun = *Shoon* (as in "should")
Sun = *Soon* (as in "book")
Wen = *Wen* as in "forgotten"
Xi = *Shee*
Xiao = *Shee-ow* (as in "shee-cow" without the "*c*")
Xin = *Shin*
Xing = *Shing*
Xiong = *Sheeoong*
Xu = *Shyeu* (as in the French "*tu*")
Yan = *Yen*
Yi = *Yee*
You = *Yo*-heave-ho
Yu = *Yew* tree (as in the French "*tu*")
Yuan = *You, Anne*
Zha = *Jar*
Zhe = *Jerrr*
Zhen = *Jurn*
Zhi = *Jirrr*
Zhou = *Joe*
Zhu = *Jew*
Zhuang = *Jwarng*
Zi = *Dzzz*
Zong = *Dzoong* (as in "book")
Zuo = *Dzore*

NOTES

1. See the annotated list of commentators beginning on p. xlix.
2. Lionel Giles spoils his book by spending so much time attacking the unfortunate Captain Calthrop, who had the audacity to produce his own translation a few years earlier, based largely on Japanese sources. Lionel clearly inherited the vitriolic tendencies of his father, the eminent sinologist Herbert Giles (1845–1935).
3. Giles, p. 124.

Suggestions for Further Reading

Chinese Military and Related Classics

The Seven Military Classics

This "canon" of military treatises was established during the reign of Emperor Shengzong (1068–85) of the Song dynasty. On these texts candidates for military promotion were examined. The order varied, but normally Master Sun's treatise was the first in rank, followed by:

Wuzi bingfa (Master Wu's Art of War)
    One of the earliest treatises (fourth century B.C.), apart from Master Sun's. In its approach it is closer to the Confucian school.
Sima fa (The Marshal's Treatise)
    Attributed to Sima Rangju of the sixth century B.C., but probably from the fourth century B.C.
Liu tao (The Six Quivers)
    According to legend, this was the "grimoire" written by Lü Shang (Taigong, or the Ancient Duke), adviser to the founder of the Zhou dynasty, King Wen.
Weiliaozi (The Book of Master Weiliao)
    Master Weiliao supposedly lived in the fourth century, and studied (like Sun Bin) under the semilegendary figure the Master of Spirit Valley.
San lüe (The Three Stratagems)
    Attributed to Lord Yellow Stone.
Li Weigong wendui (Duke Li's Dialogue)
    Military treatise in the form of a dialogue between Li Jing (571–649) and the Tang Emperor Taizong. Li Jing is also reputed to have been the author of his own *Art of War* in eight chapters and a work entitled *The Mirror of War*.

Other Military and Strategic Classics

Baizhan qilüe/qifa (The Hundred Unusual Strategies)
  Attributed to Liu Ji (Liu Bowen), early Ming dynasty. Translated by
  Ralph Sawyer (see below).
Guiguzi (The Master of Spirit Valley)
  Perhaps a work of the fourth century B.C. Sometimes classified as a mil-
  itary treatise, but more accurately regarded as a work on the strategic
  aspects of diplomacy.
Sanshiliu ji (The Thirty-six Stratagems)
  First mentioned in *History of Southern Qi*, possibly written by Tan Daoji
  (d. 436), but first made into a book in Ming/Qing times. "Rediscovered"
  in 1941.
Shangjun shu (The Book of Lord Shang)
  The classic statement of Legalist political ideas, which includes warfare
  among its subjects, and refers to Master Sun as its authority. Written
  in ?fourth century B.C. Translation by J.J.L. Duyvendak: *The Book of
  Lord Shang* (London: Probsthain, 1928).
Sun Bin bingfa (Sun Bin's Art of War)
  Referred to in early bibliographies, subsequently lost. Rediscovered in
  the Shandong excavation of 1972. In many respects a development of
  Master Sun's treatise. Recent translation by D.C. Lau and Roger Ames
  (see below).

Other Classic Chinese Works Referred to in the Commentary, with Recommended Translations

Daodejing (The Way and Its Power)
  The Taoist classic attributed to Master Lao (Laozi, or Lao Tzu). Of un-
  certain date and authorship. Excellent translation by Arthur Waley: *The
  Way and Its Power: The Tao Te Ching and Its Place in Chinese Thought* (Lon-
  don: Allen and Unwin, 1934).
Hanshu (History of the Former Han)
  Translated by Homer Dubs: *History of the Former Han Dynasty* (3 vols.,
  Baltimore: Waverly Press, 1938–55).
Houhanshu (History of the Later Han)
  No complete translation.

Huainanzi (The Book of Master Huainan)
No complete translation. See John S. Major, *Heaven and Earth in Early Han Thought* (Albany: New York University Press, 1993).
Mengzi (The Book of Mencius)
Translations by James Legge: *The Works of Mencius* (London: Trübner, 1861), and D. C. Lau: *Mencius* (London: Penguin, 1970).
Mozi (The Book of Master Mo)
Translation by Mei Yi-pao: *The Ethical and Political Works of Mo Tzu* (London: Probsthain, 1919).
Sanguo yanyi (The Romance of the Three Kingdoms)
Translations by C. H. Brewitt-Taylor: *Romance of the Three Kingdoms* (Shanghai: Kelly & Walsh, 1925), and Moss Roberts: *Three Kingdoms: A Historical Novel* (Berkeley: University of California Press, 1991).
Shiji (Records of the Grand Historian)
Translation by Burton Watson: *Records of the Grand Historian* (3 vols., rev. ed., Hong Kong and New York: Renditions Books/Columbia University Press, 1993).
Yijing (The Book of Changes)
Translations by Richard Wilhelm (English trans. Cary F. Baynes): *The I Ching or Book of Changes* (3rd ed, Princeton: Princeton University Press, 1967), and Richard Lynn, *The Classic of Changes* (New York: Columbia University Press, 1994).
Zhuangzi (The Book of Master Zhuang)
Translations by Herbert Giles: *Chuang Tzu, Taoist Philosopher and Chinese Mystic* (rev. ed., London: Allen and Unwin, 1926), and Burton Watson: *The Complete Works of Chuang Tzu* (New York: Columbia University Press, 1968).
Zuozhuan (The Zuo Commentary)
Translations by James Legge: *The Ch'un Ts'eu with the Tso Chuen* (London, Trübner, 1872), and Burton Watson: *The Tso Chuan, Selections from China's Oldest Narrative History* (New York: Columbia University Press, 1989).

Books and Articles in Western Languages

Translations

Ames, Roger T., *Sun-tzu: The Art of Warfare* (New York: Ballantine, 1993).
This edition has the Chinese text and an extensive scholarly apparatus.

xliv   Suggestions for Further Reading

Especially good on the archaeological finds (the Bamboo Strips), and valuable for Ames's philosophical interpretations.

Amiot, Jean-Joseph-Marie, *Les Treize Articles sur l'Art Militaire, ouvrage composé en Chinois par Sun-tse* (Paris: Chez Nyon, 1782).

This is the edition in the seventh volume of the Jesuit series *Mémoires concernant l'histoire, les sciences, les arts, les moeurs, les usages &c., des Chinois.* There was an earlier (now rare) edition "Chez Didot l'aîné," Paris 1772. Amiot was a prolific writer on things Chinese and also composed a Manchu grammar and dictionary.

Calthrop, E. F. (Captain, RFA), *The Book of War* (London: John Murray, 1908).

This is the version excoriated by Lionel Giles.

Cleary, Thomas, *The Art of War: Sun-tzu* (Boston: Shambhala, 1988).

This contains a selection of the traditional commentaries.

Giles, Lionel, *Sun Tzu on the Art of War* (London: Luzac, 1910).

Still considered the "standard" version by Joseph Needham in 1994. Marred by Giles's frequent and ill-tempered attacks on the unfortunate Captain Calthrop.

Griffith, Samuel B., *Sun Tzu: The Art of War* (Oxford: Clarendon Press, 1963).

Written by an ex–Marine Corps brigadier general, as a doctoral dissertation at Oxford, under the guidance of the eminent Chinese scholar Wu Shichang.

Lau, D. C., and Roger T. Ames, *Sun Pin, The Art of Warfare* (New York: Ballantine, 1996).

Lévi, Jean, *Sun Tzu, L'art de la Guerre* (Paris: Hachette, 2000).

Fascinating for its rich selection of accompanying texts and for its refreshing viewpoint.

Low, C. C., and Associates, *Sun Zi's Art of War* (Singapore: Canfonian, 1995).

Cartoon-style illustrated version, in four volumes, with countless historical examples of the Art of War, translated from the original published in China by Zhejiang People's Arts Publishing House, Hangzhou.

Machell-Cox, E., *Principles of War by Sun Tzu* (Colombo, Ceylon: Royal Air Force, 1943).

Sawyer, Ralph D., *The Complete Art of War: Sun Tzu, Sun Pin* (Boulder, Colo.: Westview Press, 1996).

Sui Yun, *Sunzi's Art of War* (Singapore: Asiapac, 1998).

One of the amusingly illustrated (by Wang Xuanming) titles in the Strategy and Leadership series, which also includes *The Thirty-six Stratagems.*

Tang Zichang, *Principles of Conflict: Recompilation and New English Translation with Annotation on Sun Zi's Art of War* (San Rafael, Calif.: T. C. Press, 1969). By a Nationalist (Kuo Min Tang) general.

Wing, R. L., *The Art of Strategy* (London: Thorsons, 1997).

Yuan Shibing, *Sun Tzu's Art of War: The Modern Chinese Interpretation by General Tao Hanzhang* (Kuala Lumpur, Malaysia: Eastern Dragon, 1991). Valuable for the commentary by Tao, a senior People's Liberation Army (PLA) general and veteran of the Long March. This is the translation reprinted in the Wordsworth Classics edition, edited with a stimulating introduction by Robert Wilkinson (Ware, England: Wordsworth, 1998).

Zhang Huimin, *Sunzi: The Art of War with Commentaries* (Peking: Panda Books, 1995). Interesting for the commentary by Xie Guoliang (another PLA general).

Other Books and Articles of Interest

Bonds, Ray, ed., *The Chinese War Machine* (London: Salamander, 1979). Out of date, but for its time a well-documented and richly illustrated portrait of the Chinese military.

Chaliand, Gérard, ed., *The Art of War in World History* (Berkeley: University of California Press, 1994). An encyclopedic compendium, translated from the French. Includes the Giles version of Master Sun (pp. 221–38).

Cleary, Thomas, trans., *Mastering the Art of War: Zhuge Liang and Liu Ji* (Boston: Shambhala, 1989).

Cowan, Connell, and Gail Parent, *The Art of War for Lovers* (New York: Pocket Books, 1998). Deals with such questions as "Why deception can be an important positive force in romance."

Deacon, Richard, *The Chinese Secret Service* (rev. ed., London: Grafton Books, 1989). Chapter 2 deals with Master Sun on espionage and "his far-reaching grasp of the essentials of national security."

Jenner, W. J. F., *The Tyranny of History* (London: Penguin, 1994). An angry historian's Swiftian pamphlet, aimed at the heart of China's darkness.

Jullien, François, *Traité de l'efficacité* (Paris: Grasset, 1997). Brilliant postmodern French philosophical treatment of ideas from Master Sun and other early strategic thinkers, side by side with the early Greeks.

Khoo Kheng-hor, *Sun Tzu & Management* (Selangor, Malaysia: Pelanduk, 1992).

Kierman, Frank A., Jr., and John K. Fairbank, eds., *Chinese Ways in Warfare* (Cambridge, Mass.: Harvard University Press, 1974).

Lau, D. C., "Some Notes on the *Sun-tzu,*" *Bulletin of the School of Oriental and African Studies* (1965:28:2), pp. 318–35.

Lévy, André, trans., *Le Sublime Discours de la Fille Candide* (Arles: Picquier, 2000).

Lewis, Mark Edward, *Sanctioned Violence in Early China* (Albany: State University of New York Press, 1990).

McNeilly, Mark, *Sun Tzu and the Art of Business* (New York: Oxford University Press, 1996).

Needham, Joseph, and Robin Yates (with Krzysztof Gawlikowski, Edward McEwen, and Wang Ling), *Science and Civilisation in China,* vol. 5, part VI: *Military Technology* (Cambridge: Cambridge University Press, 1994).
Contains one of the most intelligent summaries of the ideas of Master Sun and other strategic thinkers of early times (pp. 1–100).

Sawyer, Ralph, *Unorthodox Strategies for the Everyday Warrior* (Boulder, Colo.: Westview Press, 1996).
A translation of the (?Yuan-Ming) work *Baizhan qilüe,* largely an exposition of ideas from the main *bingfa* classics.

Seagrave, Sterling, *Lords of the Rim* (London: Corgi Books, 1996).
Fascinating study of the Overseas Chinese. Frequent references to Master Sun, the "role model for every ambitious Overseas Chinese."

van Gulik, Robert, *Erotic Colour Prints of the Ming Period, with an Essay on Chinese Sex Life from the Han to the Ch'ing Dynasty* (Tokyo: Privately published, 1951).
The lengthy "Historical Survey of Erotic Literature" contains full translations of selections from the sex handbooks, which were couched in the language of military treatises.

Yates, Robin D. S. "New Light on Ancient Chinese Military Texts," *T'oung Pao* (1988:64), pp. 211–48.

Books in Chinese

Bingshu sizhong zhuzi suoyin (Hong Kong: Commercial Press, 1992).
Invaluable concordance to four classics: *Master Sun's Art of War, Master Weiliao, Master Wu,* and *The Marshal's Treatise.* Produced by the Institute

of Chinese Studies of the Chinese University of Hong Kong, under the general editorship of D. C. Lau and Chen Fong Ching.

Shiyijia zhu Sunzi fu jinyi (Hong Kong: Zhonghua, 1973; reprint of 1985).
A convenient modern edition of the traditional eleven commentaries, with *baihua* translation of the main text by Guo Huaruo (see below).

Sunzi shijia zhu (Shanghai: Zhonghua, ?1927).
This is the Sibu beiyao edition, based on Sun Xingyan. My copy belonged to Neville Whymant and has the Giles translation interleaved with the Chinese text.

Guo Huaruo, *Sunzi yizhu* (Shanghai: Guji, 1984).
Recent revised reprint of 1957 *baihua* translation and annotated text by veteran Communist military strategist and general (born 1907), graduate of Whampoa Military Academy. Guo was a staff officer in the Red Army in Jiangxi in 1931. His Master Sun researches began in 1939 with a study published in the military journal *Junzheng zazhi*. This was adopted for use as a military textbook in Communist-controlled areas.

Li Ling, *Wu Sunzi fawei* (Peking: Zhonghua, 1997).
Incorporates the latest findings (readings, fragmentary extra materials, etc.) from the excavations of the 1970s. Each chapter has a *baihua* translation and illuminating notes.

Li Ling, *Sunzi guben yanjiu* (Peking: Peking University, 1995).
Collection of scholarly essays relating to various aspects of Master Sun.

Liu Yin, ed., *Wujing qishu zhijie* (Changsha: Yueli, 1992).
Convenient modern reprint of Ming-dynasty annotated version of Seven Military Classics, with appended essay, "How to Read the Military Classics."

Niu Guoping and Wang Fucheng, *Sunzi shiyi fu yundu* (Lanzhou: Gansu Renmin, 1991).
Modern edition with notes and translation. Especially interesting for its appendix with rhyme schemes.

Wu Jiulong, et al., eds., *Sunzi jiaoshi* (Peking: Junshi, 1990).
Well-annotated text, with *baihua* translation, incorporating much modern archaeological research. An appendix contains complete translations into English, French, Russian, Japanese, and Italian.

Wu Renjie, *Xinyi Sunzi duben* (Taipei: Sanmin, 1996).

A List of Chinese Commentators

and of Other Authorities Referred to
by Commentators

Pre-Qin philosophers are often called "Master So-and-so." In Chinese this is indicated by the suffix *zi* (*tzu* in the old Wade-Giles spelling). So Master Sun is Sunzi or Sun Tzu. The eleven commentators in the traditional canon are indicated by an asterisk (*). Entries are arranged alphabetically within each section and period, unless otherwise stated.

Traditional (Pre-Tang)

Cao Cao (155–220):* The famous general of the Three Kingdoms period and founder of the Wei dynasty. See Giles, pp. xxxv–xxxvi: "One of the greatest military geniuses that the world has seen, and Napoleonic in the scale of his operations, he was especially famed for the marvellous rapidity of his marches, which has found expression in the line 'Talk of Cao Cao, and Cao Cao will appear.' [cf. Talk of the devil . . .] According to Ouyang Xiu (Song dynasty), 'It is recorded that whenever a council of war was held by Wei on the eve of a far-reaching campaign, Cao Cao had all his calculations ready [cf. Master Sun, Chapter 1]; those generals who made use of them did not lose one battle in ten; those who ran counter to them in any particular saw their armies incontinently beaten and put to flight.' His commentary is frequently obscure; it furnishes a clue, but does not fully develop the meaning. His notes are models of brief austerity. Sometimes owing to extreme compression, they are scarcely intelligible, and stand no less in need of commentary than the text itself."

Lord Yellow Stone: Legendary figure, supposed author of *The Three Strata-gems (San lüe),* one of the Seven Military Classics (see page xli). *Records of the Grand Historian,* Chapter 55, tells the story of how Zhang Liang received a treatise from a mysterious old man, whom he met thirteen years later in the form of a yellow stone. . . . It was this treatise that enabled Zhang to help Liu Bang establish the Han dynasty.

Master Wang: No longer extant, but quoted in commentaries.

Master Weiliao (?fourth century B.C.**):** According to legend, studied under the famous Master of Spirit Valley.

Master Wu, Wu Qi (d. 381 B.C.**):** See *Master Wu's Art of War.*

Meng:* Nothing is known of him, except that he lived during the Liang dynasty (502–57).

Tang Dynasty (618–907)

Chen Hao:* Contemporary of Du Mu.

Du Mu (803–52):* Famous poet, who ended his official career as a secretary in the Grand Council. Despite his popular image as a writer of lyrical verse and a "drifter in the blue houses" (brothels) of Yangzhou, he was genuinely interested in military and political affairs all his life.

Du You (735–812):* Rose to be President of the Board of Works and Grand Guardian. Author of an encyclopedic treatise on the constitution, *Tongdian,* from which his notes on Master Sun are taken. He often repeats Cao and Meng and possibly quotes from the no-longer-extant Master Wang. His notes were added to the previous canon of ten commentators by Ji Tianbao in the Song dynasty. Grandfather of Du Mu.

Jia Lin:* Little is known about this commentator.

Li Jing (571–649): Famous general of the early Tang dynasty.

Li Quan (eighth century):* Li regularly uses anecdotes from Chinese history. He was himself the author of various works on warfare.

Song Dynasty (960–1279)

It is no accident that the four Song commentators come from the same period. They lived in the aftermath of Zhao Yuanhao's Tangut rebellion
(1034–43), when "the Court made strenuous enquiry for men skilled in war,
and military topics became the vogue amongst all the high officials." It was
the Emperor Shengzong of the Song dynasty (r. 1068–85) who designated
the Seven Military Classics for official study.

He Yanxi:* Chiefly remarkable for the extensive extracts he gives, in
adapted form, from the dynastic histories and other sources.

Ji Tianbao (late Northern Song, ca. 1100): Responsible for the edition
with ten commentators that remained widely accepted as a standard
text until the nineteenth century.

Mei Yaochen (1002–60):* Well-known poet, famous for the breadth of his
subject matter and his quality of *pingdan,* "plainness" or *fadeur.*

Wang Xi:* According to Wu Jiulong (1990), Wang consulted rare old texts
for his commentary.

Zhang Yu:* His commentary is often an expansion and elucidation of Cao
Cao's. Giles (p. xl): "Without Zhang Yu, it is safe to say that much of
Cao Cao's commentary would have remained cloaked in its pristine ob-
scurity and therefore valueless."

Ming Dynasty (1368–1644)

Liu Yin (fl. 1371): Editor of the *Wujing qishu zhijie,* an annotated version of
the Seven Military Classics.

Qing Dynasty (1644–1911)

Bi Yixun: Author of the *Sunzi xulu* (Citations from Master Sun), an important collection of materials relating to Master Sun.

Sun Xingyan (1753–1818): A prominent scholar and bibliophile, who compiled the standard Qing-dynasty edition of Master Sun's *Art of War* with the traditional commentators.

Chronologies

Dynasties

SUI	581–618
TANG	618–907
FIVE DYNASTIES	907–960
LIAO	916–1125
SONG	960–1279
Northern Song	960–1126
Southern Song	1115–1234
JIN (Jurched)	1115–1234
YUAN (Mongol)	1260–1368
MING	1368–1644
QING (Manchu)	1644–1911

Historical Events

Below are some important events in early Chinese history until the end of the period of the Three Kingdoms. Dates given are based on Jacques Gernet, *Chinese Civilisation* (Cambridge, 1982).

B.C.

771	Western Zhou leave capital in valley of Wei, and make their residence in Luoyang.
722	First year of *Spring and Autumn Annals.*
704	Expansion of southern kingdom of Chu (present-day Hunan and Hubei).
667	Beginning of hegemony of state of Qi (present-day Shandong).
632	Hegemony of Jin (present-day Shanxi).
597	King Zhuang of Chu recognized as leader of confederacy.
589	Major battle between states of Qi and Jin.
ca. 551	Birth of Confucius.
ca. 544	Birth of Sun Wu, Master Sun.
506	Offensive by Wu against Chu. Wu occupies Ying, capital of Chu.
ca. 496	Death of Master Sun. Death of He Lü, king of Wu.
494	Kingdom of Yue recognizes Wu as overlord.
481	End of Spring and Autumn period.
ca. 479	Death of Confucius. Birth of Master Mo.

473	Wu crushed by Yue, under Gou Jian. Death of the Wu king, Fu Chai, son of He Lü.
453	Division of Jin into three states of Han, Wei, and Zhao. Some consider this the start of Warring States period.
445	Expansion eastward of state of Chu, at expense of Wu.
ca. 430	Birth of Master Wu (Wu Qi).
ca. 381	Death of Master Mo. Death of Master Wu.
ca. 380	Birth of Sun Bin ("Cripple" Sun), author of Sun Bin's *Art of War.*
ca. 371	Birth of Mencius.
361	Lord Shang arrives in Qin and begins Legalist reforms.
354–51	Siege of Handan, capital of Zhao (in southwestern Hebei Province).
341	Battle of Maling.
338	Execution of Lord Shang.
334	Chu absorbs Yue (lower Yangtze and northern Zhejiang).
325	Prince of Qin takes title of king.
ca. 316	Death of Sun Bin.
ca. 300	Death of Taoist philosopher Master Zhuang.
ca. 289	Death of Mencius.
279	Tian Dan of Qi defeats Yan force at Jimo.
278–77	Qin expands at expense of Chu in Hubei and Hunan.
270	Qin attacks Han and is routed by Zhao.
259–57	Qin besieges Handan, capital of Zhao.
257	Death of Bo Qi, Qin general.
256	Qin puts an end to royal house of Zhou.
246	Accession of King Zheng of Qin, later to become first Emperor of Qin dynasty.
230–21	Qin annexes Han, Zhao, Wei, Chu, Yan, and Qi.
227	Jing Ke's unsuccessful assassination attempt on future first Emperor.
221	Foundation of Qin Empire.
220	Reconstruction of Great Walls, begun about 300 B.C.
210	Death of first Emperor.
207	Assassination of second Emperor.
206	End of Qin dynasty. Founding of Former or Western Han, capital at Chang'an.
203	Xiang Yu (king of Chu) and Liu Bang (king of Han) divide the kingdom. Han Xin's exploits as Liu Bang's general.

202	Liu Bang eliminates Xiang Yu and is proclaimed Emperor of Han.
179	Accession of Emperor Wen of Han.
141	Accession of Emperor Wu of Han.
122	Death of Liu An, Master of Huainan.
122–109	Expansion of the Han toward the south.
ca. 92	Death of Sima Qian, author of *Historical Records*.
87	Death of Emperor Wu.
73	Accession of Emperor Xuan.
48	Accession of Emperor Yuan.
32	Accession of Emperor Cheng.
6	Accession of Emperor Ai.

A.D.

9–25	Wang Mang's short-lived Xin dynasty. Founding of Latter or Eastern Han dynasty, capital at Luoyang.
27–28	Rebellion of Red Eyebrows.
ca. 125	Han begin to reestablish domination of Central Asia.
157	Census: 56,486,856 individuals.
169	Great Chinese victory over the proto-Tibetan Qiang.
184	Rebellion of Yellow Turbans.
189	Sack of Luoyang by Dong Zhuo.
190	Beginning of power of Cao Cao.
201	Cao Cao virtual master of North China.
208	Alliance between Liu Bei (Shu/Han) and Sun Quan (in lower Yangtze) against Cao Cao. Battle of Red Cliff, on the Yangtze, in which Cao Cao is defeated.
220	Death of Cao Cao. His son Cao Pei becomes first Emperor of Wei. End of Han dynasty.
221	Liu Bei proclaimed Emperor of Shu/Han in Western China.
222	Sun Quan proclaimed Emperor of Wu. Beginning of period of Three Kingdoms.
223	Death of Liu Bei.
234	Death of Zhuge Liang, strategic adviser to Shu/Han.
249	Coup d'état by Sima Yi in Wei.
263	End of Shu/Han (annexed by Wei).
265	Sima Yan founds Jin dynasty at Luoyang.

THE ART OF WAR

孫

子

Chapter One

Making of Plans

Master Sun said:

> War is
> A grave affair of state;
> It is a place
> Of life and death,
> A road
> To survival and extinction,
> A matter
> To be pondered carefully.

There are Five Fundamentals
    For this deliberation,
    For the making of comparisons
    And the assessing of conditions:
    The Way,
    Heaven,
    Earth,
    Command,
    Discipline.

The Way
    Causes men
    To be of one mind
    With their rulers,

To live or die with them,
And never to waver.

Heaven is
Yin and Yang,
Cold and hot,
The cycle of seasons.

Earth is
Height and depth,
Distance and proximity,
Ease and danger,
Open and confined ground,
Life and death.

Command is
Wisdom,
Integrity,
Compassion,
Courage,
Severity.

Discipline is
Organization,
Chain of command,
Control of expenditure.

Every commander is aware
Of these
Five Fundamentals.
He who grasps them
Wins;
He who fails to grasp them
Loses.

For this deliberation,
    For the making of comparisons,
    And the assessing of conditions,
    Discover:

    Which ruler
    Has the Way?

    Which general
    Has the ability?

    Which side has
    Heaven and Earth?

    On which side
    Is discipline
    More effective?

    Which army
    Is the stronger?

    Whose officers and men
    Are better trained?

    In which army
    Are rewards and punishments
    Clearest?

From these
    Can be known
    Victory and defeat.

Heed my plan,
    Employ me,
    And victory is surely yours;
    I will stay.

Do not heed my plan,
    And even if you did employ me,
    You would surely be defeated;
    I will depart.

Settle on the best plan,
    Exploit the dynamic within,
    Develop it without,

Follow the advantage,
    And master opportunity:
    This is the dynamic.

The Way of War is
    A Way of Deception.

    When able,
    Feign inability;

    When deploying troops,
    Appear not to be.

    When near,
    Appear far;

    When far,
    Appear near.

Lure with bait;

Strike with chaos.

If the enemy is full,
Be prepared.
If strong,
Avoid him.

If he is angry,
Disconcert him.

If he is weak,
Stir him to pride.

If he is relaxed,
Harry him;

If his men are harmonious,
Split them.

Attack
Where he is
Unprepared;
Appear
Where you are
Unexpected.

This is
Victory in warfare;
It cannot be
Divulged
In advance.

Victory belongs to the side
    That scores most
    In the temple calculations
    Before battle.
Defeat belongs to the side
    That scores least
    In the temple calculations
    Before battle.
Most spells victory;
    Least spells defeat;
    None, surer defeat.
I see it in this way,
    And the outcome is apparent.

Chapter Two

Waging of War

Master Sun said:

In War,
    For an army of
    One thousand
    Four-horse swift chariots,
    One thousand
    Hide-armored wagons,
    For one hundred thousand
    Mail-clad soldiers,
    With provisions for
    Four hundred miles;
Allowing for
    Expenses at home and at the front,
    Dealings with envoys and advisers;
    Glue and lacquer,
    Repairs to chariots and armor;
    The daily cost of all this
    Will exceed
    One thousand taels of silver.

In War,
    Victory should be
    Swift.
    If victory is slow,

Men tire,
Morale sags.
Sieges
Exhaust strength;
Protracted campaigns
Strain the public treasury.

If men are tired,
Morale low,
Strength exhausted,
Treasure spent;
Then the feudal lords
Will exploit the disarray
And attack.
This even the wisest
Will be powerless
To mend.

I have heard that in war
Haste can be
Folly
But have never seen
Delay that was
Wise.

No nation has ever benefited
From a protracted war.

Without a full understanding of
The harm
Caused by war,
It is impossible to understand

The most profitable way
Of conducting it.

The Skillful Warrior
    Never conscripts troops
    A second time;
    Never transports provisions
    A third.

    He brings equipment from home
    But forages off the enemy.
    And so his men
    Have plenty to eat.

Supplying an army
    At a distance
    Drains the public coffers
    And impoverishes
    The common people.

Where an army is close at hand,
    Prices rise;
    When prices rise,
    The common people
    Spend all they have;
    When they spend all,
    They feel the pinch of
    Taxes and levies.

Strength is depleted
    On the battlefield;
    Families at home
    Are destitute.

The common people
    Lose seven-tenths
    Of their wealth.
    Six-tenths of the public coffers
    Are spent
    On broken chariots,
    Worn-out horses,
    Armor and helmets,
    Crossbows and arrows,
    Spears and bucklers,
    Lances and shields,
    Draft animals,
    Heavy wagons.

So a wise general
    Feeds his army
    Off the enemy.
    One peck
    Of enemy provisions
    Is worth twenty
    Carried from home;
    One picul
    Of enemy fodder
    Is worth twenty
    Carried from home.

The killing of an enemy
    Stems from
    Wrath;
The fighting for booty
    Stems from
    A desire for reward.

In chariot fighting,
>   When more than ten
>   Enemy chariots are captured,
>   The man to take the first
>   Should be rewarded.

Change the enemy's
>   Chariot flags and standards;
>   Mingle their chariots
>   With ours.

Treat prisoners of war kindly,
>   And care for them.
>   Use victory over the enemy
>   To enhance your own strength.

In War,
>   Prize victory,
>   Not a protracted campaign.

The wise general
>   Is a Lord of Destiny;
>   He holds the nation's
>   Peace or peril
>   In his hands.

Chapter Three

Strategic Offensive

Master Sun said:

In War,
    Better take
    A state
    Intact
    Than destroy it.

Better take
    An army,
    A regiment,
    A detachment,
    A company,
    Intact
    Than destroy them.

Ultimate excellence lies
    Not in winning
    Every battle
    But in defeating the enemy
    Without ever fighting.
    The highest form of warfare
    Is to attack
    Strategy itself;

The next,
    To attack
    Alliances;

    The next,
    To attack
    Armies;

The lowest form of war is
    To attack
    Cities.
    Siege warfare
    Is a last resort.

In a siege,
    Three months are needed
    To assemble
    Protective shields,
    Armored wagons,
    And sundry
    Siege weapons and equipment;
    Another three months
    To pile
    Earthen ramps.

The general who cannot
    Master his anger
    Orders his troops out
    Like ants,
    Sending one in three
    To their deaths,
    Without taking the city.
    This is the calamity
    Of siege warfare.

The Skillful Strategist
    Defeats the enemy
    Without doing battle,
    Captures the city
    Without laying siege,
    Overthrows the enemy state
    Without protracted war.

He strives for supremacy
    Under heaven
    Intact,
    His men and weapons
    Still keen,
    His gain
    Complete.
    This is the method of
    Strategic attack.

In War,
    With forces ten
    To the enemy's one,
    Surround him;
    With five,
    Attack him;
    With two,
    Split in half.
    If equally matched,
    Fight it out;
    If fewer in number,
    Lie low;
    If weaker,
    Escape.

A small force
    Obstinately fighting
    Will be captured
    By a larger force.

The general is the prop
    Of the nation.
When the prop is solid,
    The nation is strong.
When the prop is flawed,
    The nation is weak.

A ruler can bring misfortune
    Upon his troops
    In three ways:

    Ordering them
    To advance
    Or to retreat
    When they should not
    Is called
    Hobbling the army;

    Ignorant interference
    In military decisions
    Confuses
    Officers and men;

    Ignorant meddling
    In military appointments
    Perplexes
    Officers and men.

When an army is confused and perplexed,
>The feudal princes
>Will cause trouble;
>>This creates
>Chaos in the ranks
>And gives away
>Victory.

There are Five Essentials
>For victory:

>Know when to fight
>And when not to fight;

>Understand how to deploy
>Large and small
>Numbers;

>Have officers and men who
>Share a single will;

>Be ready
>For the unexpected;

>Have a capable general,
>Unhampered by his sovereign.

These five
>Point the way to
>Victory.

Hence the saying
    "Know the enemy,
    Know yourself,
    And victory
    Is never in doubt,
    Not in a hundred battles."

    He who knows self
    But not the enemy
    Will suffer one defeat
    For every victory.

    He who knows
    Neither self
    Nor enemy
    Will fail
    In every battle.

Chapter Four

Forms and Dispositions

Master Sun said:

Of old,
    The Skillful Warrior
    First ensured
    His own
    Invulnerability;
    Then he waited for
    The enemy's
    Vulnerability.

Invulnerability rests
    With self;
    Vulnerability,
    With the enemy.

The Skillful Warrior
    Can achieve
    His own
    Invulnerability;
    But he can never bring about
    The enemy's
    Vulnerability.

Hence the saying
 "One can know
 Victory
 And yet not achieve it."

Invulnerability is
 Defense;
 Vulnerability is
 Attack.

Defense implies
 Lack;
 Attack implies
 Abundance.

A Skillful Defender
 Hides beneath
 The Ninefold Earth;
 A Skillful Attacker
 Moves above
 The Ninefold Heaven.

Thus they achieve
 Protection
And victory
 Intact.

To foresee
 The ordinary victory
 Of the common man
 Is no true skill.

To be victorious in battle
    And to be acclaimed
    For one's skill
    Is no true
    Skill.

To lift autumn fur
    Is no
    Strength;
To see sun and moon
    Is no
    Perception;
To hear thunder
    Is no
    Quickness of hearing.

The Skillful Warrior of old
    Won
    Easy victories.

The victories
    Of the Skillful Warrior
    Are not
    Extraordinary victories;
    They bring
    Neither fame for wisdom
    Nor merit for valor.

His victories
    Are
    Flawless;
His victory is
    Flawless

Because it is
Inevitable;
He vanquishes
An already defeated enemy.

The Skillful Warrior
Takes his stand
On invulnerable ground;
He lets slip no chance
Of defeating the enemy.

The victorious army
Is victorious first
And seeks battle later;
The defeated army
Does battle first
And seeks victory later.

The Skillful Strategist
Cultivates
The Way
And preserves
· The law;
Thus he is master
Of victory and defeat.

In War,
There are Five Steps:

Measurement,
Estimation,
Calculation,
Comparison,
Victory.

Earth determines
    Measurement;
    Measurement determines
    Estimation;
    Estimation determines
    Calculation;
    Calculation determines
    Comparison;
    Comparison determines
    Victory.

A victorious army
    Is like a pound weight
    In the scale against
    A grain;
A defeated army
    Is like a grain
    In the scale against
    A pound weight.

A victorious army
    Is like
    Pent-up water
    Crashing
    A thousand fathoms
    Into a gorge.

This is all
    A matter of
    Forms and
    Dispositions.

Chapter Five

Potential Energy

Master Sun said:

Managing many
    Is the same as
    Managing few;
    It is a question of
    Division.

Fighting with many
    Is the same as
    Fighting with few;
    It is a matter of
    Marshaling men
    With gongs,
    Identifying them
    With flags.

With a combination of
    Indirect and
    Direct,
    An army
    Can hold off the enemy
    Undefeated.

With an understanding of
    Weakness and
    Strength,
    An army
    Can strike
    Like a millstone
    Cast at an egg.

In warfare,
    Engage
    Directly;
    Secure victory
    Indirectly.

The warrior skilled
    In indirect warfare
    Is infinite
    As Heaven and Earth,
    Inexhaustible
    As river and sea,
    He ends and begins again
    Like sun and moon,
    Dies and is born again
    Like the Four Seasons.

There are but
    Five notes,
    And yet their permutations
    Are more
    Than can ever be heard.

There are but
    Five colors,
    And yet their permutations

Are more
Than can ever be seen.

There are but
    Five flavors,
    And yet their permutations
    Are more
    Than can ever be tasted.

In the dynamics of War,
    There are but these two—
    Indirect
    And direct—
    And yet their permutations
    Are inexhaustible.
    They give rise to each other
    In a never-ending,
    Inexhaustible circle.

A rushing torrent
    Carries boulders
    On its flood;
    Such is the energy
    Of its momentum.

A swooping falcon
    Breaks the back
    Of its prey;
    Such is the precision
    Of its timing.

The Skillful Warrior's energy is
 Devastating;
 His timing,
 Taut.

His energy is like
 A drawn crossbow,
 His timing like
 The release of a trigger.

In the tumult of battle,
 The struggle may seem
 Pell-mell,
 But there is no disorder;
 In the confusion of the melee,
 The battle array may seem
 Topsy-turvy,
 But defeat is out of the question.

Disorder is founded
 On order;
 Fear,
 On courage;
 Weakness,
 On strength.

Orderly disorder
 Is based on
 Careful division;
 Courageous fear,
 On potential energy;
 Strong weakness,
 On troop dispositions.

The warrior skilled at
    Stirring the enemy
    Provides a visible form,
    And the enemy is sure to come.
    He proffers the bait,
    And the enemy is sure
    To take it.
    He causes the enemy
    To make a move
    And awaits him
    With full force.

The Skillful Warrior
    Exploits
    The potential energy;
    He does not hold his men
    Responsible.
He deploys his men
    To their best
    But relies on
    The potential energy.

Relying on the energy,
    He sends his men into battle
    Like a man
    Rolling logs or boulders.
    By their nature,
    On level ground
    Logs and boulders
    Stay still;
    On steep ground
    They move;
    Square, they halt;

Round, they roll.
Skillfully deployed soldiers
Are like round boulders
Rolling down
A mighty mountainside.

These are all matters
    Of potential energy.

Chapter Six

Empty and Full

Master Sun said:

First on the battlefield
    Waits for the enemy
    Fresh.

Last on the battlefield
    Charges into the fray
    Exhausted.

The Skillful Warrior
    Stirs
    And is not stirred.

    He lures his enemy
    Into coming
    Or obstructs him
    From coming.

    Exhaust
    A fresh enemy;
    Starve
    A well-fed enemy;
    Unsettle
    A settled enemy.

Appear at the place
    To which he must hasten;
    Hasten to the place
    Where he least expects you.

March hundreds of miles
    Without tiring,
    By traveling
    Where no enemy is.

Be sure of victory
    By attacking
    The undefended.

Be sure of defense
    By defending
    The unattacked.

The Skillful Warrior attacks
    So that the enemy
    Cannot defend;
    He defends
    So that the enemy
    Cannot attack.

Oh, subtlety of subtleties!
    Without form!
Oh, mystery of mysteries!
    Without sound!
    He is master of
    His enemy's fate.

He advances
  Irresistibly,
  Attacking emptiness.

He retreats,
  Eluding pursuit,
  Too swift
  To be overtaken.

If I wish to engage,
  Then the enemy,
  For all his high ramparts
  And deep moat,
  Cannot avoid the engagement;
  I attack that which
  He is obliged
  To rescue.

If I do not wish to engage,
  I can hold my ground
  With nothing more than a line
  Drawn around it.
  The enemy cannot
  Engage me
  In combat:
  I distract him
  In a different direction.

His form is visible,
  But I am
  Formless;
  I am concentrated,
  He is divided.

I am concentrated
    Into one;
    He is divided
    Into ten.
    I am
    Ten
    To his one;
    Many
    Against
    His few.

Attack few with many,
    And my opponent
    Will be weak.

The place I intend to attack
    Must not be known;
    If it is unknown,
    The enemy will have to
    Reinforce many places;
    The enemy will
    Reinforce many places,
    But I shall attack
    Few.

By reinforcing his vanguard,
    He weakens his rear;
By reinforcing his rear,
    He weakens his vanguard.
By reinforcing his right flank,
    He weakens his left;

By reinforcing his left,
    He weakens his right.
By reinforcing every part,
    He weakens every part.

Weakness
    Stems from
    Preparing against attack.
Strength
    Stems from
    Obliging the enemy
    To prepare against an attack.

If we know
    The place and the day
    Of the battle,
    Then we can engage
    Even after a march
    Of hundreds of miles.

But if neither day
    Nor place
    Is known,
    Then left cannot
    Help right,
    Right cannot
    Help left,
    Vanguard cannot
    Help rear,
    Rear cannot
    Help vanguard.
    It is still worse

If the troops
Are separated
By a dozen miles
Or even by a mile or two.

According to my assessment,
    The troops of Yue
    Are many,
    But that will avail them little
    In the struggle.
    So I say
    Victory
    Is still possible.

The enemy may be many,
    But we can prevent
    An engagement.

Scrutinize him,
    Know the flaws
    In his plans.

Rouse him,
    Discover the springs
    Of his actions.

Make his form visible,
    Discover his grounds
    Of death and life.

Probe him,
    Know his strengths
    And weaknesses.

The highest skill
    In forming dispositions
    Is to be without form;
    Formlessness
    Is proof against the prying
    Of the subtlest spy
    And the machinations
    Of the wisest brain.

Exploit the enemy's dispositions
    To attain victory;
    This the common man
    Cannot know.
    He understands
    The forms,
    The dispositions
    Of my victory;
    But not
    How I created the forms
    Of victory.

Victorious campaigns
    Are unrepeatable.
    They take form in response
    To the infinite varieties
    Of circumstance.

Military dispositions
    Take form like water.
    Water shuns the high
    And hastens to the low.
    War shuns the strong
    And attacks the weak.

Water shapes its current
    From the lie of the land.
The warrior shapes his victory
    From the dynamic of the enemy.

War has no
    Constant dynamic;
    Water has no
    Constant form.

Supreme military skill lies
    In deriving victory
    From the changing circumstances
    Of the enemy.

Among the Five Elements
    There is no one
    Constant supremacy.
The Four Seasons
    Have no
    Fixed station;
There are long days
    And short;
    The moon
    Waxes
    And it
    Wanes.

Chapter Seven

The Fray

Master Sun said:

In War,
   The general
   Receives orders
   From his sovereign,
   Assembles troops,
   And forms an army.
   He makes camp
   Opposite the enemy.
   The true difficulty
   Begins with
   The fray itself.

The difficulty of the fray
   Lies in making
   The crooked
   Straight
   And in making
   An advantage
   Of misfortune.

Take a roundabout route,
   And lure the enemy
   With some gain;

Set out after him,
    But arrive before him;
    This is to master
    The crooked
    And the straight.

The fray can bring
    Gain;
    It can bring
    Danger.

Throw your entire force
    Into the fray
    For some gain,
    And you may still
    Fail.

Abandon camp and
    Enter the fray
    For some gain,
    And you may lose
    Your equipment.

Order your men to
    Carry their armor
    And make forced march,
    Day and night,
    Without halting,
    March thirty miles
    At double speed
    For some gain,
    And you will lose
    All your commanders.

The most vigorous men
Will be in the vanguard;
The weakest,
In the rear.
One in ten
Will arrive.

March fifteen miles
For some gain,
And the commander
Of the vanguard
Will fall;
Only half the men
Will arrive.

March ten miles
For some gain,
And two in three men
Will arrive.

Without its equipment,
An army is lost;
Without provisions,
An army is lost;
Without base stores,
An army is lost.

Without knowing the plans
Of the feudal lords,
You cannot
Form alliances.

Without knowing the lie
    Of hills and woods,
    Of cliffs and crags,
    Of marshes and fens,
    You cannot
    March.

Without using local guides,
    You cannot
    Exploit
    The lie of the land.

War
    Is founded
    On deception;
    Movement is determined
    By advantage;
    Division and unity
    Are its elements
    Of Change.

Be rushing as a wind;
    Be stately as a forest;
Be ravaging as a fire;
    Be still as a mountain.
Be inscrutable as night;
    Be swift as thunder or lightning.

Plunder the countryside,
    And divide the spoil;
Extend territory,
    And distribute the profits.

Weigh the situation carefully
    Before making a move.

Victory belongs to the man
    Who can master
    The stratagem of
    The crooked
    And the straight.

This is the
    Art of the Fray.

The Military Primer says:

When ears do not hear,
    Use gongs and drums.
When eyes do not see,
    Use banners and flags.

Gongs and drums,
    Banners and flags
    Are the
    Ears and eyes
    Of the army.

With the army focused,
    The brave will not
    Advance alone,
    Nor will the fearful
    Retreat alone.

This is the Art of
    Managing Many.

In night fighting,
    Use torches and drums;
In daylight,
    Use banners and flags;
    So as to transform
    The ears and eyes
    Of the troops.

A whole fighting force
    Can be robbed
    Of its spirit;
A general
    Can be robbed
    Of his presence of mind.

The soldier's spirit
    Is keenest
    In the morning;
    By noon
    It has dulled;
    By evening
    He has begun
    To think of home.

The Skillful Warrior
    Avoids the keen spirit,
    Attacks the dull
    And the homesick;
    This is
    Mastery of Spirit.

He confronts chaos
    With discipline;
He treats tumult
    With calm.
    This is
    Mastery of Mind.

He meets distance
    With closeness;
He meets exhaustion
    With ease;
He meets hunger
    With plenty;
This is
    Mastery of Strength.

He does not intercept
    Well-ordered banners;
He does not attack
    A perfect formation.
This is
    Mastery of Change.

These are axioms
    Of the Art of War:
    Do not advance uphill.
    Do not oppose an enemy
    With his back to a hill.
    Do not pursue an enemy
    Feigning flight.
    Do not attack
    Keen troops.

Do not swallow
A bait.
Do not thwart
A returning army.

Leave a passage
For a besieged army.

Do not press
An enemy at bay.

This is
The Art of War.

Chapter Eight

The Nine Changes

Master Sun said:

In War,
    The general
    Receives orders
    From his sovereign,
    Then assembles troops
    And forms an army.

On intractable terrain,
    Do not encamp;
On crossroad terrain,
    Join forces with allies;
On dire terrain,
    Do not linger;
On enclosed terrain,
    Make strategic plans;
On death terrain,
    Do battle.

There are roads
    Not to take.
There are armies
    Not to attack.

There are towns
    Not to besiege.
There are terrains
    Not to contest.
There are ruler's orders
    Not to obey.

The general
    Who knows the gains
    Of the Nine Changes
    Understands War.

The general
    Ignorant of the gains
    Of the Nine Changes
    May know the lie of the land,
    But he will never reap
    The gain
    Of that knowledge.

The warrior
    Ignorant of the Art
    Of the Nine Changes,
    May know
    The Five Gains
    But will not get the most
    From his men.

The wise leader
    In his deliberations
    Always blends consideration
    Of gain
    And harm.

By tempering thoughts of
    Gain,
    He can accomplish
    His goal;

By tempering thoughts of
    Harm,
    He can extricate himself
    From calamity.

He reduces the feudal lords
    To submission
    By causing them
    Harm;

He wears them down
    By keeping them
    Constantly occupied;

He precipitates them
    With thoughts of
    Gain.

The Skillful Warrior
    Does not rely on the enemy's
    Not coming,
    But on his own
    Preparedness.

    He does not rely on the enemy's
    Not attacking,
    But on his own
    Impregnability.

There are Five Pitfalls
     For a general:

Recklessness,
     Leading to
     Destruction;
Cowardice,
     Leading to
     Capture;
A hot temper,
     Prone to
     Provocation;
A delicacy of honor,
     Tending to
     Shame;
A concern for his men,
     Leading to
     Trouble.

These Five Excesses
     In a general
     Are the
     Bane of war.

If an army is defeated
     And its general slain,
     It will surely be because of
     These Five Perils.
They demand the most
     Careful consideration.

Chapter Nine

On the March

Master Sun said:

In taking up position
    And confronting the enemy:

Cross mountains,
    Stay close to valleys;
    Camp high,
    And face the open;
    Fight downhill,
    Not up.
These are positions in
    Mountain warfare.

Cross rivers,
    Then keep a distance
    From them.
    If the enemy crosses a river
    Toward you,
    Do not confront him
    In midstream.
    Let half his troops cross
    Before you strike.
    If you wish to do battle,
    Do not confront the enemy

Close to the river.
Occupy high ground,
And face the open.
Do not advance
Against the flow.
These are positions in
River warfare.

Cross salt marshes
Rapidly;
Never linger.
If you must do battle
In a salt marsh,
Keep water plants
Close by
And trees
Behind you.
These are positions in
Salt marshes.

On level ground,
Occupy easy terrain.
Keep high land
To the right and rear:
Keep death in front
And life to the rear.
These are positions on
Level ground.

Observation of
These four types of positions
Enabled the Yellow Emperor
To defeat
The Four Emperors.

Armies prize high ground,
    Shun low;
    They esteem Yang,
    Avoid Yin.

Nurture life,
    Occupy solid ground.
    Your troops will thrive,
    Victory will be sure.

On mound,
    Hill,
    Bank,
    Or dike,
    Occupy the Yang,
    With high ground
    To right and rear.
Use the lie of the land
    To the troops' benefit.

When rains upstream
    Have swollen the river,
    Let the water subside
    Before crossing.

If you come to
    Heaven's Torrents,
    Heaven's Wells,
    Heaven's Prisons,
    Heaven's Nets,
    Heaven's Traps,
    Heaven's Cracks:

Quit such places
With all speed.
Do not go near them.
Keep well away,
Let the enemy
Go near them.
Keep them in front;
Let him have them
At his rear.

If you march by
    Ravine,
    Swamp,
    Reedy marshland,
    Mountain forest,
    Thick undergrowth:
    Beware,
    Explore them diligently.
    These are places
    Of ambush,
    Lairs for spies.

When the enemy is
    Close at hand
    And makes no move,
    He is counting on
    A strong position;

If he is
    At a distance
    And provokes battle,
    He wants his opponent
    To advance.

If he is
    On easy ground,
    He is luring us.

If trees move,
    He is coming.

If there are many screens
    In the grass,
    He wants
    To perplex us.

Birds rising in flight
    Are a sign
    Of ambush;

Beasts startled
    Are a sign
    Of surprise attack.

Dust high and peaking
    Is a sign
    Of chariots approaching;

Dust low and spreading
    Is a sign
    Of infantry approaching;

Dust in scattered strands
    Is a sign
    Of firewood's being collected;

Dust in drifting pockets
    Is a sign
    Of an army encamping.

Humble words, coupled with
    Increased preparations,
    Are a sign
    Of impending attack;

Strong words, coupled with
    An aggressive advance,
    Are a sign
    Of impending retreat.

Light chariots
    Emerging first
    On the wings
    Are a sign
    Of battle formation.

Words of peace,
    But no treaty,
    Are a sign
    Of a plot.

Much running about
    And soldiers parading
    Are a sign
    Of expectation.

Some men advancing
    And some retreating
    Are a sign
    Of a decoy.

Soldiers standing
    Bent on their spears
    Indicate great
    Hunger.

Bearers of water
    Drinking first
    Indicate great
    Thirst.

An advantage perceived,
    But not acted on,
    Indicates utter
    Exhaustion.

Birds gather
    On empty ground.

Shouting at night
    Is a sign
    Of fear.

Confusion among troops
    Is a sign
    That the general
    Is not respected.

Banners and flags moving
    Are a sign
    Of disorder.

If officers
    Are prone to anger,
    The men become weary.

If they feed
> Grain to their horses
> And meat to their men;

If they fail to
> Hang up their pots
> And do not
> Return to their quarters;
> Then they are
> At bay.

Men whispering together,
> Huddled in small groups,
> Are a sign
> Of disaffection.

Excessive rewards
> Are a sign
> Of desperation.

Excessive punishments
> Are a sign
> Of exhaustion.

If a general is by turns
> Tyrannical
> And in terror
> Of his own men,
> It is a sign of
> Supreme incompetence.

Envoys
> With words of conciliation
> Desire cessation.

Protracted, fierce
   Confrontation,
   With neither engagement
   Nor retreat,
   Must be regarded
   With great vigilance.

In War,
   Numbers
   Are not the issue.
It is a question of
   Not attacking
   Too aggressively.
   Concentrate your strength,
   Assess your enemy,
   And win the confidence of your men:
   That is enough.

Rashly underestimate your enemy,
   And you will surely be
   Taken captive.

Discipline troops
   Before they are loyal,
   And they will be
   Refractory
   And hard to put to good use.
   Let loyal troops
   Go undisciplined,
   And they will be altogether
   Useless.

Command them
    With civility,
    Rally them
    With martial discipline,
    And you will win their
    Confidence.

Consistent and effective orders
    Inspire obedience;
    Inconsistent and ineffective orders
    Provoke disobedience.

When orders are consistent
    And effective,
    General and troops
    Enjoy mutual trust.

Chapter Ten

Forms of Terrain

Master Sun said:

There are different forms of terrain:

>   Accessible terrain,
>   Entangling terrain,
>   Deadlock terrain,
>   Enclosed terrain,
>   Precipitous terrain,
>   Distant terrain.

"Accessible" means that
>   Both sides
>   Can come and go freely.
>   On accessible terrain,
>   He who occupies
>   High Yang ground
>   And ensures
>   His line of supplies
>   Will fight
>   To advantage.

"Entangling" means that
>   Advance is possible,
>   Withdrawal hard.

On entangling terrain,
If the enemy is unprepared,
Go out and defeat him.
But if he is prepared,
And our move fails,
It will be hard to retreat.
The outcome will not be
To our advantage.

"Deadlock" means that
Neither side finds it
Advantageous
To make a move.
On deadlock terrain,
Even if our enemy
Offers a bait,
We do not make a move;
We lure him out;
We retreat.
And when half his troops
Are out,
That is our moment
To strike.

On enclosed terrain,
If we occupy it first,
We must block it
And wait for the enemy.
If he occupies it first
And blocks it,
Do not go after him;
If he does not block it,
Then go after him.

On precipitous terrain,
    If we occupy it first,
    We should hold the Yang heights
    And wait for the enemy.
    If the enemy occupies it first,
    Do not go after him,
    But entice him out
    By retreating.

On distant terrain,
    When strengths are matched,
    It is hard to provoke battle,
    And an engagement
    Will not be advantageous.

These six constitute
    The Way of Terrain.
    It is the general's duty
    To study them diligently.

In War,
    The following are not
    Natural calamities,
    But the fault
    Of the general:

    Flight,
    Impotence,
    Decay,
    Collapse,
    Chaos,
    Rout.

If relative strengths are matched,
But one army faces another
Ten times its size,
The outcome is
Flight.

When troops are strong
But officers weak,
The result is
Impotence.

When officers are strong
But troops weak,
The result is
Decay.

When superior officers are angry
And insubordinate
And charge into battle
Out of resentment,
Before their general can judge
The likelihood of victory,
Then the outcome is
Collapse.

When the general is weak
And lacking in severity,
When his orders
Are not clear,
When neither officers nor men
Have fixed rules
And troops

Are slovenly,
The outcome is
Chaos.

When a general
    Misjudges his enemy
    And sends a lesser force
    Against a larger one,
    A weaker contingent
    Against a stronger one;
    When he fails to pick
    A good vanguard,
    The outcome is
    Rout.

These six constitute
    The Way of Defeat.
    It is the general's duty
    To study them diligently.

The form of the terrain
    Is the soldier's ally;

Assessment
    Of the enemy
    And mastery of victory;
    Calculating the difficulty,
    The danger,
    And the distance
    Of the terrain;
    These constitute the Way
    Of the Superior General.

He who knows this
     And practices it in battle
     Will surely be
     Victorious.
     He who does not know it
     And does not practice it
     Will surely be
     Defeated.

If an engagement is sure
     To bring victory,
     And yet the ruler
     Forbids it,
     Fight;
     If an engagement is sure
     To bring defeat,
     And yet the ruler
     Orders it,
     Do not fight.

He who advances
     Without seeking
     Fame,
     Who retreats
     Without escaping
     Blame,
     He whose one aim is
     To protect his people
     And serve his lord,
     This man is
     A Jewel of the Realm.

He regards his troops
    As his children,
    And they will go with him
    Into the deepest ravine.
He regards them
    As his loved ones,
    And they will stand by him
    Unto death.

If he is generous
    But cannot command,
If he is affectionate
    But cannot give orders,
If he is chaotic
    And cannot keep order,
Then his men
    Will be like
    Spoiled children,
    And useless.

If we know that our own troops
    Are capable of attacking
    But fail to see
    That the enemy
    Is not vulnerable,
    We have only
    Half of victory.

If we know that the enemy
    Is vulnerable
    But fail to see
    That our own troops

Are incapable of attacking,
We have only
Half of victory.

If we know that the enemy
Is vulnerable,
And know that our own troops
Are capable of attacking,
But fail to see
That the terrain
Is unfit for attack,
We still have only
Half of victory.

The Wise Warrior,
When he moves,
Is never confused;
When he acts,
Is never at a loss.

So it is said:
"Know the enemy,
Know yourself,
And victory
Is never in doubt,
Not in a hundred battles."

Know Heaven,
Know Earth,
And your victory
Is complete.

Chapter Eleven

The Nine Kinds of Ground

Master Sun said:

In War,
> There are
> Nine Kinds of Ground:

> Scattering ground,
> Light ground,
> Strategic ground,
> Open ground,
> Crossroad ground,
> Heavy ground,
> Intractable ground,
> Enclosed ground,
> Death ground.

When the feudal lords
> Fight on home territory,
> That is
> Scattering ground.

When an army enters
> Enemy territory,
> But not deeply,
> That is
> Light ground.

When the ground
      Offers advantage
      To either side,
      That is
      Strategic ground.

When each side
      Can come and go freely,
      That is
      Open ground.

When the ground
      Borders
      Three states
      And the first to take it
      Has mastery
      Of the empire,
      That is
      Crossroad ground.

When an army enters
      Enemy territory deeply
      And holds
      Several fortified towns
      In its rear,
      That is
      Heavy ground.

When an army travels through
      Mountains and forests,
      Cliffs and crags,
      Marshes and fens,
      Hard roads,

These are
Intractable ground.

Ground reached
   Through narrow gorges,
   Retreated from
   By twisting paths,
   Where a smaller force of theirs
   Can strike our larger one,
   That is
   Enclosed ground.

Ground where mere survival
   Requires
   A desperate struggle,
   Where without
   A desperate struggle
   We perish,
   That is
   Death ground.

On scattering ground,
   Do not fight.
On light ground,
   Do not halt.
On strategic ground,
   Do not attack.
On open ground,
   Do not block.
On crossroad ground,
   Form alliances.
On heavy ground,
   Plunder.

On intractable ground,
    Keep marching.
On enclosed ground,
    Devise stratagems.
On death ground,
    Fight.

The Skillful Warrior of old
    Could prevent
    The enemy's vanguard
    From linking with his rear,
    Large and small divisions
    From working together,
    Crack troops
    From helping poor troops,
    Officers and men
    From supporting one another.
    The enemy,
    Once separated,
    Could not
    Reassemble;
    Once united,
    Could not
    Act in concert.

When there was some gain
    To be had,
    He made a move;
    When there was none,
    He halted.

To the question
    "How should we confront
    An enemy,

Numerous and well arrayed,
    Poised to attack?"
My reply is
    "Seize something
    He cherishes,
    And he will do your will."

Speed
    Is the essence of War.
    Exploit the enemy's unpreparedness;
    Attack him unawares;
    Take an unexpected route.

The Way of Invasion is this:
    Deep penetration
    Brings cohesion;
    Your enemy
    Will not prevail.

Plunder fertile country
    To nourish your men.
    Cherish your troops,
    Do not wear them out.
    Nurture your energy;
    Concentrate it.

Move your men about;
    Devise stratagems
    That cannot be fathomed.
    Throw your men
    Where there is no escape,
    And they will die
    Rather than flee.

Men who have
Faced death
Can achieve anything;
They will give
Their last drop of strength,
Officers and men alike.

Troops in desperate straits
    Know no fear.
    Where there is no escape,
    They stand firm;
    When they have entered deep,
    They persist;
    When they see no hope,
    They fight.

They are alert
    Without needing
    Discipline;
    They act
    Without needing
    Instructions;
    They are devoted
    Without needing
    A compact;
    They are loyal
    Without needing
    Orders.

Forbid the consulting of omens,
    Cast out doubts,
    And they will go on
    To the death.

Our men have no excess
    Of worldly goods,
    And yet they do not
    Disdain wealth;
    They do not expect
    To live long,
    And yet they do not
    Disdain long life.

On the day
    They are ordered into battle,
    They sit up and weep,
    Wetting their clothes with their tears;
    They lie down and weep,
    Wetting their cheeks.

But throw them
    Where there is no escape,
    And they will fight
    With the courage
    Of the heroes
    Zhu and Gui.

The Skillful Warrior
    Deploys his troops
    Like the *shuairan* snake
    Found on Mount Heng.
    Strike its head,
    And the tail lashes back;
    Strike its tail,
    And the head fights back;
    Strike its belly,
    And both head and tail

Will attack you.
To the question
"Can an army be
Like the *shuairan* snake?"
I reply,
"Yes, it can."
Take the men of Wu
And the men of Yue.
They are enemies,
But if they cross a river
In the same boat
And encounter a wind,
They will help each other,
Like right hand and left.

It is not enough
 To tether horses
 And to bury
 Chariot wheels.

There must be a single courage
 Throughout:
 This is the Way
 To manage an Army.

Strong and weak,
 Both can serve,
 Thanks to the principle
 Of ground.

The Skillful Warrior
 Directs his army
 As if it were
 A single man.

He leaves it no choice
    But to obey.

It is the business of the general
    To be still
    And inscrutable,
    To be upright
    And impartial.

He must be able
    To keep his own troops
    In ignorance,
    To deceive their eyes
    And their ears.

He changes his ways
    And alters his plans
    To keep the enemy
    In ignorance.

He shifts camp
    And takes roundabout routes
    To keep the enemy
    In the dark.

He leads his men into battle
    Like a man
    Climbing a height
    And kicking away the ladder;
    He leads them
    Deep into the territory
    Of the feudal lords
    And releases the trigger.

He burns his boats,
He breaks his pots.
He is like a shepherd
Driving his sheep
This way and that;
No one knows
Where he is going.

He assembles his troops
    And throws them
    Into danger;
    This is the business
    Of the commander.

These things must be studied:
    The Variations
    Of the Nine Kinds of Ground;
    The Advantages
    Of Flexible Maneuver;
    The Principles
    Of Human Nature.

The Way of Invasion is this:
    Deep penetration
    Brings cohesion;
    Shallow penetration
    Brings scattering.

When you leave your own territory
    And lead your men
    Across the border,
    You enter dire terrain.

When there are lines of communication
>On all four sides,
>You are on
>Crossroad terrain.

When you penetrate deeply,
>You are on
>Heavy terrain.

When you penetrate superficially,
>You are on
>Light terrain.

When there are strongholds to your rear
>And narrow passes in front,
>You are on
>Enclosed terrain.

When there is no way out,
>You are on
>Death terrain.

On scattering ground,
>We unite the will of our men.

On light ground,
>We keep them connected.

On strategic ground,
>We bring up our rear.

On open ground,
>We see to our defenses.

On crossroad ground,
   We strengthen our alliances.

On heavy ground,
   We ensure continuity of supplies.

On intractable ground,
   We keep on the move.

On enclosed ground,
   We block the passes.

On death ground,
   We demonstrate
   The desperateness
   Of the situation.

It is in the soldier's nature that
   When surrounded,
   He resists;
   When all seems lost,
   He struggles on;
   When in danger,
   He obeys orders.

Without knowing the plans
   Of the feudal lords,
   You cannot
   Form alliances.

Without knowing the lie
   Of hills and woods,
   Of cliffs and crags,

Of marshes and fens,
    You cannot
    March.

Without using local guides,
    You cannot
    Exploit
    The lie of the land.

Ignorance of any one
    Of these points
    Is not characteristic
    Of the army of a great king.

When the army of a great king
    Attacks a powerful state,
    He does not allow the enemy
    To concentrate his forces.
    He overawes the enemy
    And undermines his alliances.

He does not strive
    To ally himself
    With all the other states;
He does not foster
    Their power;
He pursues
    His own secret designs,
    Overawing his enemies.
Thus he can capture
    The enemy's cities
    And destroy
    The enemy's state.

Distribute rewards
    Without undue respect for rules;
    Publish orders
    Without undue regard for precedent;

Deal with a whole army
    As if it were a single man.
    Apply them to their task
    Without words of explanation.
    Confront them with the advantage,
    But do not explain the danger.

Throw them into
    Perilous ground,
    And they will survive;
    Plunge them into
    Death ground,
    And they will live.

When a force
    Has fallen into danger,
    It can
    Snatch victory
    From defeat.

Success in war
    Lies in
    Scrutinizing
    Enemy intentions.
    And going with them.

Focus on the enemy,
    And from hundreds of miles
    You can kill their general.

This is
Success
Through cunning.

On the day
    You decide to attack,
    Close the passes,
    Destroy the tallies,
    Break off intercourse
    With envoys;
    Be firm in the temple council
    For the execution of
    Your plans.

If the enemy opens a door,
    Rush in.
    Seize what he holds dear,
    And secretly contrive
    An encounter.

Discard rules,
    Follow the enemy,
    To fight
    The decisive battle.

At first,
    Be like a maiden;
    When the enemy opens the door,
    Be swift as a hare;
    Your enemy will not
    Withstand you.

Chapter Twelve

Attack by Fire

Master Sun said:

> There are Five Ways to
> Attack by Fire.
>
> The first is to burn
> Men;
>
> The second is to burn
> Supplies;
>
> The third is to burn
> Equipment;
>
> The fourth is to burn
> Warehouses;
>
> The fifth is to burn
> Lines of communication.
>
> Attack by fire
> Requires means;
> The material
> Must be ready.

There is a season
    For making a fire;
    There are days
    For lighting a flame.

The proper season is
    When the weather is
    Hot and dry;

The proper days are
    When the moon is in
    Sagittarius,
    Pegasus,
    Crater,
    Corvus.
    These are the
    Four Constellations
    Of Rising Wind.

When attacking with fire,
    Adapt to
    These Five Changes of Fire:

If fire breaks out
    Within the enemy camp,
    Respond at once
    From without.

If fire breaks out
    But the enemy remains calm,
    Wait,
    Do not attack.
    Let the fire reach

Its height,
And follow up
If at all possible;
If not,
Wait.

If fire attack is possible
From without,
Do not wait
For fire to be started
Within;
Light
When the time is right.

When starting a fire,
Be upwind;
Never attack
From downwind.

A wind that rises
During the day
Lasts long;
A night wind
Soon fails.

In War,
Know these
Five Changes of Fire,
And be vigilant.

Fire
Assists an attack
Mightily.

Water
    Assists an attack
    Powerfully.

Water
    Can isolate,
    But it cannot
    Take away.

To win victory,
    To complete an objective,
    But not to follow through,
    Is a disastrous
    Waste.

Hence the saying
    "The enlightened ruler
    Considers deeply;
    The effective general
    Follows through."

Never move
    Except for gain;
Never deploy
    Except for victory;
Never fight
    Except in a crisis.

A ruler
    Must never
    Mobilize his men
    Out of anger;
    A general

Must never
Engage battle
Out of spite.

Move
    If there is gain;
Halt
    If there is no gain.

Anger
    Can turn to
    Pleasure;
Spite
    Can turn to
    Joy.
But a nation destroyed
    Cannot be
    Put back together again;
    A dead man
    Cannot be
    Brought back to life.

So the enlightened ruler
    Is prudent;
The effective general
    Is cautious.
This is the Way
    To keep a nation
    At peace
    And an army
    Intact.

Chapter Thirteen

Espionage

Master Sun said:

> Raising an army
> Of a hundred thousand men
> And marching them
> Three hundred miles
> Drains the pockets
> Of the common people
> And the public treasury
> To the daily sum of
> A thousand taels of silver.
> It causes commotion
> At home and abroad
> And sets countless men
> Tramping the highways
> Exhausted.
> It keeps seven hundred thousand families
> From their work.

> Two armies may
> Confront each other
> For several years,
> For a single
> Decisive battle.

It is callous
        To begrudge the expense of
        A hundred taels
        Of silver
        For knowledge
        Of the enemy's situation.

Such a miser is
        No commander of men,
        No support to his lord,
        No master of victory.

Prior information
        Enables wise rulers
        And worthy generals
        To move
        And conquer,
        Brings them success
        Beyond that of the multitude.

This information
        Cannot be obtained
        From spirits;
        It cannot be deduced
        By analogy;
        It cannot be calculated
        By measurement.

It can be obtained only
        From men,
        From those who know
        The enemy's dispositions.

There are Five Sorts of Spies:

> Local,
> Internal,
> Double,
> Dead, and
> Live.

When these five sorts of espionage
>Are in operation,
>No one knows
>The Way of it.
>It is called
>The Mysterious Skein,
>The Lord's Treasure.

Local spies
>Come from among our enemy's
>Fellow countrymen;

Internal spies,
>From among our enemy's
>Officials,

Double spies,
>From among our enemy's
>Own spies.

Dead spies
>Are those for whom
>We deliberately create
>False information;
>They then pass it on
>To the enemy.

Live spies
    Are those who return
    With information.

In the whole army,
    None should be closer
    To the commander
    Than his spies,
    None more highly rewarded,
    None more confidentially treated.

Without wisdom,
    It is impossible
    To employ spies.

Without humanity and justice,
    It is impossible
    To employ spies.

Without subtlety and ingenuity,
    It is impossible
    To ascertain
    The truth of their reports.

Subtlety of subtleties!
    Spies have
    Innumerable uses.

If confidential information
    Is prematurely divulged,
    Both spy and recipient
    Must be put to death.

In striking an army,
    In attacking a city,
    In killing an individual,
    It is necessary to know beforehand
    The names of the general
    And of his attendants,
    His aides,
    His doorkeepers,
    His bodyguards.
    Our spies must be instructed
    To discover all of these
    In detail.

Enemy spies,
    Come to spy on us,
    Must be sought out,
    Bribed,
    Won over,
    Well accommodated.
    Then they can be
    Employed as
    Double agents.

From the double agent
    We discover
    Local and internal spies.

From the double agent
    We learn how best
    To convey misinformation
    To the enemy.

From the double agent
    We know how and when
    To use
    Live spies.

The ruler
    Must know all five of these
    Sorts of spies;
    This knowledge must come
    From the double agent;
    So the double agent
    Must be
    Treated generously.

Of old,
    The rise of the Yin dynasty
    Was due to Yi Zhi,
    Who had served under the Xia;
    And the rise of the Zhou dynasty
    Was due to Lü Ya,
    Who had served under the Yin.

Only the enlightened ruler,
    The worthy general,
    Can use
    The highest intelligence
    For spying,
    Thereby achieving
    Great success.

Spies
Are a key element
In warfare.
On them depends
An army's
Every move.

THE ART OF WAR

with Commentary

Chapter One

Making of Plans

Cao Cao: Planning means choosing generals, assessing the enemy, surveying the terrain, counting troops, measuring distances, and knowing the lie of the land: all this takes place in the ceremonial temple.

Du Mu: Planning is all a matter of calculation, conducted in the ceremonial temple in terms of the Five Fundamentals listed below. We calculate our own strengths and weaknesses, and the enemy's, in terms of these Five Fundamentals, and from this calculation we can infer victory or defeat. Then, and only then, do we mobilize our troops. This is the most important stage of all in military strategy, and therefore occupies first place in the treatise.

Master Sun said:

Li Ling (1997): This formula, found in other early philosophical classics, points to the likelihood that the text of *The Art of War* was compiled by disciples of the Master.

War is
A grave affair of state;

***The Zuo Commentary*, Duke Cheng, Thirteenth Year:** The two grave affairs of state are Ritual and War.

It is a place
Of life and death,
A road
To survival and extinction,

A matter
To be pondered carefully.

Li Quan: War is an instrument of ill omen. It brings life and death, survival and extinction. A grave endeavor indeed, and one that men, alas, undertake too lightly.

Sun Bin's Art of War, **Chapter 2:**   Victory in war can restore a state that has perished, it can revive extinct lineages. But failure to gain victory can lose territory, it can bring danger to the altars. So war must be pondered carefully. The man who takes pleasure in war will perish. He who benefits from victory incurs dishonor. War is not a thing to be enjoyed. Victory is not something to benefit from.

The Way and Its Power, **Chapter 31:**   War and its weapons are instruments of misfortune. One who has the Way does not deal with them. They are not the instruments proper to the true gentleman, who uses them only as a last resort, esteeming instead peace and tranquillity. He sees no beauty in victory. To see beauty in victory is to rejoice in the killing of others.

The Book of Master Mo **(?479–?381 B.C.), Chapter 17, "Against Offensive War":**   Murdering one man is considered wrong and is punished with the death penalty. According to this argument, murdering ten men should be ten times more wrong and receive ten death penalties. And likewise with murdering a hundred men. The gentlemen of the world know these acts to be wrong. But the great wrong of attacking a state, *that* they do not find wrong but praise it and call it right. They are not even aware that it is wrong.

The Book of Mencius **(371–289 B.C.), I, xiv, 2–3:**   When men fight because of a struggle for a city, they slaughter men till the city is filled with them. This is like leading the monster of the land to devour human flesh. Death is not enough for such a crime. And so Skillful Warriors should suffer the highest punishment.

The Book of Mencius, **VII, ii, 4:**   There are men who say, "I am skillful at marshaling troops, I am a Skillful Warrior." They are great criminals. If the ruler of a state loves benevolence, he will have no enemy in the whole empire.

Translator: Or, as the poet Edward Young (1683–1765) expressed it in his poem "Love of Fame":

One to destroy, is murder by the law;
And gibbets keep the lifted hand in awe;
To murder thousands, takes a specious name,
War's glorious art, and gives immortal fame.

There are Five Fundamentals
  For this deliberation,
  For the making of comparisons
  And the assessing of conditions:
  The Way,
  Heaven,
  Earth,
  Command,
  Discipline.

Zhang Yu: The order here is clear. When troops are raised to put down an offending force, the ceremonial temple council first considers the compassion and good faith of the ruler [the Way]; next it looks into the favorable juncture or otherwise of the seasons [heaven]; then the ease or danger of the terrain [earth]. Once these three aspects have been thoroughly examined, the council proceeds to choose a general to take command of the campaign [command]. Finally, once the troops have crossed the border, the authority to give orders rests with the commanding general [discipline]. This is the correct order.

The Way
  Causes men
  To be of one mind
  With their rulers,
  To live or die with them,
  And never to waver.

Zhang Yu: Govern with compassion and good faith, with integrity [the Way] and righteousness, and the army will be of one mind, it will rejoice in its task. As *The Book of Changes* says [Hexagram 58, *Dui,* The Joyous]: Lead the people into danger with joy, and they will forget death.

Sun Bin's Art of War, Chapter 20:   What determines victory or defeat, is the Way.

The Way and Its Power, Chapter 32:   All under heaven will be drawn to the Way, as streams and torrents flow into a great river or sea.

The Book of Zhuangzi (fourth century B.C.), Chapter 12, "Heaven and Earth":   Look at distinctions in the light of the Way— and the duty of sovereign and subject will be clear. . . . The rulers of ancient times were without desire and the world was satisfied, they were without action and the Ten Thousand Things were transformed. They were deep and silent and the Hundred Clans were at rest.

The Book of Lord Shang (d. 338 B.C.), Chapter 10, "Methods of Warfare":   All methods of war must be based in successful government. With this, men will not contend with one another, and not contending, they will have no thought of self-interest, but will regard their ruler's interests as their own.

The Book of Master Huainan (ca. 179–122 B.C.), Chapter 15:   An army that has lost the Way is weak, but if it possesses the Way, it will be strong. If a general loses the Way, he will be powerless, but if he has the Way, he will be efficacious. If a country is imbued with the Way, it will abide; if it loses the Way, it will perish.

Guo Huaruo (1984):   The Way here refers to the politics of government as practiced by the ruling landlord class. The "men" are the laboring masses, the serfs and slaves. When the government is relatively enlightened, then the men and the government are of one mind and cooperate.

Translator: This is the first occurrence of the fundamental term *dao,* traditionally romanized as Tao, the Way. The word can have an almost infinite range of meanings. Every field of human endeavor (war, statesmanship, archery, calligraphy, to name the first four that leap to mind) has its Way. But every particularized, limited Way is also encompassed within a greater, cosmic Way, the Way of Heaven and Earth. So "the Way that can be spoken of is not the true Way" (the famous opening words of that wonderful Taoist work *The Way and Its Power,* Chapter 1). Here it is clear that we are talking of the Way of Good Government, where subjects can relate to their rulers as "having the Way." Despite the frequently repeated charge that Master Sun is an opportunist, a proponent of the "dirtiest form of statecraft, with unspeakable depths of duplicity" (see Griffith, p. 172, quoting James Murdoch's *History of Japan* [London, 1949]), it is to be noted that here, at the very beginning of the treatise attributed to him, pride of place is given to the Way, to the importance of the value system of any body politic when it contemplates war. It is debatable how much Master Sun's Way has in common with the mystical Way of *The Way and Its Power.* The great Qing-dynasty scholar Yu Yue (1821–1907) saw a close affinity between Master Sun and Taoism and affirmed the popular saying that the "writers of Military Treatises all had their source in *The Way and Its Power*" (Wu, 1990, p. 5). Master Sun is dealing with military success, and his Way of War is in a sense a knack, a skill, a "virtue" similar to the Taoist Way leading to spiritual "success." But here he is simply reminding his disciples that (empirically speaking) moral power bestows military power. In this respect he is echoed by Napoleon: "In war, moral considerations make up three quarters of the game; the real balance of power accounts only for the remaining quarter." (*Observations sur les affaires d'Espagne,* 1808).

Heaven is
  Yin and Yang,
  Cold and hot,
  The cycle of seasons.

Cao Cao: *The Marshal's Treatise* says, Do not mobilize troops in winter or summer, out of love for the common people.

Meng: Warfare models itself on the movement of Heaven. Yin and Yang alternate hard and soft, waxing and waning. A Yin tactic is hidden, empty, static, and still; a Yang tactic is light, swift, sudden, and forceful. In retreat, one uses Yin; in attack, one uses Yang. . . . The two take forms that are forever changing. Thus the warrior models himself on Heaven.

Zhang Yu: Here Yin and Yang have nothing to do with the calculations of divination [as they often did]. Warfare has its own particular sense of Yin and Yang. As Fan Li [the great minister of Gou Jian, king of the state of Yue in the fifth century B.C.] put it: "Use Yin last; use Yang first. Exhaust the enemy's Yang energy, nurture your own yin energy, and thus prevail." Humans have their Yin and Yang, female and male; Heaven has its Yin and Yang, morning and evening; [in warfare] the variations of soft and hard, of indirect and direct strategy, are the intermingling of human and celestial Yin and Yang.

Cold and hot refer to winter and summer. In the Han dynasty, during the campaign against the Xiongnu barbarians [of the northern steppes], many soldiers lost their fingers; and when Ma Yuan led a campaign against the [southern] Man barbarians [A.D. 43], many of his troops went down with plague. This was because they fought during winter and summer. The movement of the seasons refers to the varying physical conditions of the annual seasonal cycle, such as flooding and drought. . . . Again, this has nothing to do with divination.

Wang Xi: This refers to the entire Way [Giles: the General Economy] of Heaven, the Five Elements, the Four Seasons, wind and cloud, and other natural phenomena. A skillful ebbing and flowing with this aids the path to victory.

The Book of Changes, **Hexagram 55,** *Feng,* **Commentary on the Judgment:**   When the sun stands at midday, it begins to set; when the moon is full, it begins to wane. The fullness and emptiness of heaven and earth wax and wane with time. How much truer is this of men, or of spirits and gods!

Translator: Master Sun introduces a second fundamental concept of early Chinese thought, that of the "complementarity" or "alternating polarity" of Yin and Yang. Every phenomenon, every process, is viewed as a particular blend of these two forces, these two modes of energy. "One Yin, one Yang, such is the Way" (Commentary on *The Book of Changes*). Indeed, the very building blocks of *The Book of Changes* itself are the broken (Yin) line and the unbroken (Yang) line. The two terms later acquired a specific range of meanings and were applied to every category of human experience, every kind of food, every bodily organ, every sickness, every terrestrial and celestial entity. But in this context, for Master Sun, they represent something simpler, the broad movement of nature, as revealed in the cycle of the seasons. "The Chinese regard the fundamental ordering of the universe as being based on the interplay of these two groups of opposite but complementary aspects of the principle of energy" (Manfred Porkert, *Chinese Medicine* [New York: Morrow, 1982], p. 68).

We have here the first statement of the importance of flexibility, the quality that enables Master Sun's warrior to adapt and respond effectively to his ever-changing environment.

Earth is
>   Height and depth,
>   Distance and proximity,
>   Ease and danger,
>   Open and confined ground,
>   Life and death.

Mei Yaochen: This refers to a knowledge of the terrain, its advantages and dangers.

Zhang Yu: In deploying troops, it is essential to know the terrain. A knowledge of the distances involved makes it possible to choose between an indirect and a direct plan of action. A knowledge of the ease or otherwise of the terrain makes it possible to choose between the use of infantry or cavalry. A knowledge of the open or confined nature of the terrain makes it possible to judge the size of the force needed. A knowledge of the "life and death" of the terrain makes it possible to decide whether to do battle or disperse.

Giles: The safety of an army (life and death) depends largely on its quickness to turn these geographical features to account.

Wu Jiulong (1990):   The first two items (height and depth) are only found in the excavated Han Bamboo Strips. Since they are meaningful details, they are added to the received text.

Translator: Terrain is one of the prime concerns of any general anywhere. Understandably it preoccupies Master Sun, and a discussion of its various aspects takes up a large part of Chapters 8, 10, and 11.

Command is
    Wisdom,
    Integrity,
    Compassion,
    Courage,
    Severity.

Cao Cao: These are the five virtues of a general.

Du Mu: The kings of old valued [the virtue of] compassion above all, but the writers on war placed wisdom at the head of the list. A wise commander recognizes change and acts in accordance with it. A commander of integrity inspires his troops never to question rewards and punishments. A compassionate commander loves his own men, has sympathy for the enemy, and values hard work. A courageous commander seizes opportunities without procrastination and thereby achieves victory. A severe commander inspires awe and discipline in his men.

Jia Lin: An excess of wisdom can lead to rebellion; untempered compassion can cause weakness; absolute integrity can cause folly; brute courage can produce violence; excessive severity can be cruel. All five virtues must be present together in a general; each must play its role.

Giles: The five cardinal [Confucian] virtues of the Chinese are Humanity, or Benevolence [here translated Compassion]; Uprightness of Mind [sometimes translated Righteousness, absent here]; Self-respect, self-control, "proper feeling" [sometimes translated as Ritual, also absent here]; Wisdom; and Sincerity or Good Faith [here translated as Integrity]. Here Wisdom and Sincerity [Integrity] are put before Compassion, and the two military virtues of Courage and Severity substituted for Uprightness of Mind and Self-respect.

Translator: The discipline of Julius Caesar (100–44 B.C.) was "truly based on mutual understanding and self-respect; and his army grew to love him as a man and a soldier, and to believe in him as a leader, just as the British troops swore by 'Corporal John' and the French adored 'le Petit Caporal.' Like Marlborough and Napoleon, Caesar knew what the morale of an army means—knew how to create it, and to sustain it. So trained, so led, troops will go anywhere and do anything . . ." (H. J. Edwards, Introduction to *The Gallic War,* Loeb Classical Library, 1958). Master Sun is here seeking to identify the elusive quality of leadership. Viscount Montgomery devoted a small book to this quality, and included in his gallery of great world leaders Master Sun's twentieth-century disciple, Mao Zedong (1893–1976). The first-century Greek strategist Onasander, in his treatise *Strategikos,* gave his own list of the qualities to be desired in a general: "I believe we must choose a general because he is temperate, self-restrained, vigilant, frugal, hardened to labour, alert (as Homer says, 'quick as a bird or a thought'), free from avarice . . ." (Chaliand, *The Art of War in World History* [Berkeley: University of California Press, 1994], p. 154).

Discipline is
   Organization,

Cao Cao: Proper organization of regiments, of flags and insignia, of gongs and drums [for retreat and attack].

Chain of command,

Cao Cao: Proper distinction between the [different spheres of responsibility of] various officers.

Control of expenditure.

Translator: Caesar again: "Moral superiority alone does not ensure success in war; soldiers are human, and armies cannot live or fight without supplies, nor move without transport. It is the mark of a good general that he appreciates and anticipates the material needs; and it is abundantly clear that Caesar's *celeritas* [swiftness] in the field was rendered possible only by the most careful and constant attention to all details of administration" (Edwards, Introduction to *The Gallic War*).

Every commander is aware
   Of these
   Five Fundamentals.
   He who grasps them
   Wins;

He who fails to grasp them
Loses.

Translator: This is Master Sun's constantly recurring dichotomy: win/lose, victory/defeat, success/failure.

For this deliberation,
    For the making of comparisons,
    And the assessing of conditions,
    Discover:

    Which ruler
    Has the Way?

Mei Yaochen: Which ruler can win the trust of his men?

    Which general
    Has the ability?

Du Mu: Which general has wisdom, integrity, compassion, courage, and severity?

    Which side has
    Heaven and Earth?

Zhang Yu: See which side is acting in accordance with the advantages of season and terrain. When Cao Cao attacked the state of Wu in the depths of winter, he made a blunder.

    On which side
    Is discipline
    More effective?

Cao Cao: Once a rule is established, it must be obeyed; any offender must be put to death.

Giles: Du Mu alludes to the remarkable story of Cao Cao, who was such a strict disciplinarian that once, in accordance with his own severe regulations against injury to standing crops, he condemned himself to death for having allowed his horse to shy into a field of corn! However, in lieu of losing his head, he was persuaded to satisfy his sense of justice by cutting off his hair.

The Romance of the Three Kingdoms, **Chapter 17:**   It was the summer, the fourth month of the third year of the period Jian-an (199 A.D.). . . . The army marched away. In the course of the march they passed through a wheat district and the grain was ready for harvesting, but the peasants had fled for fear and the corn was uncut. Cao Cao caused it to be known all about that he was sent on the expedition by command of the Emperor to capture a rebel and save the people. He could not avoid moving in the harvest season but if anyone trampled down the corn he should be put to death. Military discipline was so strict that the people need fear no damage. The people were very pleased and lined the road, wishing success to the expedition. When the soldiers passed wheatfields, they dismounted and pushed aside the stalks so that none were trampled down.

One day, when Cao Cao was riding through the fields, a dove suddenly got up, startling the horse so that he swerved into the standing grain and a large patch was trampled down. Cao at once called the Provost Marshal and bade him decree the sentence for the crime of trampling down corn.

"How can I deal with your crime?" asked the Provost Marshal.

"I made the rule and I have broken it. Can I otherwise satisfy public opinion?"

He laid hold of the sword by his side and made to take his own life. All hastened to prevent him, and Guo Jia said, "In ancient Spring and Autumn days, the laws were not applied to the persons of the most honorable. You are the supreme leader of a mighty army and must not wound yourself."

Cao Cao pondered for a long time. At last he said, "Since there exists the reason just quoted I may perhaps escape the death penalty." Then with his sword he cut off his hair and threw it on the ground, saying, "I cut off the hair as touching the head." . . . This deed was a stimulus to discipline all through the army so that not a man dared be disobedient [trans. C. H. Brewitt-Taylor].

> Which army
> Is the stronger?

Zhang Yu: In which army are the chariots most solid, the horses fittest, the officers bravest, the weapons keenest; in which camp does the drum for attack inspire shouts of joy and the gong for retreat provoke cries of indignation?

> Whose officers and men
> Are better trained?

Du You: Master Wang said, "Without constant training, the officers will be fearful and undecided when confronting the enemy; without constant training, the general will be wavering and irresolute when faced with the crisis."

> In which army
> Are rewards and punishments
> Clearest?

Du Mu: Neither should be excessive.

Giles: That is, on which side is there the most absolute certainty that merit will be rewarded and misdeeds summarily punished?

> From these
> Can be known
> Victory and defeat.

Mei Yaochen: By unraveling the true circumstances [assessing conditions], the outcome—whether it be victory or defeat—can be known.

Zhang Yu: If all seven of these factors are favorable, then victory is certain before battle has been engaged; if they are unfavorable, then defeat is equally certain. This is the "knowing" referred to.

> Heed my plan,
> Employ me,
> And victory is surely yours;
> I will stay.

Do not heed my plan,
>   And even if you did employ me,
>   You would surely be defeated;
>   I will depart.

Zhang Yu: Master Sun is trying to persuade the king of Wu to employ his services.

Guo Huaruo: It was a unique characteristic of the Warring States period that military advisers could pick and choose where to serve—like Wu Qi in the state of Wei, and Yue Yi in the state of Yan.

Settle on the best plan,
>   Exploit the dynamic within,
>   Develop it without,

Cao Cao: Beyond the regular rules.

Mei Yaochen: Settle on the [basic] plan within, develop it strategically without, thus helping to bring about victory.

Jia Lin: Calculate the advantages, settle on a plan, then assess the enemy and develop ruses to exploit the situation strategically. These maneuvers include attacks from the flank or ambuscades on the enemy's rear, to supplement straightforward, direct confrontation.

Translator: This is the first occurrence of the key word *shi*, dynamic, potential energy of the situation, which will be explored at greater length in Chapter 5.

Follow the advantage,
>   And master opportunity:
>   This is the dynamic.

Cao Cao: The mastery comes from the opportunity itself; the opportunity is mastered through events.

Du Mu: These are the strategic initiatives "beyond the regular rules" [referred to by Cao Cao]. The strategic situation cannot be seen in advance. Sometimes what is to the enemy's disadvantage reveals our own advantage, and vice versa. These are the elements that enable us to master the opportunity and achieve victory.

Giles: Master Sun, as a practical soldier, will have none of the "bookish theoric." He cautions us here not to pin our faith to abstract principles. "For," as Zhang Yu puts it, "while the main laws of strategy [the regular rules] can be stated clearly enough for the benefit of all and sundry, you must be guided by the actions of the enemy in attempting to secure a favourable position in actual warfare." On the eve of the battle of Waterloo, Lord Uxbridge, commanding the cavalry, went to the Duke of Wellington in order to learn what his plans and calculations were for the morrow, because, as he explained, he might suddenly find himself Commander-in-chief and would be unable to frame new plans in a critical moment. The Duke listened quietly and then said: "Who will attack the first tomorrow—I or Bonaparte?" "Bonaparte," replied Lord Uxbridge. "Well," continued the Duke, "Bonaparte has not given me any idea of his projects; and as my plans will depend on his, how can you expect me to tell you what mine are?" (Sir W. Fraser, *Words on Wellington*).

Translator: Along with the pair *sheng/bai* (victory/defeat), the pair *li/hai* (advantage/disadvantage, gain/harm) plays a very large part in Master Sun's thinking.

> The Way of War is
>   A Way of Deception.

Cao Cao: In war, there is nothing constant. The Way lies in deception and cunning.

Zhang Yu: War must be based upon righteousness, but victory depends on deception and cunning.

Li Quan: In war, there cannot be too much cunning.

Mei Yaochen: Without cunning, it is impossible to master opportunity and defeat the enemy.

Giles: The truth of this pithy and profound saying [of Master Sun's] will be admitted by every soldier. Colonel Henderson [1854–1903] tells us that Wellington, great in so many military qualities, was especially distinguished by "the extraordinary skill with which he concealed his movements and deceived both friend and foe."

Translator: As François Jullien points out (pp. 167–68), this is more than a trite piece of advice to be tricky for the sake of it. On this basis of deception, of dissimulation and concealment, is built the whole principle of "manipulation" of the enemy, which lies at the heart of Master Sun's strategic thinking. It is a question of unsettling the enemy, getting him into a weak situation (*ébranler l'adversaire*), or of getting him to get himself into such a situation, rather than of directly confronting him and "fighting it out" (the heroism of action). By these means we gradually erode the enemy's capacity to resist.

> When able,
> Feign inability;

Zhang Yu: When in reality strong, appear to be weak; when in reality full of courage, appear to be fearful.

> When deploying troops,
> Appear not to be.

Du Mu: Conceal the true situation with cunning. Keep it hidden from the enemy. If the enemy can observe the true state of affairs, he will know how to react. As the *Historical Records* have it [in the biography of Gou Jian, king of Wu]: "A hawk must keep out of sight before it swoops."

> When near,
> Appear far;
>
> When far,
> Appear near.

Mei Yaochen: So that the enemy cannot predict your movements.

> Lure with bait;

Du Mu: The Zhao general Li Mu [d. 229 B.C.; charged with defending the northern frontier against the nomadic Xiongnu] released large numbers of cattle and their herders into open country, which induced the Xiongnu barbarians to advance a little. General Li then pretended to retreat, leaving a few thousand stragglers as a decoy. The khan of the Xiongnu when he learned of this was overjoyed and advanced into the open at the head of a large force of men. General Li then took them by surprise and attacked with a pincer formation from left and right, crushing them and killing over a hundred thousand of their cavalry.

> Strike with chaos.

Zhang Yu: Feign chaos, lure the enemy out, and then strike. In the war between Wu and Yue, Wu used three thousand criminals, to give an appearance of disorder and to draw out the Yue forces. The criminals ran [chaotically] hither and thither or surrendered. As a result, Yue engaged battle, only to be defeated by Wu.

> If the enemy is full,
> Be prepared.
> If strong,
> Avoid him.

Zhang Yu: As the classic says, "In engaging the enemy, discover where he is abundant and where deficient." Abundant means full or solid. Deficient means empty or weak. Wherever the enemy's situation is solid, we should adopt a plan for dealing with an invincible foe and not act lightly. In the words of Li Jing's *Mirror of War*, "Observe emptiness and advance; observe fullness and halt."

Du You: When his stores are well stocked and full and his troops keen, retreat and wait for him to become weak and lax; observe the change and respond to it.

Translator: For the pivotal pair empty/full, see Chapter 6.

> If he is angry,
> Disconcert him.

Zhang Yu: When he is [by nature] obstinate and irascible, insult him and make him angry. He will be provoked and confused and will advance recklessly, without thought for the consequences.

He Yanxi: As when the Han troops succeeded by dint of repeated taunts and insults in provoking the Chu forces under [the grand marshal] Cao Jiu into the battle of the river Si. [In 203 B.C., Cao Jiu, provoked to a fit of rage, disobeyed the orders of his sovereign Xiang Yu and led a fatal sortie from the city of Chenggao. His troops were halfway across the river when the Han army fell on them and routed them. Cao Jiu subsequently cut his own throat. This historical incident is a favorite with the commentators. See Chapter 3.]

> If he is weak,
> Stir him to pride.

Du You: When the enemy mobilizes his troops and advances in anger, make an outward show of weakness and docility and thereby heighten his ambition; wait for him to slacken and then strike. Master Wang of old said that the Skillful Tactician plays with his adversary as a cat plays with a mouse, pitting his wisdom against the enemy, first feigning weakness and immobility, then suddenly pouncing on him.

Translator: Du You took this sentence in a different sense: "Pretend to be weak yourself. . . ." Often different commentators took the same passage to mean radically different things. Here I have included Du You's comment because of Master Wang's memorable cat comparison.

> If he is relaxed,
> Harry him;

Zhang Yu: Keep your own strength intact; let him wear himself out.

Wang Xi: Employ a large number of surprise tactics. When the enemy comes out, retreat; when the enemy retreats, come out; when he comes to the rescue of his left flank, go for his right; when he reinforces his right flank, go for his left; harry him in this way.

> If his men are harmonious,
> Split them.

Cao Cao: Send spies to split his forces.

Li Quan: Break their understanding, split lord from subject, and then attack. When the state of Qin was launching an attack on the state of Zhao
[260 B.C.], the minister of Qin, the marquis of Ying, sent spies to the king
of Zhao, saying, "We men of Qin are afraid that you will put Zhao Gua in
command; Lian Po [the current commander] would be easier for us to deal
with." The king of Zhao fell for this little ruse and replaced Lian Po with
Zhao Gua. As a result, at the Battle of Changping, four hundred thousand
troops from Zhao surrendered and were killed. [See *Records of the Grand
Historian*, Chapter 73, biographies of Bo Qi and Wang Jian.]

Zhang Yu: Split lord from subject, split ally from ally; split them, and
then attack them.

> Attack
> Where he is
> Unprepared;
> Appear
> Where you are
> Unexpected.

Meng: Attack the void [the weakest point]; take him where he is slack-
est; never let the enemy know where to prepare his defense. Hence the saying "In war, the knack lies in being without form [invisible]." As the Ancient
Duke said, "The most effective movement is the one that is unexpected.
The best plan is the one that is unknown."

> This is
> Victory in warfare;
> It cannot be
> Divulged
> In advance.

Cao Cao: Like a secret. War has no constant dynamic, just as water has
no constant form. It is a matter of adapting flexibly to the changing circumstances of the enemy, and these cannot be [known, let alone] divulged in

advance. Hence the saying "Measure the enemy in your mind, spot the opportunity with your eye."

Mei Yaochen: It is when one is face-to-face with the enemy that one has to respond to changing circumstances and decide strategies. How can such things be talked of in advance?

> Victory belongs to the side
>> That scores most
>> In the temple calculations
>> Before battle.
> Defeat belongs to the side
>> That scores least
>> In the temple calculations
>> Before battle.
> Most spells victory;
>> Least spells defeat;
>> None, surer defeat.
> I see it in this way,

Cao Cao: According to the Art of War.

> And the outcome is apparent.

***The Book of Lord Shang*, Chapter 10, "Methods of Warfare":** By estimating the strength of the enemy and by examining one's own forces, victory or defeat may be known beforehand. . . . If the policy originates in the temple calculations, then it will lead to victory, be the leader good or inferior.

***Records of the Grand Historian*, Chapter 8:**   The First Emperor of Han said to Wang Ling, "I know how to plan campaigns with counting-rods in the headquarters tent."

Zhang Yu: In ancient times, before the beginning of a campaign, the general would conduct ceremonial deliberations in his field temple and make calculations. With deep and far-sighted strategies, planning achieves a great deal, and in this way victory is won before battle is joined. With superficial planning, little is gained, and defeat is certain. Much planning spells victory; less planning, a less certain outcome; no planning, certain defeat. Hence the saying "The victorious army is victorious first and seeks battle later; the defeated army does battle first and seeks victory later. [See Chapter 4, p. 156.] Victory and defeat lie in the presence or absence of planning."

Li Ling (1997):   Many examples of early calculating devices (counting-rods) using bamboo or wooden tallies of a fixed length have been found in recent excavations. In this chapter calculations with such rods are meant, whereby the relative advantages of the opposing forces are measured (our own strengths and weaknesses, and those of the enemy). This use of calculation to determine a course of action is of very ancient origin, and ethnographers have uncovered many relics of it. The Chinese words signifying calculate *(suan)*, measure *(chou)*, scheme *(ce)*, and plan *(ji)* all have the Bamboo Radical, and are all linked with this form of counting.

Wang Xi: Anxious lest the student be perplexed by his earlier statement "Victory cannot be divulged in advance," Master Sun here restates the broad principles of his first section on planning.

Translator: Several contemporary commentators have compared this prewar temple council of Master Sun's time to a form of early war game: a careful simulation, assessing a range of different factors and calculating from them the underlying dynamic of the situation (and the almost certain outcome). At the end of his first chapter, Master Sun returns to the crucial importance of such deliberations.

Chapter Two

Waging of War

Cao Cao: The warrior wishing to wage war must first calculate the cost and should always feed his men off the enemy.

Zhang Yu: Once planning and calculation are completed, chariots and horses must be made ready, weapons honed and equipment prepared, provisions transported, expenses estimated, all in preparation for battle. So this section follows "Making of Plans."

Master Sun said:

In War,
    For an army of
    One thousand
    Four-horse swift chariots,
    One thousand
    Hide-armored wagons,

Zhang Yu: The lighter, swift chariots were used for combat; the heavier, hide wagons for defense.

    For one hundred thousand
    Mail-clad soldiers,

Li Quan: Foot soldiers.

    With provisions for
    Four hundred miles;

Cao Cao: Four hundred miles beyond the frontier.

> Allowing for
>> Expenses at home and at the front,
>> Dealings with envoys and advisers;

Translator: As Niu Guoping and Wang Fucheng (1991) point out, among the advisers whose expenses had to be met would have been such individuals as Master Sun himself (a native of the northeastern state of Qi), and Wu Zixu (a native of the central southern state of Chu), both employed as advisers by the southeastern state of Wu.

> Glue and lacquer,
> Repairs to chariots and armor;
> The daily cost of all this
> Will exceed
> One thousand taels of silver.

Zhang Yu: A round figure for the heavy expenses involved, not including the money required for paying bribes [for the purposes of intelligence?].

***Records of the Grand Historian*, Chapter 112:**   It is said in *The Art of War*, "For an army of a hundred thousand soldiers, one must spend a thousand taels of silver a day." The Qin forces were constantly raising large numbers of troops, several hundreds of thousands at a time. Although they succeeded in defeating armies, slaying generals, and taking prisoners from among the barbarians, this only had the effect of stirring up bitter hatred and deep resentment toward Qin; it did not make up for the huge costs to the country. To empty the state coffers and to wear out the common people, simply in order to have one's way with a foreign nation, is not a sound policy.

> In War,
>> Victory should be
>> Swift.

Translator: Julius Caesar again: "The keynote of Caesar's generalship was speed (*celeritas*). He was swift to calculate and decide, swift to move—

and by movement to keep the initiative, to surprise the enemy, and divide his strength; swift, in the hour of battle, to seize the tactical opportunity, to remedy the tactical mistake; swift always in pursuit, knowing full well that only he who pursues till he can go no further secures the full fruit of victory. Such speed in war as Caesar's was no gift of fortune: it depended on certain conditions in himself and his army. He had an energy which was invincible and irresistible: he had that courage which ignores fear or danger, but which refuses to be foolhardy. In his expeditions he combined boldness and caution; he fought his battles not only of design, but as opportunity offered" (Edwards, quoting Suetonius, in his Introduction to *The Gallic War*).

If victory is slow,
Men tire,
Morale sags.
Sieges
Exhaust strength;

Zhang Yu: When a campaign is protracted in order to secure victory, the men become weary and their morale sags. Laying siege to a city hundreds of miles from home inevitably exhausts one's strength.

Translator: (As narrated in an episode from the popular novel *The Romance of the Three Kingdoms,* Cao Cao resorted to a characteristically cold-blooded ruse in order to raise the sagging morale of his troops and bring to a successful conclusion the siege of Shouchun.)
Cao Cao's besieging army of a hundred seventy thousand required vast stores of grain, but the surrounding districts, stricken by drought, could offer no aid. Cao pressed for battle, but General Li Feng kept within the confines of the camp. After another month Cao Cao, faced with dwindling supplies, borrowed a hundred thousand bushels of grain from Sun Ce. But he did not distribute it. During the emergency, the commissariat chief Ren Xun and the granary officer Wang Hou petitioned Cao Cao: "There is not enough to feed so many. What shall we do?" Cao Cao ordered him to find a way of "tiding us over." "And if they complain?" asked Wang Hou. "I have a plan for that eventuality," Cao Cao assured him. [Mao Zong'gang comments, "He was certainly not going to tell Wang his plan at this stage."] The officer gave out reduced rations as ordered. Meanwhile, Cao Cao sent his men around to the camps and learned that soldiers were accusing him of

cheating them. He then secretly summoned Wang Hou, the granary officer, and said, "There is something of yours I would like to borrow to pacify the soldiers. I hope you will not begrudge it." [Mao Zong'gang: "He was unlikely to begrudge the loan. But it would be a once-only transaction."] "What do I have," Wang Hou answered, "that could be of use to Your Excellency?" "Your head," Cao replied. "To show the men." "But I have committed no crime!" cried the terrified officer. "I know that," Cao said. "But I must put you to death, or the army will revolt. I will look after your family personally, so have no concern on their account." Before Wang Hou could say more, the executioners had received their orders and were already pushing him out. They cut off his head and stuck it on a pole with a signboard reading, "Wang Hou: Duly Punished by Military Law for Purposefully Assigning Short Rations and Stealing from the Granary." This measure improved the troops' morale (cf. Brewitt-Taylor, p. 180).

> Protracted campaigns
> Strain the public treasury.

Zhang Yu: With a daily expense of one thousand taels, if the campaign is protracted, of course the public treasury will be insufficient. Emperor Wu of the Han dynasty [r. 141–87 B.C.] embarked on a policy of extensive exploration and protracted expansion of the empire that exhausted the public treasury. He lived to regret it.

***History of the Former Han*, Chapter 94:**   The adviser Yan You [first century A.D.] gave the following counsel to [the usurper] Wang Mang [on the inherent difficulty of supplying troops in extended campaigns against the Xiongnu barbarians]: "On average, for a three-hundred-day journey, one soldier needs to consume eighteen bushels of rice, which has to be transported by ox. The ox itself also needs to be fed, which adds another twenty pecks to the weight. Given that the nature of the Xiongnu terrain is desert, with little water or grass, the ox will not survive a hundred days. The remaining quantity of food will be too heavy for a soldier to carry.

> If men are tired,
>> Morale low,
>> Strength exhausted,
>> Treasure spent;

Then the feudal lords
   Will exploit the disarray
   And attack.
   This even the wisest
   Will be powerless
   To mend.

Zhang Yu: As when the state of Wu attacked Chu [506 B.C.], took the city of Ying, and stayed there a long time without returning home. During the army's protracted absence, the forces of Yue invaded Wu. Even counselors of the distinction of Wu Zixu and Master Sun were powerless to save Wu from the disastrous consequences.

Translator: "Feudal lords" was an expression used collectively for the various rival states into which the feudal Zhou kingdom disintegrated during the Spring and Autumn (722–481 B.C.) and Warring States (403–221 B.C.) periods.

I have heard that in war
   Haste can be
   Folly;
   But have never seen
   Delay that was
   Wise.

Chen Hao: As the saying goes, a clap of thunder leaves no time to cover the ears; a flash of lightning strikes before the eyes can blink.

Du Mu: In obtaining victory, it is supreme speed that counts, even if the tactics are foolish. Speed avoids the twin pitfalls of expense and exhaustion. *This* is wisdom.

He Yanxi: Haste may be foolish, but at least it does not expend energy and treasure; protracted operations may be very wise, but they may also bring calamity in their train.

Zhang Yu: So long as victory is achieved, foolish haste is better than wise delay.

Giles: What Master Sun says is that while speed may sometimes be injudicious, tardiness can never be anything but foolish—if only because it means impoverishment to the nation. The classic example of Fabius Cunctator [Quintus Fabius Maximus, "the Delayer," Roman general in the Second Punic War against Hannibal, d. 203 B.C.] will inevitably occur to the mind. That general [famous for his cautious "delaying tactics"] deliberately measured the endurance of Rome against that of Hannibal's isolated army, because it seemed to him that the latter was more likely to suffer from a long campaign in a strange country. [See the famous line of Ennius, *Annals* xii: "Unus homo nobis cunctando restituit rem," "One man, by delaying, saved the state for us."] But it is a moot question whether his tactics would have proved successful in the long run.

> No nation has ever benefited
> From a protracted war.

Li Quan: The *Spring and Autumn Annals* says, "War is like fire. Those who cannot bring hostilities to a close, burn themselves out."

Translator: As John Dryden (1631–1701) observed in the play *Tyrannic Love*, "All delays are dangerous in war." According to the Chinese general Tao Hanzhang, General Westmoreland quoted this very sentence from Master Sun as his argument for withdrawing his troops from Vietnam.

> Without a full understanding of
> The harm
> Caused by war,
> It is impossible to understand
> The most profitable way
> Of conducting it.

Giles: That is, with rapidity. Only one who knows the disastrous effects of a long war can realise the supreme importance of rapidity in bringing it to a close.

Du You: When planning a campaign, if one does not consider the potential disasters, one will not be able to reap the benefits.

> The Skillful Warrior
> Never conscripts troops
> A second time;
> Never transports provisions
> A third.

Cao Cao: Seize victory when you first draft your troops. Do not return to raise more men.

Giles: Once war is declared, he will not waste precious time in waiting for reinforcements, nor will he turn his army back for fresh supplies, but crosses the enemy's frontier without delay. This may seem an audacious policy to recommend, but with all great strategists, from Julius Caesar to Napoleon Bonaparte, the value of time—that is, being a little ahead of your opponent—has counted for more than either numerical superiority or the nicest calculations with regard to commissariat.

> He brings equipment from home
> But forages off the enemy.
> And so his men
> Have plenty to eat.

Zhang Yu: Large quantities of food are difficult to transport. If the army has to have its grain transported over a distance of four hundred miles, the troops will have a hungry look about them.

Records of the Grand Historian, Chapter 92, biography of Han Xin, marquis of Huaiyin: [The troops of Han were threatening the state of Zhao.] Li Zuoche, lord of Guangwu, advised Chen Yu, minister of the king of Zhao, "I have heard it said that, when provisions must be transported four hundred miles, the soldiers have a hungry look and, when fuel must be gathered before the mess is prepared, the army seldom sleeps with a full stomach. . . . On a march of several hundred miles under such circumstances, their provisions are sure to be in the rear. I beg you to lend me a force of thirty thousand surprise troops, which I can lead by a secret route to cut off their supply wagons. . . ."

> Supplying an army
>   At a distance
>   Drains the public coffers
>   And impoverishes
>   The common people.

Zhang Yu: Of course it does, if the strength of seven hundred thousand households has to be used to supply food for an army of a hundred thousand men at a distance of four hundred miles.

Du Mu: *The Book of Master Guan* [ca. 250 B.C.] says, "Transporting grain a hundred miles uses up a year's stocks of grain; a hundred and fifty miles, two years; two hundred, and the common people begin to look hungry."

> Where an army is close at hand,
>   Prices rise;
>   When prices rise,
>   The common people
>   Spend all they have;
>   When they spend all,
>   They feel the pinch of
>   Taxes and levies.

> Strength is depleted
>   On the battlefield;
>   Families at home
>   Are destitute.

Translator: Here I follow the Bamboo Strip text from Shandong, as advocated by Li Ling (1997, p. 43) and Wu Jiulong (pp. 28–29).

The common people
   Lose seven-tenths
   Of their wealth.
   Six-tenths of the public coffers
   Are spent
   On broken chariots,
   Worn-out horses,
   Armor and helmets,
   Crossbows and arrows,
   Spears and bucklers,
   Lances and shields,
   Draft animals,
   Heavy wagons.

So a wise general
   Feeds his army
   Off the enemy.
   One peck
   Of enemy provisions
   Is worth twenty
   Carried from home;
   One picul
   Of enemy fodder
   Is worth twenty
   Carried from home.

Zhang Yu: Because twenty cartloads will be consumed in the process of transporting one cartload to the front—or even more, if the terrain is difficult.

Translator: I have taken a certain liberty with the exact measurements, since Master Sun is more concerned with relative amounts. At this point in the text, the commentators ancient and modern write at inordinate length on the exact quantities indicated by the terms used.

The killing of an enemy
   Stems from
   Wrath;

Du Mu: As when the Qi general Tian Dan was defending the city of Jimo and deliberately caused the Yan army to cut off the noses of their Qi prisoners and to exhume the bodies of the Qi dead.

He Yanxi (amplifying Du Mu):   When the Yan army surrounded the city of Jimo in the state of Qi [279 B.C.], they cut off the noses of all their Qi prisoners. [In the story as related by Sima Qian in his *Records of the Grand Historian*, Chapter 82, which for the most part He Yanxi is repeating verbatim, it is in fact the Qi general Tian Dan's own cunning stratagem to *suggest* this nasty idea to the men of Yan.] The men of Qi were enraged by this, and as a result defended the city all the more courageously. Tian Dan then sent a double agent to misinform the Yan troops, saying, "Our people fear that you will dig up the graves outside the city walls and dishonor our ancestors. The very thought makes us tremble with horror!" Sure enough, the Yan soldiers went ahead and dug up the graves, then burned the corpses. The inhabitants of Jimo witnessed this desecration from the city walls and wept with rage. Now they wished to go out and do battle, their wrath kindled tenfold. Tian Dan knew that his troops were ready and proceeded to inflict a crushing defeat on the army of Yan.

Translator: In the *Records of the Grand Historian*, Tian Dan is credited with several other cunning ruses, including the idea of launching through breaches in the city walls a thousand bulls swathed in red silk and painted in bright colors to look like dragons, their tails soaked in oil and blazing. The Grand Historian, Sima Qian, comments, quoting Master Sun (Chapter 5), "In warfare, engage directly; secure victory indirectly. The Skillful General uses both direct and indirect with infinite variety. Tian Dan's tactics were unorthodox: at first, he was yielding like a young virgin; then swift as an escaping hare." This whole historical episode is referred to again and again by Master Sun's traditional commentators.

Zhang Yu: In the [military classic] *Master Weiliao*, it says, "What stirs the people to make war is their spirit [*qi*]." When their spirit is kindled to wrath, then they will do battle.

The fighting for booty
>Stems from
>A desire for reward.

Du You: If the men know that victory will be richly rewarded, they will brave any danger and gladly enter the fray. Such is the beguiling force of material reward.

In chariot fighting,
>When more than ten
>Enemy chariots are captured,
>The man to take the first
>Should be rewarded.
Change the enemy's
>Chariot flags and standards;

Cao Cao: Make them the same as ours.

Mingle their chariots
>With ours.

Zhang Yu: They should not be sent into battle in a formation of their own.

Treat prisoners of war kindly,
>And care for them.

Zhang Yu: Treat prisoners of war with compassion and good faith, and they will be all the more useful.

Use victory over the enemy
>To enhance your own strength.

He Yanxi: Use the enemy to defeat the enemy, and be all the stronger.

In War,
> Prize victory,
> Not a protracted campaign.

Meng: Prize a swift victory, and a speedy return.

Mei Yaochen: Swiftness saves expense, and spares the people.

The wise general
> Is a Lord of Destiny;
> He holds the nation's
> Peace or peril
> In his hands.

He Yanxi: The general is responsible for the destiny and well-being of the nation. The scarcity of fine generals has always been a source of calamity.

Chapter Three

Strategic Offensive

Du Mu: Planning and calculation have taken place in the ceremonial temple: equipment and provisions have been prepared; now is the time for strategic offensive.

Master Sun said:

In War,
> Better take
> A state
> Intact
> Than destroy it.

Li Quan: Do not prize the taking of life.

He Yanxi: To cause the enemy to surrender through the sheer psychological impact [literally, the energy dynamic] of one's strategy is the best of all strategies.

Zhang Yu: In *Master Weiliao* it says, "Victory through the Tao consists in assessing the enemy, then causing him to lose heart and his army to disperse. He remains externally intact but powerless to act. Victory through force involves combat, killing, destruction, and pillage." "To take a state intact" is victory through the Tao, and to "destroy it" is victory through force.

Jia Lin: To take the enemy state intact and at the same time to maintain one's own state intact, this is the best of all.

Better take
   An army,
   A regiment,
   A detachment,
   A company,
   Intact
   Than destroy them.

Wang Xi: However great or small the entity involved, be it state, army, regiment, detachment, or company, taking it intact enhances prestige and power; destroying it lessens prestige and power.

Ultimate excellence lies
   Not in winning
   Every battle

Zhang Yu: Victory through battle entails great loss of life. That is why it is not excellent.

But in defeating the enemy
   Without ever fighting.

Cao Cao: The enemy surrenders without a battle's having been fought.

Du Mu: Defeating the enemy through planning.

Chen Hao: General Han Xin [a self-confessed student of Master Sun's *Art of War*] adopted Li Zuoche's plan and [rather than sending his already exhausted troops into battle again] sent an envoy with a letter to the king of Yan [describing in persuasive terms his own army's huge superiority], whereupon Yan surrendered without a battle.

The Way and Its Power, **Chapter 68:**   The most Skillful Warrior is never warlike; the most Skillful Warrior is never angered; the most skilled at defeating the enemy never strives.

The Way and Its Power, **Chapter 73:**   The Way of Heaven is to be skilled at winning without striving.

Giles: No modern strategist but will approve the words of the old Chinese. General Moltke's greatest triumph, the capitulation of the huge French army at Sedan [1870], was won practically without bloodshed.

Translator: This famous axiom of Master Sun's lies at the very heart of his treatise. It is admirably restated by Mark Lewis (1990, pp. 116–17): "The principle that the true commander conquered without fighting, or worked out the victory in his mind before giving battle, appears in most of the military treatises and epitomized the new art of command. . . . Battle was no longer the testing ground of prowess or honor for the glory of the lineage, but rather a blackboard on which the sage commander gave lessons to his less-gifted peers." The Marxist military theoretician Guo Huaruo (1984, p. 100) has a more skeptical view of the subject: "Victory without fighting a battle is sometimes the result of a long preceding period of preparatory fighting. . . . For example, we would not have been able to take Peking without a fight during the War of Liberation, unless we had already won the Battle of Tientsin [January 1949] that came before it. . . . And the subsequent 'bloodless' surrender of six provincial capitals may also have seemed on the surface like 'victory without fighting,' but in fact it was the fruits of twenty-two years of war. . . ." The American China-policy guru J. K. Fairbank offers a biting contemporary summary: "As Master Sun's *Art of War* makes plain, violence is only one part of warfare and not even the preferred part. The aim of war is to subdue an opponent, in fine, to change his atittude and induce his compliance. The most economical means is the best: to get him—through deception, surprise, and his own ill-conceived pursuit of infeasible goals—to realize his own inferiority, so that he surrenders or at least retreats without your having to fight him. . . . The author of the *Art of War* would smile at the American exaltation of firepower, which too easily makes a means into an end in itself" ("Varieties of the Chinese Military Experience," in Kierman and Fairbank, eds., *Chinese Ways in Warfare* [Cambridge, Mass.: Harvard University Press, 1974]).

The highest form of warfare
Is to attack
Strategy itself;

Cao Cao: While the enemy is still formulating his strategy, it is easy to attack.

Li Quan: Attack strategy at its very source. During the Later Han dynasty, Kou Xun besieged Gao Jun. Gao sent out his strategic adviser, Huangfu Wen, to negotiate with Kou. Huangfu was rude and ill mannered, and Kou had him beheaded. Kou himself reported this to Gao, saying, "Your minister was ill mannered. I have beheaded him. If you are willing to surrender, do so at once. If not, then defend yourself well." That very day Gao opened his city gates and surrendered. Kou's generals said to him, "May we ask, sire? You killed his envoy, and yet he surrendered his city? How did this come about?" Kou's reply was "Huangfu was Gao's closest minister, his most trusted strategist. Had I spared him, Huangfu would have achieved his goals. By killing him, I destroyed the very seat of Gao's courage. This is what it means to say that the best form of warfare is to attack strategy." "We did not know this," replied his generals.

He Yanxi: While the enemy is formulating his initial plan of attack against us, we must anticipate him by delivering our own attack first. This is easy. We must sound out the drift of the enemy's plans, deploy troops accordingly, and attack his very thinking.

Mei Yaochen: Victory through wisdom.

Du Mu: Duke Ping of Jin [r. 557–532 B.C.] wanted to attack the state of Qi and sent Fan Zhao there to observe the state of affairs. Duke Jing of Qi offered him a goblet of wine; Fan Zhao, when he had become somewhat tipsy, asked if he could drink out of the ruler's special goblet. Duke Jing ordered his personal goblet to be brought in for his guest. Fan Zhao was already drinking from it when Master Yan [a work bearing his name has been found among the Bamboo Strip texts excavated in Shandong] took the goblet away from him and replaced it with another one. Fan Zhao pretended to be drunk and rose unhappily to dance. He asked the music master: "Can you play the music of Zhengzhou for me? I wish to dance to it." To which the music master replied, "I am afraid I am not familiar with that music." Whereupon Fan Zhao strode out.

   "Jin is a great state," said Duke Jing. "This man came here to observe our government; now you have angered the envoy of a neighboring state. What are we to do?" Master Yan said, "I could see that Fan Zhao understood the rules of propriety but wanted to offend us deliberately. I would not go along with this." The music master said, "The music of Zhengzhou is the music of the Son of Heaven. Only the ruler can dance to it. Fan Zhao is a mere subject, and yet he wished to dance to the music of the Son of Heaven. I refused to play it for him."

When Fan Zhao returned to Jin, he reported to Duke Ping, "We cannot attack Qi. I wished to insult their ruler, but Master Yan knew [what I was doing]. I wished to behave contrary to their rules of propriety, and the music master knew." Confucius later said, "To go no further than one's own banquet hall and yet to shatter the enemy from a thousand miles away: this refers to Master Yan." [In other words, by "knowing," i.e., by attacking or undermining strategy itself, Master Yan and the music master defused the hostile intentions toward Qi.]

Du You: The highest form of warfare is to overcome the enemy while he is still making his plans and mobilizing his troops. As the Ancient Duke said, "The best way to avert misfortune is to deal with it before it is born; the best way to defeat an enemy is when his troops are still without form."

The Romance of the Three Kingdoms, **Chapter 87:**   In war it is best to attack minds, not cities; psychological warfare is better than fighting with weapons. [Mao Zong'gang: These words are not to be found in *The Art of War*. They are the very summit of the art, superior even to the teachings of Master Sun and Master Wu.]

> The next,
>> To attack
>> Alliances;

Li Quan: Attack when alliances are first being formed.

Mei Yaochen: Victory through intimidation.

Wang Xi: If it is impossible to foil his strategy, then drive a wedge in his alliances and cause them to fall apart.

Giles: Isolate the enemy from his allies. We must not forget that Master Sun, in speaking of hostilities, always has in mind the numerous states or principalities into which the China of his day was split up.

Translator: But the destruction of alliances can be costly. Li Ling (1997, p. 50), quotes the Song scholar Zheng Youxian: "Destroying strategy brings victory at no cost; destroying alliances can be very costly, without achieving victory."

> The next,
> To attack
> Armies;

Cao Cao: When troops have already been drawn up.

Mei Yaochen: Victory through battle.

Li Quan: To fight it out in battle is a lower form of war.

Jia Lin: The Ancient Duke said, "To wrest victory from the clashing of blades is not the mark of a great general."

> The lowest form of war is
> To attack
> Cities.
> Siege warfare
> Is a last resort.

Du You: Besieging cities and massacring the population is a low form of offensive. It entails excessive casualties.

Mei Yaochen: A prodigious waste of material and human resources.

Wang Xi: It involves extensive casualties and may not even lead to the capture of the city.

Translator: Giles's illustration of this maxim reflects the mood of his time: "Another sound piece of military advice. Had the Boers acted upon it in 1899, and refrained from dissipating their strength before Kimberley, Mafeking, or even Ladysmith, it is more than probable that they would have been masters of the situation before the British were ready seriously to oppose them." One of Giles's favorite strategists, the vicomte de Turenne (1611–75), Louis XIV's marshal, echoed Master Sun's sentiments on this matter: "Strategic caution and logistic accuracy, combined with brilliant dash in small combats and constancy under all circumstances of success or failure may perhaps be considered the salient points of Turenne's genius for war. Great battles he avoided. 'Few sieges and many combats' was his own maxim" (*Encyclopaedia Brittanica*, Eleventh Edition [1910–11], vol. 27, p. 414).

In a siege,
>Three months are needed
>To assemble
>Protective shields,

Li Quan: Used to protect the soldiers' heads as they scale the city ramparts.

>Armored wagons,

Li Quan: Four-wheeled, wooden, missile-proof mobile tanks, propelled from inside, each carrying ten men, used for the purpose of filling up the encircling moat of a city with earth.

>And sundry
>Siege weapons and equipment;

Li Quan: Such as scaling towers and cloud-ladders.

>Another three months
>To pile
>Earthen ramps.

Cao Cao: To pile high earthen ramps up against the city walls.

The general who cannot
>Master his anger
>Orders his troops out
>Like ants,
>Sending one in three

To their deaths,
Without taking the city.
This is the calamity
Of siege warfare.

Cao Cao: If a general is too angry to wait for the siege equipment to be got ready and sends his men clambering over the city ramparts, like ants swarming up a wall, many of them will die or be wounded.

Du Mu: As when a general is insulted by the enemy and cannot preserve his sangfroid. The Emperor Taiwu of the Northern Wei [Tuoba Tao, A.D. 408–52] led a force of ten thousand men against Zang Zhi of the southern kingdom of Song, at the city of Yutai. The Emperor asked Zang for a ritual goblet of wine, whereupon Zang filled a wine-jar with urine and presented it to him. The Emperor flew into a mighty rage and proceeded to attack the city forthwith. His men engaged in close combat, without armor, and attempted to scale the walls of the city in successive waves. No sooner were they repulsed than they surged recklessly forward again and were cut down and lay in piles on the city walls. This went on for thirty days, until more than half their number were dead. Others were dying of sickness. Finally the Emperor gave the order for the retreat. A saying has it that a single woman can hold a besieged city against ten men. This story suggests that the saying is an understatement.

Translator: The Greek historian Polybius (ca. 202–ca. 120 B.C.) has this to say about irascible generals: "Rashness, temerity, and uncalculating impetuosity, as well as foolish ambition and vanity, give an easy victory to the enemy" (*The Histories,* translated by Evelyn Shuckburgh [London: Macmillan, 1889], vol. I, p. 238). Giles speaks for his own time in his comment on siege warfare: "We are reminded of the terrible losses of the Japanese before Port Arthur, in the most recent siege which history has to record."

The Skillful Strategist
Defeats the enemy
Without doing battle,

Li Quan: He defeats him through planning, he does not subdue him through battle.

Captures the city
Without laying siege,

Li Quan: He captures it by planning. During the Later Han dynasty, Zang Gong, marquis of Zan, besieged the "demon" rebels in Yuanwu but was unable to take the city for several months. His own officers and men fell ill and suffered from ulcers. The prince of Donghai said to him, "Here you are with your troops surrounding an enemy determined to fight to the death. There is no planning in this. You should abandon the siege and offer them a visible escape route. They will surely flee and scatter, and then the merest constable will be able to take them." The marquis followed his advice and took Yuanwu.

Overthrows the enemy state
Without protracted war.

Li Quan: He overthrows the state by guile, and it soon collapses.

Du Mu: He sees the potential dynamic of a situation, a weakness in the enemy camp, and seizes the opportunity. It is like pushing over a rotten tree.

Jia Lin: He overthrows the state, but does no harm to its people. When King Wu attacked Yin, the people of Yin hailed him as their father and mother.

He strives for supremacy
Under heaven
Intact,
His men and weapons
Still keen,
His gain
Complete.
This is the method of
Strategic attack.

Cao Cao: Without engaging the enemy in battle, he achieves his goal entire and intact, is victorious "under heaven," and has not subjected his troops to blood and sword.

Translator: This central thesis of Master Sun's is closely paralleled by Nasir al-Din al-Tusi (1201–74), *wazir* of Hülegü, the Mongol khan responsible for the sack of Baghdad in 1258: "It is not prudent to have recourse to arms, if it is possible to disperse and annihilate the enemy through ruse and stratagem. Ardashir said: 'Do not use a stick where a whip will do or a sword where a mace suffices.' War must be the last resort. . . . To break the unity of the enemy and disperse his troops, ruses, deceit, fabrication, and the use of lies are not reprehensible, but recourse to treachery is never permissible. The most important dispositions to take for any war are to be alert and send out spies and scouts" (quoted by Chaliand [1994], p. 445).

> In War,
>> With forces ten
>> To the enemy's one,
>> Surround him;

Du Mu: Surrounding involves having men massed on all four sides, so that the enemy cannot escape. The encirclement has to be at a certain distance from the town under siege, and it has to occupy a considerable space. A strict guard has to be mounted, and without a large number of men, there are bound to be gaps. That is why tenfold forces are needed.

Zhang Yu: When our men are ten to his one, surround him on four sides and take him. This is the case when both sides are evenly matched in every other respect. If, however, we are strong and the enemy weak, there is no need for such numerical superiority before encircling him. As Master Wei-liao said, "In defense, one man can resist ten, ten can resist a hundred, a hundred can resist a thousand." In other words, it takes a hundred to surround ten. The idea is the same.

Amiot: Totally surround the enemy, making sure that he can neither escape nor receive the slightest reinforcements.

> With five,
> Attack him;

Cao Cao: This allows for three direct maneuvers and two indirect.

Du Mu: Divide our troops into five parts. Use three of those parts to mount an attack, and keep two in readiness for a surprise assault on a crack in the enemy's defenses.

Zhang Yu: When our troops are five to his one, we can surprise him in the front and fall upon his rear; assault him from the east and attack him from the west. Without fivefold superiority, it is impossible to adopt such a [many-pronged] plan.

> With two,
> Split in half.

Cao Cao: When our troops are twice the enemy's, use a double strategy: direct attack on the one hand, surprise attack on the other.

Zhang Yu: Divide our troops into two, using one half for a frontal assault, the other to attack the enemy's rear. If the enemy responds at the front, then attack the rear; if he responds at the rear, then attack the front. This is what Cao Cao means by double strategy.

> If equally matched,
> Fight it out;

Mei Yaochen: If potential strengths are matched, then fight.

Zhang Yu: Use subterfuge; use direct as indirect, use indirect as direct, play infinite variations, bewilder the enemy. Use every surprise method to gain the victory.

> If fewer in number,
> Lie low;

Li Quan: If you are weaker than the enemy, strengthen your defenses and do not expose yourself. Wait for his zeal to slacken before sallying out and attacking him. This was what the Qi general Tian Dan did when he was besieged at Jimo. He used the stratagem of the blazing oxen to destroy the troops of Yan.

Du Mu: If your troops are fewer, temporarily avoid his onslaught, wait for an opening, then surge forward decisively and take the victory. This requires patience and forbearance in the face of the enemy's provocations, which was beyond the ability of the Chu general Cao Jiu at the river Si [who in 203 B.C. was provoked by the Han into impetuously sending his men across the river, where they were cut down].

Jia Lin: When the enemy is numerous and you are few, keep your troop dispositions hidden from the enemy. Meanwhile lay an ambush for them, confuse them with subterfuge and ruse; this, too, can lead to victory. Another interpretation: Hide your troop dispositions, and keep the enemy in the dark as to your plans. They may suspect some ruse and flee themselves.

> If weaker,
> Escape.

Zhang Yu: When weaker in every way, in terms of troops, strategy, morale, then the thing to do is to withdraw and wait for a new opportunity.

Mei Yaochen: When the enemy is numerous and we are few, get away; do not give battle.

> A small force
> Obstinately fighting
> Will be captured
> By a larger force.

Du Mu: An obstinate refusal to withdraw or escape will lead to capture.

Meng: A small force cannot withstand a large one. What this means is that if a small state does not assess its own strength properly and dares to oppose a large one, whatever measures it may take to defend itself, it will end up being taken captive. As the *Spring and Autumn Annals* say, "They could not be strong, nor did they know how to be weak, and so they were defeated."

Li Quan: If a small force fails to assess its own strength and insists on fighting, it is sure to be taken captive by a larger force. When the Han commander Li Ling pitched his five thousand infantry against a force of a hundred thousand Xiongnu, he was annihilated.

Giles: In other words: "C'est magnifique; mais ce n'est pas la guerre" [Marshal Bosquet's famous comment on the Charge of the Light Brigade, 1854].

> The general is the prop
>   Of the nation.
> When the prop is solid,
>   The nation is strong.
> When the prop is flawed,
>   The nation is weak.

Jia Lin: When the general is a solid support to his sovereign, the nation is strong; when there is the slightest division between general and sovereign, the nation is weak.

Translator: Guo Huaruo (1984, p. 107) comments predictably, "This undue emphasis on the importance of the individual commander is not in accordance with dialectical materialism." The duke of Wellington did not agree: "I used to say of Napoleon that his presence on the field made the difference of forty thousand men" (Stanhope, *Life of Wellington*, p. 9, quoted by Giles).

> A ruler can bring misfortune
>   Upon his troops
>   In three ways:
>
>   Ordering them
>   To advance
>   Or to retreat
>   When they should not
>   Is called
>   Hobbling the army;

Li Quan: Not knowing when to advance or retreat leads to sure defeat. It is like tying together the legs of a thoroughbred; it cannot gallop.

Jia Lin: The decision whether to advance or retreat must be taken by the general flexibly, in response to a changing situation. Nothing is more disastrous than for the sovereign to issue orders from the seclusion of the court. As the Ancient Duke said, "The nation cannot be governed from the field; nor can war be directed from court."

Wang Xi: To get rid of this crippling misfortune, the general must be given unrestricted power, which makes it all the more imperative to appoint a general who is both loyal and gifted.

Ignorant interference
In military decisions
Confuses
Officers and men;

Cao Cao: The military and the civil are distinct spheres; you cannot direct an army in terms of ritual.

Zhang Yu: Compassion and righteousness are the principles on which to govern a state, but not an army; tactical flexibility is a military rather than a civic virtue. This is only proper.

Ignorant meddling
In military appointments
Perplexes
Officers and men.

Mei Yaochen: Making appointments without a knowledge of the art of strategy causes perplexity.

Giles: That is, the ruler is not careful to use the right man in the right place.

When an army is confused and perplexed,
The feudal princes

Will cause trouble;
    This creates
Chaos in the ranks
And gives away
Victory.

Mei Yaochen: We ourselves create the chaos; we ourselves give away the victory.

    There are Five Essentials
      For victory:

      Know when to fight
      And when not to fight;

Zhang Yu: If you can fight, advance and take the offensive; if you cannot fight, retreat and remain on the defensive. He who can determine which is appropriate, the offensive or the defensive, will invariably be the victor.

Du Mu: This is the same as the "knowing of self" and the "knowing of the enemy" that Master Sun discusses later.

Meng: Victory comes from correctly assessing the enemy, from examining his strengths and weaknesses.

      Understand how to deploy
      Large and small
      Numbers;

Zhang Yu: According to the Art of War, a lesser force can defeat a greater, and vice versa. The secret lies in making the appropriate judgments and not letting the right moment slip by.

      Have officers and men who
      Share a single will;

Be ready
For the unexpected;

Have a capable general,
Unhampered by his sovereign.

Du You: A Skillful General, well versed in military strategy, should be given full rein by his sovereign. As Master Wang said, "The sovereign gives broad instructions, the general makes battle decisions."

Giles: Napoleon undoubtedly owed much of his extraordinary success to the fact that he was not hampered by any central authority—that he was, in fact, general and sovereign in one.

These five
    Point the way to
    Victory.

Hence the saying
    "Know the enemy,
    Know yourself,
    And victory
    Is never in doubt,
    Not in a hundred battles."

Zhang Yu: These words refer to both attack and defense. Knowing the enemy, you can take the appropriate offensive; knowing yourself, you can adopt the appropriate defensive strategy. Attack is the secret of defense; defense is the planning of attack. Know this, and you will never fail, not in a hundred battles.

The Way and Its Power, Chapter 33:   To know others is wisdom; to understand oneself is enlightenment. To conquer others requires force; to conquer oneself shows strength.

Translator: The Greek historian Polybius said of Hannibal, "It is mere blind ignorance to believe that there can be anything of more vital importance to a general than the knowledge of the character and disposition of one's opponent" (*Histories,* quoted by Chaliand, p. 113).

This, one of Master Sun's most famous maxims, was endorsed by Mao Zedong: "This saying of the great Chinese military thinker of ancient times, Master Sun, includes [under knowledge] the stages of both theoretical knowledge and practice; it includes the observation of the laws of development of objective practice, and the process of determining one's own actions in accordance with those laws, so as to overcome the present enemy. We must not underestimate [the wisdom of] this saying" (*Selected Works,* p. 166).

> He who knows self
> But not the enemy
> Will suffer one defeat
> For every victory.

Li Quan: If one is aware of one's own strength and yet one has not estimated the enemy properly, victory is not assured. The prince of Qin, Fu Jian, in A.D. 383 led an army of a million soldiers south against the forces of Jin. Someone commented that the Jin had men of the caliber of Xie An and Huan Chong and that he should not underestimate them. To which Fu Jian replied, "I have the assembled forces of eight provinces in my army, a million horses and men. They could dam the Yangtze River itself by merely throwing their whips into it. What have I to fear?" He was subsequently heavily defeated.

> He who knows
> Neither self
> Nor enemy
> Will fail
> In every battle.

Chapter Four

Forms and Dispositions

Cao Cao: Military dispositions. Marching and countermarching, each army endeavoring to discover the other's true condition.

Du Mu: It is through outward dispositions [forms] that the true condition of an army may be discovered. If you are "without form" [your dispositions are not visible], your true condition will remain secret. Once your dispositions are known, your true condition becomes transparent. Being secret brings the victory; being transparent, defeat.

Wang Xi: The Skillful Warrior can secure victory by adapting his own dispositions to those of the enemy.

Zhang Yu: This refers to the dispositions of both armies, in attack and defense. So long as one's own are hidden, the enemy cannot know them. Once they are visible, the enemy can exploit the slightest crack or opportunity. Since dispositions become manifest in attack and defense, this chapter follows the chapter on "Strategic Offensive."

Translator: The word used in the title of this chapter, *xing*, has the fundamental meaning of "form, shape, appearance," and is used in the traditional language of Chinese geomancy (*fengshui*) to refer to the configurations of the earth, the ways in which the shapes of the earth, its hills and rivers, reveal and express its underlying dynamic (*shi*). Here it refers to the military formations and positions that equally reveal the underlying strength or weakness of an army. But in Master Sun's strategic thinking, the philosophical implications of form [i.e., military dispositions] are subtler than those to be found in a more mechanical strategist such as von Clausewitz (1780–1831). At times there is an unmistakable Taoist tinge to Master Sun. One is reminded of the fundamental Taoist notion of "nonaction" (*wuwei*), of minimal interference and maximum spontaneity, according to which things will "come out right to the extent that people are aware of their circumstances and of each other" (Angus Graham, *Disputers of the Tao* [La Salle, Ill.: Open Court, 1989], p. 233). "The greatest carver does the least cutting" (*The Way and Its Power*, Chapter 28). "The Way constantly does nothing, yet there is nothing it does not do" (Chapter 37). "If I do nothing, of themselves the people are transformed" (Chapter 57). At times the Skillful Warrior resembles the almost invisible Taoist sage. In Chapter 6, for example, we are reminded, "The highest skill in forming dispositions is to be without form; formlessness is proof against the prying of the subtlest spy and the machinations of the wisest brain."

Master Sun said:

Of old,
  The Skillful Warrior
  First ensured
  His own
  Invulnerability;

Zhang Yu: In other words, he knew himself.

Then he waited for
The enemy's
Vulnerability.

Zhang Yu: He knew his enemy.

Mei Yaochen: Kept dispositions hidden within and waited for the other's weakness or lapses.

Translator: Throughout this passage, the words I have translated as "invulnerability" and "vulnerability" (*bukesheng*, literally "unbeatable," and *kesheng*, "beatable") can be more widely understood as "strength" and "weakness."

Invulnerability rests
  With self;

Vulnerability,
With the enemy.

Cao Cao: One should cultivate oneself and wait for a lapse on the part of the enemy.

The Skillful Warrior
Can achieve
His own
Invulnerability;

Zhang Yu: He can achieve this by concealing the disposition of his troops, by covering up his tracks, and by taking strict precautions. These things are within his sphere of action.

But he can never bring about
The enemy's
Vulnerability.

Du Mu: If my enemy presents no visible disposition, no lapse that can be exploited, then even if I myself may have perfected every tool for victory, how can I defeat him?

Hence the saying
"One can know
Victory
And yet not achieve it."

Du Mu: All I can know is whether my own strength is sufficient to defeat the enemy. I cannot cause the enemy to slacken and provide me with the opening necessary for victory.

Du You: This is because the enemy has taken precautions. If I can assess the enemy correctly and observe his dispositions, then victory can be known. But if the enemy is secretive and keeps his dispositions invisible, I cannot force him into defeat. Hence the saying of Fan Li: "If the time is not right, matters cannot be forced; if the affair is not ready, it cannot be hastened to completion."

> Invulnerability is
>   Defense;

Cao Cao: It is a matter of keeping dispositions hidden.

Du Mu: If I have not been able to observe the enemy's dispositions and vulnerability, I can at least keep my own dispositions hidden; I can keep myself invulnerable and defend myself.

Mei Yaochen: It is a matter of waiting.

> Vulnerability is
>   Attack.

Cao Cao: If the enemy attacks me, then he becomes vulnerable.

Du Mu: Once the enemy reveals a vulnerable disposition, go out and attack him.

Mei Yaochen: It is a matter of spotting the lapse.

> Defense implies
>   Lack;
>   Attack implies
>   Abundance.

Cao Cao: I defend because I am lacking in strength; I attack because I have an abundance of strength.

> A Skillful Defender
>   Hides beneath
>   The Ninefold Earth;

Cao Cao: Taking advantage of the shelter provided by mountains, rivers, and other natural features.

Du You: The Skillful Defender must take advantage of the obstructions caused by mountains and rivers and lesser hills, so that the enemy does not know where to attack. He hides secretly "beneath the Ninefold Earth."

> A Skillful Attacker
> Moves above
> The Ninefold Heaven.

Cao Cao: Taking advantage of the changing weather.

Du You: The Skillful Attacker must take advantage of the transformations of weather and terrain, using flood and fire according to the situation, so that the enemy does not know where to prepare. He moves like a bolt of lightning "above the Ninefold Heaven."

> Thus they achieve
> > Protection
> And victory
> > Intact.

> To foresee
> > The ordinary victory
> > Of the common man
> > Is no true skill.

Cao Cao: One must see the subtler origins.

Li Quan: Foreseeing an ordinary victory is no skill at all. When General Han Xin destroyed the state of Zhao [a truly extraordinary victory], he marched out of Well Ravine without so much as eating breakfast, saying to his men, "We will feast after destroying Zhao." His generals were aghast but mumbled a perfunctory agreement. Han drew up his men with their backs to the river [a "deadly" position and an obvious breach of tactical rules], and when the men of Zhao looked down and saw this from the battlements of the city, they roared with laughter, saying that Han Xin knew nothing of warfare. But sure enough he defeated Zhao [by means of a subtle stratagem], and his men had their feast. This was because General Han could see beyond the common man.

Translator: This story, a favorite with the commentators, is recounted in much greater detail toward the end of Chapter 11.

> To be victorious in battle
>> And to be acclaimed
>> For one's skill
>> Is no true
>> Skill.

Cao Cao: It is just winning.

Li Quan: Winning a combat by sheer force is highly visible, but not skillful.

Du Mu: Acclaimed by the "common man" already referred to. This is the sort of victory that involves wiping out an army and eliminating its generals. My idea of skill involves subtle planning, secret movements, targeting the enemy's "mind," attacking strategy—a bloodless victory.

Jia Lin: Solid defense, decisive attack, protecting oneself intact, a clear knowledge of victory and defeat before either occurs—these are the signs of the genuine military adept, the warrior of true subtlety and insight. These are far beyond the ordinary victory of the common man.

***The Way and Its Power,* Chapter 22:**   Therefore the Sage embraces Unity and makes it the Measure of All-Under-Heaven. He does not exhibit himself and is seen; he does not assert himself and is manifest; he does not boast and therefore succeeds; he is not proud and therefore becomes the leader. It is because he does not contend that no one Under Heaven can contend with him.

> To lift autumn fur
>> Is no
>> Strength;

Zhang Yu: The fur of the hare, finest (and lightest) in autumn.

> To see sun and moon
>> Is no
>> Perception;
> To hear thunder
>> Is no
>> Quickness of hearing.

Zhang Yu: These are things everyone is capable of. They suggest the ordinary victory of the common man.

He Yanxi: These are the ordinary attainments of the common man. Wu Huo could lift a tripod of a thousand *jun* [one *jun* weighed thirty catties, or Chinese pounds]—now, *that* was strength; Li Zhu could tell apart objects the size of a grain of mustard at a hundred paces—*that* was perception; Shi Kuang the Blind Musician could hear a mosquito or an ant move—*that* was hearing.

Li Quan: The truly wise and capable general is deeply inscrutable, engrossed in his stratagems. As Master Sun said [Chapter 7], "He is as inscrutable as night."

> The Skillful Warrior of old
>> Won
>> Easy victories.

Cao Cao: The easy victory lies in subtleties, in attacking the vulnerable, not the invulnerable.

Mei Yaochen: Seeing the obvious makes for a difficult victory; seeing the subtle makes for an easy victory.

***The Way and Its Power*, Chapter 63:**   It [the Way] acts without action, does without doing, finds taste in the tasteless. It makes the little great and the few many. . . . It tackles the hard in the easy, the great in the small. The difficult affairs of the empire are dealt with when they are easy; the great affairs of the empire are dealt with when they are small. So the Sage never acts big but always succeeds in being big.

The victories
   Of the Skillful Warrior
   Are not
   Extraordinary victories;

Translator: The words "are not extraordinary victories" are not present in the accepted text but are found in the Bamboo Strips. See Wu (1990), p. 59.

They bring
   Neither fame for wisdom
   Nor merit for valor.

Du Mu: His victories are based on seeing the "subtler origins," so the world at large knows nothing of them, and they bring no fame for wisdom. The enemy surrenders, the victory is won without bloodshed, and the victorious general receives no credit for his valor.

The Way and Its Power, **Chapter 17:**   The highest [statesmen, sages] were those of whom nothing was known. . . . The task was accomplished, and the common people considered it to have happened to them of itself.

The Way and Its Power, **Chapter 20:**   The world is full of those that shine; I alone am dark. . . .

His victories
      Are
      Flawless;

Chen Hao: He plans no superfluous moves, he devises no futile strategies.

Zhang Yu: He who conquers by brute strength, skillful though he may be, is also liable on occasion to be defeated; whereas he who can look into the unseen and discern conditions that are not yet manifest will be victorious every time. His victory will have no flaw in it.

His victory is
  Flawless
  Because it is
  Inevitable;
He vanquishes
  An already defeated enemy.

Zhang Yu: His victories are flawless because he detects the inevitable dispositions of defeat within the enemy camp, before deploying his troops.

The Skillful Warrior
  Takes his stand
  On invulnerable ground;
  He lets slip no chance
  Of defeating the enemy.

Du Mu: Invulnerable ground means an invulnerable strategy, a strategy that denies the enemy the slightest chance of victory. Letting slip no chance means keeping a close watch on every slightest crack in the enemy's guard, not missing the tiniest shred of a chance.

The victorious army
  Is victorious first
  And seeks battle later;
  The defeated army
  Does battle first
  And seeks victory later.

Du Mu: As Master Guan said, "The seasons of Heaven, the advantages of Earth, the counting of troop numbers, all of these elements must form part of the planning." Careful planning must precede any dispatching of troops beyond the borders.

He Yanxi: In warfare, first lay plans that will ensure victory, and then lead your army into battle; if you have no stratagem but rely on brute strength, victory is by no means certain.

The Skillful Strategist
>   Cultivates
>   The Way
>   And preserves
>   The law;
>   Thus he is master
>   Of victory and defeat.

Du Mu: The Way is the way of compassion and righteousness; the law is the sum of the rules of military organization.

Zhang Yu: He cultivates the Way of War; he preserves the law of mastering the enemy. Thus he is sure of victory.

Translator: This is one of Master Sun's frequent evocations of the Warrior Adept. The wisdom of the Art of War was a mental skill that could be verbally formulated and taught. The strategists transmitted and taught an "esoteric wisdom that expressed divine patterns inherent in the cosmos" (Lewis, 1990, p. 98), and it was the Warrior Adept's mastery of this "warfare of the mind" that enabled him to lead his troops to victory (Lewis, p. 104).

In War,
>   There are Five Steps:

>   Measurement,

Jia Lin: Of terrain.

>   Estimation,

Jia Lin: Of strength in numbers and of supplies in granaries.

>   Calculation,

Jia Lin: In terms of numbers. The many as opposed to the few, the strong as opposed to the weak.

Comparison,

Jia Lin: Having calculated the numbers, ascertaining the relative weight and ability of the two sides.

Wang Xi: Weighing with a steelyard balance.

Translator: The word *cheng* refers to the Chinese "suspended steelyard of unequal arms," used since ancient times for weighing.

Victory.

Zhang Yu: This refers to the [likely victorious outcome consequent on having a] proper arrangement of camp and battle formations. As Duke Li said, "Training troops is like placing pieces on a Go board. If there is no designated path, how can you deploy your men?"

Earth determines
Measurement;

Cao Cao: We measure according to the outward form *[xing]* and dynamic energy *[shi]* of the earth *[terrain]*.

Measurement determines
Estimation;

Du Mu: Once the earth *[terrain]* has been properly measured, then we can estimate the enemy's relative strength.

Estimation determines
Calculation;

Du Mu: Calculation of the best strategic use of opportunity.

Calculation determines
Comparison;

Du Mu: Comparison of the relative chances of ourselves and the enemy.

Comparison determines
Victory.

Du Mu: Once we have made the comparison, the victory will be self-
evident.

The Way and Its Power, Chapter 25:   Man is patterned on earth;
earth is patterned on heaven; heaven is patterned on the Tao; the Tao is patterned on the natural.

Translator: Joseph Needham (1994, p. 47) comments that this passage
(which he thinks is probably a quotation from a very ancient text, older than
Master Sun's Art of War) "was not fully understood and has always puzzled
commentators." He himself understands it in the following way: "According to the principle of war the first measurement is Distance, the second
measurement is Volume, the third is Number, the fourth is Weight, the fifth
is Victory. . . ." Or, as he paraphrases it, "Territory determines physical distances and contours [my "measurement"], and these determine the necessary strength for an army ["estimation"], because there are potentially
strong and weak areas which indicate the number of troops which should
be used in particular places. The distribution of troops determines the
might that can be mustered at any particular place ["calculation"], and this
in turn affects the balance of power ["comparison"]; this last factor is the
one that determines victory."

A victorious army
    Is like a pound weight
    In the scale against
    A grain;
A defeated army
    Is like a grain
    In the scale against
    A pound weight.

A victorious army
    Is like
    Pent-up water

Crashing
A thousand fathoms
Into a gorge.

This is all
A matter of
Forms and
Dispositions.

Zhang Yu: By its nature, water avoids the high and hastens to the low. When a dam bursts, the water comes crashing out with irresistible force. Now, the forms and dispositions of an army resemble that of water. Take advantage of the enemy's unpreparedness; attack him when he least expects it; avoid his strength and strike his weakness. Then you are like water, and nothing can oppose you.

Chapter Five

Potential Energy

Cao Cao: In war, rely on the potential energy of the situation.

Wang Xi: This refers to the permutations of accumulated potential energy. The Skillful Warrior, by relying on potential energy to obtain victory, never exhausts his own strength.

Translator: The word used in the title of this chapter, *shi,* lies at the very heart of *The Art of War.* I have already touched on this in my Introduction. It means literally "situation," and so the inherent power or dynamic of a situation or moment in time (for good or bad), the strength or weakness of a location (in terms of *fengshui,* or Chinese geomancy). But it is also used in a wide range of domains: it is the word for a sexual position as described in the Chinese sex handbooks (Chapter 2 of the *Wonderful Disquisition of the Plain Girl,* for example, is entitled "The Nine Positions [or *Shi*]"); for the lines of force in the contours of a landscape (which reveal to the eye of the landscape painter the inner energy of the landscape, at a deeper level than do its outer forms); for the inherent force of brushstrokes in Chinese calligraphy; for the tendency or style of a work of literature (Chapter 30 of *The Literary Mind and the Carving of Dragons* is entitled "Establishing a Style [or *Shi*]"). In the context of *The Art of War,* it means the potential energy, or strategic advantage, within a particular configuration of space and time. Thence it comes to mean the resulting might or influence of a person or group of people and so, in a strictly military context, "the power imparted to an army by the circumstances of the campaign" (Lewis, 1990, p. 117). As the great French sinologist Marcel Granet has written in his masterful study *La Pensée Chinoise* (new edition, Paris: Albin Michel, 1988, p. 351), "The various situations and conditions of time and space contain latent within themselves opportunities whose influence and power we must enable ourselves to exploit, if we are to make the utmost of what fate offers us." This fragile equilibrium between action and nonaction, between sensitivity to the signs of what is and the will to engage with it, expresses a fundamental dichotomy that underlies so much of early Chinese thinking about the management of human affairs in general, be they military, civil, or personal, be the philosophical standpoint Taoist, Confucian, or some other "nondenominational" strand in Chinese philosophy. It finds its earliest expression in that monumental repository of early Chinese thought *The Book of Changes,* whose entire premise is that it is possible to see into potential changes before they occur, to grasp the subtle configurations of Yin and Yang and thus attune oneself to the energy at work in the world around us. "The Master said, 'To know the pivots [the springs or mechanism of opportunity] is divine indeed. . . . The pivots are the first, imperceptible beginning of movement, the first trace of good or bad fortune that shows itself. The superior man perceives the pivot and immediately acts. He does not wait even for a day'" (Lewis, p. 119, quoting the Great Treatise from the Wilhelm/Baynes version of the *Changes,* 1967 edition, p. 342).

Writing of the warlords of the chaotic Warring States period in which Master Sun lived, Granet adds, "They lived in a state of constant revolutionary expectancy. They were preparing themselves to occupy the seat of the Son of Heaven, that is to say, to impose a new order on civilization. And so the slightest change could mean total change; and seizing the slightest sign of change was tantamount to seizing the opportunity of bringing about total change" (p. 351).

Master Sun said:

Managing many
　　Is the same as
　　Managing few;
　　It is a question of
　　Division.

Du Mu/Giles: This is achieved by organizing the regimental sections and carefully delegating authority and responsibility. In this way I only have a few men under my actual command. The First Han Emperor once said to his general Han Xin, "How large an army do you think I could lead?" To which Han Xin replied, "Not more than a hundred thousand men, Your Majesty." "And you?" asked the Emperor. "The more the better," replied Han Xin.

Fighting with many
>Is the same as
>Fighting with few;
>It is a matter of
>Marshaling men
>With gongs,
>Identifying them
>With flags.

Zhang Yu: When many troops are deployed and the distances between them are great, they cannot see or hear each other; with the use of gongs as a signal for retreat and flags as a signal for attack, the brave do not find themselves advancing in isolation, and the fearful do not end up retreating alone. [Compare Chapter 7.]

With a combination of
>Indirect and
>Direct,
>An army
>Can hold off the enemy
>Undefeated.

Cao Cao: Going straight out into battle is direct; appearing from the rear is indirect.

Li Quan: Confrontation is direct; lateral excursions are indirect. Without indirect tactics [or surprise troops], victory is unattainable.

Jia Lin: Face-to-face with the enemy, use direct formations; but react with indirect tactics [or surprise troops] on the flanks and to the fore and rear, and victory is assured.

He Yanxi: Troop configurations are infinite in their variety; they are all potentially direct and indirect. . . . Inasmuch as the enemy comes to see our direct tactics as indirect and our indirect tactics as direct, then the direct becomes indirect and the indirect direct. When General Han Xin arrayed his men with their backs to the river, at the same time sending a surprise force around the hill, taking the Zhao standards and destroying their state, he was using both kinds of tactics—direct (backs to the river) and indirect (around the hill). The same general assembled his troops outside the city of Linjin, feigning a frontal assault, and simultaneously launched a surprise attack, using wooden tubs, by way of Xiayang, and took the king of Wei prisoner. The frontal formation at Linjin was direct, the attack via Xiayang indirect. The combination of direct and indirect is the key to victory. [Compare *Historical Records,* Chapter 167; *History of the Former Han,* Chapter 34.]

Zhang Yu: Different people have different ideas of the meaning of direct and indirect. Master Weiliao said that direct tactics prized frontal attack, while indirect tactics preferred attack from the rear. This was also Cao Cao's way of thinking. Duke Li held a similar view. All of these thinkers treated direct and indirect as two separate things, failing to see how the two are interlocked, how they merge and transform into one another. Emperor Taizong of the Tang dynasty was the only person to grasp this: "Turn an indirect maneuver into a direct one by causing the enemy to see it as direct; in this way, a frontal attack becomes indirect. And vice versa. The secret lies in utterly confusing the enemy, so that he cannot fathom our intent."

Giles: To put it perhaps a little more clearly: any attack or other operation is "direct" on which the enemy has had his attention fixed; whereas that which is "indirect" takes him by surprise or comes from an unexpected quarter. If the enemy perceives a movement which is meant to be "indirect," it immediately becomes "direct."

Translator: This is the first appearance in *The Art of War* of the pair of terms *zheng* and *qi,* "direct" and "indirect," which are so central to Master Sun's strategic ideas. They could also be translated as "orthodox" and "unorthodox," "regular" and "irregular," "straightforward" and "surprise," "overt" and "covert." What Master Sun has in mind is the complementarity of the fixed assault and the flexible maneuver. As Brigadier General Sam Griffith puts it (pp. 34–35), "The science (or art) of tactics was born. The enemy, engaged by the *zheng* (orthodox) force, was defeated by the *qi* (unorthodox, unique, rare, wonderful) force or forces; the normal pattern was a holding or fixing effort by the *zheng* while *qi* groups attacked the deep flanks and rear. Distraction assumed great importance and the enemy's communications became a primary target." The French translator Jean Lévi (pp. 177–78), like He Yanxi, illustrates the point with one of Han Xin's exploits, going on to expound the point with characteristically French brilliance and wit: "General Han Xin, by repairing the suspended mountain walkways between Chang'an and Sichuan, deluded his enemy into thinking that this (normally 'indirect') route was the one he had chosen, and therefore into regarding it as the 'direct' mode of operation, and preparing against it. Meanwhile, General Han was in fact planning to attack the enemy via Chencang, and this (otherwise perfectly 'normal') route now became his 'surprise' attack. . . . When the frontal attack is the norm, a flanking attack becomes the exception; when the flanking attack is the norm, the frontal attack becomes the exception. Both norm and exception depend on what the other party is expecting. It is on the basis of the other's expectations that one has to make decisions, and surprise him with his guard down. One must always be one step ahead, and guess what he is guessing about our own plans, in order to turn his own calculations against him. This dialectic of the 'direct' and the 'indirect' brings us face-to-face with the infinite modalities of the paradox of the liar. Sometimes an excess of 'scheming' can cause one to blunder, whereas the total absence of 'scheming' is the supreme 'scheming.' If one is scheming against an enemy who is not scheming at all, one may end up the victim of one's own cleverness, having incorrectly assumed that he was scheming. Thus subtlety and stupidity become one. One can understand why certain generals in despair resorted to consulting *The Book of Changes* for their decisions." (My translation.)

> With an understanding of
>   Weakness and
>   Strength,
>   An army
>   Can strike
>   Like a millstone
>   Cast at an egg.

Cao Cao: By attacking that which is weakest with that which is strongest.

He Yanxi: In warfare, a knowledge of the weakness and strength in the potential energy of the situation ensures victory.

Zhang Yu: In assembling the troops, first be sure of the proper division of units; then perfect the banners and other forms of communication; then be clear about the direct and indirect tactics; once these elements are discerned, then the strength and weakness of the situation will be apparent.

Translator: Strictly speaking, the stone referred to is a large grindstone; millstone seems to convey better the relative size and weight.

> In warfare,
>> Engage
>> Directly;
>> Secure victory
>> Indirectly.

Cao Cao: Confront the enemy directly; attack indirectly from the flank where least expected.

Zhang Yu: First engage the enemy directly, at the same time steadily developing an indirect assault, either by pounding the enemy's flanks or falling on his rear.

Giles: A brilliant example of "indirect tactics" which decided the fortunes of a campaign was Lord Roberts' night march round the Peiwar Kotal in the second Afghan war.

The Way and Its Power, Chapter 57:   Rule the state directly; wage war indirectly; gain the empire through "nonaction."

> The warrior skilled
>> In indirect warfare
>> Is infinite
>> As Heaven and Earth,

Li Quan: In the variations and alternations of his movement and stillness.

>> Inexhaustible
>> As river and sea,

Li Quan: Infinitely flexible and mobile.

Zhang Yu: Infinitely resourceful in launching indirect attacks in response to the changing situation.

> He ends and begins again
> Like sun and moon
> Dies and is born again
> Like the Four Seasons.

Li Quan/Du You/Zhang Yu: Sun and moon revolve through their phases, they set and rise again, wax and wane; the seasons alternate, they move through cycles of hot and cold; the infinite variations of direct and indirect are like the setting and rising of the sun and moon, like the alternations of the seasons.

***Sun Bin's Art of War*, Chapter 31, "Direct and Indirect":**   The fundamental pattern of Heaven and Earth is such that when something has reached its apogee, it goes around [its cycle] again; when it has waxed, it wanes. . . . This is seen in the sun and moon, it is seen in the Four Seasons. . . . War is victory through form. . . . The changes of victory through form are as infinite as the changes of Heaven and Earth.

> There are but
>   Five notes,

Li Quan: *Gong, shang, jue, zhi, yu* [the five notes of the old pentatonic scale].

> And yet their permutations
> Are more
> Than can ever be heard.

Li Quan: Played on instruments of the eight sounds [gourd, clay, hide, wood, stone, metal, silk, and bamboo], they constitute an infinite repertoire of music.

> There are but
>   Five colors,

Li Quan: Blue, yellow, red, white, and black.

> And yet their permutations
> Are more
> Than can ever be seen.

> There are but
>   Five flavors

Li Quan: Sour, pungent, salty, sweet, bitter.

> And yet their permutations
> Are more
> Than can ever be tasted.

Li Quan: This is the art of the chef.

Zhang Yu: These are analogies of the infinite variations of direct and indirect.

> In the dynamics of War,
>   There are but these two—
>   Indirect
>   And direct—
>   And yet their permutations
>   Are inexhaustible.
>   They give rise to each other
>   In a never-ending,
>   Inexhaustible circle.

Wang Xi: Indirect and direct are the key to the door in warfare, the pivotal force in gaining victory. They revolve in an inexhaustible circle. Breaking that circle means defeat.

Zhang Yu: Indirect is also direct; direct is also indirect. In their infinite permutations, they give rise to one another [like Yin and Yang], like a circle that has neither beginning nor end; it cannot be exhausted.

A rushing torrent
  Carries boulders
  On its flood;
  Such is the energy
  Of its momentum.

Du You: The nature of water is soft and yielding, the nature of stone is hard and heavy; and yet water can roll great boulders downstream, by virtue of the torrential flood of its momentum.

Translator: The one word *shi* takes on different shades of meaning in different sections of this chapter and of the whole work: potential energy, dynamic, momentum. All are connected.

A swooping falcon
  Breaks the back
  Of its prey;
  Such is the precision
  Of its timing.

Giles: This seems to me to denote that instinct of self-restraint which keeps the bird from swooping on its quarry until the right moment, together with the power of judging when the right moment has arrived. [Compare Du Mu's note in Chapter 1, where he quotes the *Historical Records*: "A hawk must keep out of sight before it swoops."]

Translator: The image of the word *jie,* which I have here translated as "timing," comes from the knots or joints in a length of bamboo, so it comes to mean a division, a juncture, notches or demarcations in time and space, the rhythm or timing (necessary for a well-judged attack).

The Skillful Warrior's energy is
   Devastating;
   His timing,
   Taut.

Wang Xi: The warrior must seize the moment [grasp the opportunity], just as the falcon does.

Giles: The analogous quality in soldiers is the highly important one of being able to reserve their fire until the very instant at which it will be most effective. When the *Victory* went into action at Trafalgar at hardly more than a drifting pace, she was for several minutes exposed to a storm of shot and shell before replying with a single gun. Nelson coolly waited until he was within close range, when the broadside he brought to bear worked fearful havoc on the enemy's nearest ships. That was a case of *jie* ["timing"].

His energy is like
   A drawn crossbow,
   His timing like
   The release of a trigger.

Giles: The force [energy] is potential, being stored up in the bent crossbow until released by the finger on the trigger.

Translator: The introduction of the powerful crossbow around 500 B.C. revolutionized Chinese warfare, and its trigger action was a potent image. *The Book of Changes* (Appended Judgments) makes use of the same image: "The words and acts of the Sage are like the mechanism of a crossbow. Honor and shame depend on the releasing of the trigger." (Compare Wilhelm/ Baynes, p. 305.) In Chapter 11, p. 289, Master Sun once again uses the release of the crossbow trigger to describe the sudden unleashing of an army's potential energy.

In the tumult of battle,
   The struggle may seem
   Pell-mell,
   But there is no disorder;

In the confusion of the melee,
The battle array may seem
Topsy-turvy,
But defeat is out of the question.

Mei Yaochen: Divisions have in fact been fixed; signals and flags have been ordained; therefore, despite all the comings and goings, the breaking and joining of ranks, though the fighting may seem disordered, it is not so. The battle array may appear to have no front or rear, everything may appear to be going around in circles, but there is no question of defeat.

Giles: It is a little difficult to decide whether the words [signifying disorder and confusion] should not be taken as imperatives: "fight in disorder (for the purpose of deceiving the enemy), and you will be secure against real disorder."

Translator: Niu and Wang (1991) do indeed take the words in this sense: "Feign disorder and confusion in the ranks, and thereby ensure victory. This is an example of using the potential energy of the situation to deceive the enemy."

Disorder is founded
    On order;
    Fear,
    On courage;
    Weakness,
    On strength.

Du Mu: In other words, if you wish to feign disorder and entice your enemy into the fray, you must first achieve a high degree of order; if you wish to feign fear and lure your enemy into a trap, you must first achieve a high degree of courage; if you wish to feign weakness and lead the enemy into hubris, you must first achieve a high degree of strength.

Orderly disorder
    Is based on
    Careful division;

Zhang Yu: Apparent disorder, masking real order, is based on sound division and organization.

Courageous fear,
On potential energy;

Zhang Yu/Du Mu/*Records of the Grand Historian*, Biography of Sun Bin: Apparent fear, masking real courage, is founded on the potential energy of a favorable situation. The Wei general Pang Juan attacked the state of Han [in 341 B.C.], and the Qi general Tian Ji went to the aid of his ally Han. Sun Bin ["Cripple" Sun, a descendant of Master Sun and a deadly enemy of Pang Juan, the man originally responsible for amputating his legs at the knees] said to General Tian, "The troops of those three western states [Wei, Han, and Zhao] have always been fierce and contemptuous of the men of Qi. In fact, with them Qi has a reputation for fear and cowardice. A Skillful Warrior will turn the potential energy of this situation to his own advantage. March the troops of Qi into the territory of Wei, and then with each succeeding night let them make a show of a dwindling number of campfires, from a hundred thousand to fifty thousand to twenty thousand, thereby making it seem as if the men of Qi are deserting in droves." The Qi expeditionary force did exactly this. When General Pang Juan heard of it, he was delighted and exclaimed, "I always knew that the men of Qi were cowards and deserters!" He pursued them hotly for several days. The men of Qi came to the narrow defile at Maling, where Sun Bin gave orders for a tree to be inscribed with the words "Pang Juan died beneath this tree." He then secretly stationed ten thousand of his crossbow archers on either side of the defile and instructed them to let loose their arrows at the first sign of the lighting of a torch. Sure enough, General Pang arrived that very night and, seeing the inscription on the tree, gave orders for a torch to be lit so that he could read it. In that instant, before he could finish reading the inscription, ten thousand crossbows discharged their arrows, and his force was annihilated. He himself took his own life with his sword, exclaiming, "Let the glory be Sun Bin's!"

Strong weakness,
On troop dispositions.

Zhang Yu: The founding Emperor of the Han dynasty, Liu Bang, wishing to attack the Xiongnu barbarians, sent a number of spies to report on the condition of their forces [in 200 B.C.]. The Xiongnu concealed their strongest men and their sleekest horses and paraded only their weakest soldiers and skinniest livestock. All the spies advised the Emperor to attack, except for Liu Jing, who said, "When two countries fight, they usually exaggerate their strength. But our spies have seen nothing but old and infirm soldiers. This must be a ruse. They are keeping their crack troops hidden. It would be inadvisable to attack." The Emperor ignored his advice, attacked, and was duly surrounded by the Xiongnu at Mount Baideng.

> The warrior skilled at
>> Stirring the enemy
>> Provides a visible form,
>> And the enemy is sure to come.

Cao Cao: Provides the outward signs of weakness.

Du Mu: Not just weakness. What this means is, if we are strong and the enemy is weak, then we should exhibit weakness, and this will cause the enemy to come; if, on the other hand, we are weak and the enemy is strong, then we should exhibit strength, and this will cause the enemy to depart. The enemy's movements all follow ours.

Translator: The Marxist strategist and scholar Guo Huaruo (1984, p. 13) quotes Chairman Mao: "We can artificially create the enemy's mistakes, just as Master Sun says, by 'providing a visible form.' We provide a sign [form] in the east, and meantime we strike in the west; this is the stratagem [the sixth of the famous *Thirty-six Stratagems*] known as Cry East Strike West" (*Selected Works*, vol. 1, p. 193).

> He proffers the bait,
> And the enemy is sure
>> To take it.

Mei Yaochen: He exhibits fear, and the enemy is sure to respond.

Zhang Yu: He entices the enemy with some small gain, and the enemy is sure to rise to the bait.

He causes the enemy
To make a move
And awaits him
With full force.

Translator: François Jullien (pp. 164–65) puts this idea very well: "Profit and danger are held out to the enemy like a trap. This is the very principle of manipulation (in Master Sun's thinking), and what makes it so fascinating. To manipulate the 'other' [the enemy], is to make him want to do 'of his own accord and will' the very thing that I want him to do, and which I predict will do him harm (but which he thinks will be to his profit). He thinks he is making his own decisions, but in fact I am the one indirectly leading him on."

The Skillful Warrior
    Exploits
    The potential energy;
    He does not hold his men
    Responsible.
He deploys his men
    To their best
    But relies on
    The potential energy.

Du Mu: He first assesses the military dynamic [potential energy] and then measures the human talent available to him. He uses his men according to their capabilities and does not demand perfection.

Relying on the energy,
    He sends his men into battle
    Like a man
    Rolling logs or boulders.
    By their nature,
    On level ground
    Logs and boulders

Stay still;
On steep ground
They move;
Square, they halt;
Round, they roll.

Cao Cao: He relies on their natural energy.

Mei Yaochen: Logs and boulders are heavy objects. It is their own energy that enables them to move with ease. To move them by force is difficult. For an army to fight with the natural energy of the situation, and not with force, is the Way of Nature [*ziran,* the "of itself" naturalness of the Tao].

Skillfully deployed soldiers
Are like round boulders
Rolling down
A mighty mountainside.

Du Mu: Their unstoppable descent is due to the mountain, not to the boulders themselves. The main drift of this chapter is the importance in war of relying on the energy of the situation itself, using speed and sudden attack. In this way, a great deal can be achieved with little expenditure of force.

Mei Yaochen: When round boulders are on the mountainside, their energy is great; one man can push them downhill, and a thousand would be unable to check their descent.

Wang Xi: The boulders cannot roll of their own accord; it is the potential energy of the mountain that makes them unstoppable.

Zhang Yu: Likewise, it is potential energy that makes an army victorious. According to Li Jing [and also *The Book of Master Huainan*], there are three kinds of potential energy in warfare. The first is when a general despises the enemy and his officers love to fight, when ambition soars into the clouds and spirits blow like the wind; this is the energy of enthusiasm. The second is when one side finds itself in a narrow defile between mountains, where paths wind and narrow openings abound, where one man can hold the place and a thousand cannot pass through; this is the energy of terrain. The third is when the enemy is lax, weary, hungry, and thirsty, when his forward camp is not yet pitched and his rear van has not yet crossed the river; if one takes advantage of this situation, this is strategic energy. Thus, to send men into battle relying on potential energy is like letting a round ball roll down a sleep slope; the slightest exertion of force can have huge results.

These are all matters
Of potential energy.

Chapter Six

Empty and Full

Li Quan: The Skillful Warrior turns the empty into the full.

Du Mu: In war, avoid the full and strong, attack the empty and weak; but first of all know your own and the enemy's empty and full points [limitations and strengths].

Niu and Wang: Empty means fearful, weak, disorderly, hungry, exhausted, few, unprepared. Full means brave, strong, well ordered, well nourished, relaxed, many, prepared.

Wu Jiulong: Empty means hollow, as when military might is dispersed and vulnerable. Full means solid, as when military might is concentrated and strong. Empty and full are opposites, and yet they evolve into each other as part of an ongoing process. This chapter explains how, through an understanding and mastery of the relationship between empty and full, the warrior can seize the initiative in the struggle; he "stirs and is not stirred."

Translator: In Chinese medicine, "full" (*shi*) refers to the Yang state of "energy abundance" or "*repletio,*" while "empty" (*xu*) refers to the Yin state of "energy exhaustion" or "*inanitas.*" (See Manfred Porkert, *Chinese Medicine* [New York, 1982], p. 71.)

Guo Huaruo summarizes the drift of this chapter (1984, p. 130): "Avoiding the full and attacking the empty is a key principle in Master Sun's strategic thinking. He expounds the importance of taking the initiative and of avoiding passivity; of creating the enemy's weakness and of forcing or enticing the enemy troops to disperse and exhaust themselves, while our own troops concentrate their might; thus we counter exhaustion with a relaxed ease. And as soon as we detect a weak point in the enemy, we respond swiftly and seize the moment to attack while he is unprepared. We gain the victory by adapting our actions to those of the enemy."

Master Sun said:

First on the battlefield
    Waits for the enemy
    Fresh.

Jia Lin: He occupies a winning position and waits for the enemy. He is well prepared. His men and horses are relaxed and fresh.

Last on the battlefield
    Charges into the fray
    Exhausted.

Jia Lin: If, on the other hand, the enemy occupies an advantageous position, then I should not advance but should withdraw my troops, seeming not to wish to confront the enemy. He will assume that I have no strategy and will surely attack. And so I end up exhausting the enemy and not myself.

The Skillful Warrior
    Stirs
    And is not stirred.

Du Mu: I stir my enemy to move toward me, while I myself nurture my strength and wait for him. I do not go toward him, for fear of exhausting myself.

Zhang Yu: I stir my enemy into combat, and he is empty; I do not engage in combat and remain full. This is the art of empty and full, mine and the enemy's.

He lures his enemy
    Into coming
    Or obstructs him
    From coming.

Du You: Go where he is bound to go, attack where he is bound to defend. Defend the crucial passes and passages, and he will not be able to get through. As Master Wang said, "A single cat guards the hole, and ten thousand rats dare not come out; a single tiger guards the ford, and ten thousand deer dare not cross."

Translator: Master Wang seems to have been rather fond of the cat as tactician! See Du You's comment toward the end of Chapter 1.

> Exhaust
> A fresh enemy;

Cao Cao: Harass him.

> Starve
> A well-fed enemy;

Cao Cao: Cut off his supplies.

> Unsettle
> A settled enemy.

Cao Cao: Attack what he holds dear, go where he must go, and he will have to come to the rescue.

> Appear at the place
> To which he must hasten;
> Hasten to the place
> Where he least expects you.

Records of the Grand Historian, **Chapter 65:**   The state of Wei attacked the state of Zhao [in 354 B.C.] and laid siege to its capital, Handan. Zhao, hard pressed, begged for help from the state of Qi. The king of Qi wished to put Sun Bin in command of his troops, but Sun Bin refused, in view of the physical mutilation [amputation to the knee] he had recently been subjected to. Instead, Tian Ji was placed in command, with Sun Bin as his strategic adviser, traveling in a curtained carriage covered with a canopy, within which he contemplated his strategies. Tian Ji was for going straight to the relief of the besieged city of Handan. But Sun Bin argued with him that just as one does not disentangle a tangled skein of silk by hitting it, so one should not go to the aid of a party embroiled in a fight by joining in the free-for-all oneself. A better course of action would be to avoid obstacles and instead exploit the empty points of weakness. That way the tangle would untangle itself. Now, since Wei was at war with Zhao, its crack troops had been dispatched beyond its own frontiers, and only the old and the frail had been left behind at home. The smartest move would therefore be to march on the Wei capital at Daliang and cut their lines of communication. The Wei army would then be forced to leave Zhao and come to the rescue of its own threatened territory. In one move, not only would the siege of Handan have been lifted but a severe blow would have been dealt to Wei itself. Tian Ji followed this plan, and the Wei army withdrew from the siege of Handan. They fought the troops of Zhao at Guiling and suffered a crushing defeat. [This stratagem, of avoiding the "full" (the besieged Zhao capital at Handan) and instead attacking the "empty" (the undefended Wei capital at Daliang), is the second of *The Thirty-six Stratagems*, Attacking Wei to save Zhao.]

> March hundreds of miles
>   Without tiring,
>   By traveling
>   Where no enemy is.

Cao Cao: Set out in the void; attack emptiness; avoid that which is defended; attack where you are not expected.

> Be sure of victory
>   By attacking
>   The undefended.

Wang Xi: Attack an empty (weak) point, one where the general is incompetent or the soldiers ineffectual; where the fortifications are not strong or the precautions not strict; where relief will come too late, or provisions are too scanty, or where the defenders are at variance among themselves.

Zhang Yu: He who is skilled in attack dashes forth from the topmost heights of the Ninefold Heaven [see Chapter 4], making it impossible for the enemy to guard against him. The places to attack are precisely those that the enemy cannot defend.

> Be sure of defense
> By defending
> The unattacked.

Zhang Yu: He who is skilled in defense hides below the Ninefold Earth, making it impossible for the enemy to estimate his whereabouts. In this way, the places that I shall hold are precisely those that the enemy cannot attack.

> The Skillful Warrior attacks
> So that the enemy
> Cannot defend;
> He defends
> So that the enemy
> Cannot attack.

Wang Xi: The Skillful Attacker waits for the enemy to exhibit a sign of vulnerability and then attacks with all speed; in this way the enemy cannot defend. The Skillful Defender ensures that he is never vulnerable; in this way the enemy can never attack.

Giles: An aphorism which puts the whole art of war into a nutshell.

Translator: Wu Jiulong (pp. 88–89) paraphrases: "The skillful attacking force succeeds by making it impossible for the enemy to know where to defend; the skillful defending force succeeds by making it impossible for the enemy to know where to attack."

> Oh, subtlety of subtleties!
> Without form!
> Oh, mystery of mysteries!
> Without sound!

He is master of
His enemy's fate.

Wang Xi: Subtle and inscrutable, so he cannot be seen; mysterious and swift, so that no response is possible. That is how he can control the enemy's fate.

He Yanxi: Master Sun's method of "empty and full" is indeed subtle and mysterious, and its results are exceedingly great. We cause the enemy to see our strength as weakness and our weakness as strength; we in our turn are able to convert the enemy's strength into weakness, and as for the enemy's weakness, we know it for what it is. So the enemy is not aware of our weakness and strength, but we are aware of his. If we wish to attack him, we know that the place he is defending must be a place of strength, and that the place he is not defending is weak; we can then avoid his strong point and attack him where he is frailest. We can go for his throat. We can home in on his most vulnerable point. . . . Thus, when we do attack, he does not know where to defend; and when we defend, he does not know where to attack. All the prodigious permutations of attack and defense arise from this method of "empty and full." . . . The Skillful Warrior is adept at these permutations and can penetrate into the inner recesses of this most subtle of mysteries. . . .

Zhang Yu: The techniques of attack and defense are subtle and ingenious, they are mysterious and secret. They are not outwardly visible or audible. It is through them that we can become the masters of our enemy's fate, of his life or death.

He advances
    Irresistibly,
    Attacking emptiness.

Translator: Like Cook Ding, in *The Book of Master Zhuang*, Chapter 3, "The Secret of Caring for Life": "What I care about is the Way, which is more advanced than mere skill. When I first began cutting up oxen, what I saw was the whole ox. After three years I no longer saw the whole ox. And now—now I approach it with my spirit and don't see it with my eyes. My senses have stopped, and my spirit moves at will. I follow the pattern of nature, I strike in the big hollows, I glide my knife through the big joints, and go with the nature of the ox. . . ." (Compare Watson, pp. 50–51.)

> He retreats,
>   Eluding pursuit,
>   Too swift
>   To be overtaken.

Zhang Yu: He comes like the wind, he goes like lightning.

> If I wish to engage,
>   Then the enemy,
>   For all his high ramparts
>   And deep moat,
>   Cannot avoid the engagement;
>   I attack that which
>   He is obliged
>   To rescue.

Du Mu: Suppose the enemy has invaded my territory; I can cut his supplies and occupy the roads by which he will have to return. If, on the other hand, I am the invader, I may direct my attack against the sovereign himself.

> If I do not wish to engage,
>   I can hold my ground
>   With nothing more than a line
>   Drawn around it.

Jia Lin: Even though I have constructed neither wall nor ditch.

> The enemy cannot
>   Engage me
>   In combat:

I distract him
In a different direction.

Li Quan: Puzzle him by strange and unusual dispositions, and so make it impossible for him to engage in battle. In the Han dynasty [144 B.C.] General Li Guang [finding his force of one hundred cavalry threatened by several thousand Xiongnu horsemen, instead of fleeing], ordered his men to dismount, undo their saddles, turn loose their horses, and lie down on the ground, thereby causing the Xiongnu to suspect an ambush [and enabling his own men to return home safely].

Du Mu/Zhang Yu: [The great general and strategist] Zhuge Liang [the Sleeping Dragon—see Introduction], when encamped at Yangping, ordered Wei Yan and other commanders of his to proceed together eastward, while he kept a small force of ten thousand men to defend the city. The opposing general, Sima Yi, observed that Zhuge Liang had few troops in the city and that his generals and officers seemed to have lost heart. In point of fact, Zhuge's spirits were high. He deliberately ordered his troops to lay down their banners and silence their drums, and he forbade them to go out. Then he threw open the four gates of the city and set men to sweeping and sprinkling the streets. General Sima suspected an ambush and drew off his army to the northern hills. Subsequently, when he learned the truth of what had happened, he felt extremely bitter about it. [This is the famous Stratagem of the Empty City, the thirty-second in *The Thirty-six Stratagems,* where it is classified as a stratagem for use in a desperate situation, a deliberate and crafty exploitation of one's own weakness, to outwit the enemy. The veracity of the story has been questioned by historians, but it has always been popular with Chinese novelists and dramatists. As it is told in Chapter 95 of the Ming-dynasty novel *The Romance of the Three Kingdoms,* the wily Zhuge Liang is calmly playing his lute on the battlements, in full view of the enemy, a smile on his face, incense burning, with no one except two page boys in attendance.]

Giles: What Master Sun is advocating here is nothing more nor less than the timely use of "bluff." [He would doubtless have been an excellent poker player.]

His form is visible,
     But I am
     Formless;

I am concentrated,
He is divided.

Zhang Yu: If the enemy's forms (dispositions) are visible, we can attack as one body; whereas, so long as our own forms (dispositions) are kept secret, the enemy will be obliged to divide his forces in order to guard against attack from every quarter.

Translator: Any disposition/form is per se a handicap; it bogs you down (through loss of dynamism); it concretizes and so reduces possibilities. By acquiring a form, the enemy becomes numb, while I, by remaining formless, also remain alert and flexible. The enemy is caught "downhill" of reality; I remain "uphill" of it and am able to manipulate the situation to my advantage. (See Jullien, p. 168.)

I am concentrated
  Into one;
  He is divided
  Into ten.
  I am
  Ten
  To his one;
  Many
  Against
  His few.

Attack few with many,
  And my opponent
  Will be weak.

Du Mu: I may use light troops and sturdy cavalry to attack him at an "empty" spot; I may use strong crossbows and archers to seize one of his key positions. I attack him left and right; I surprise him in front and rear. By day I confuse him with flags; by night I confuse him with beacons and drums. So my opponent is filled with fear, divides his forces in order to defend himself. I know his dispositions, but he does not know mine. I am united, he is divided. I am sure of victory.

> The place I intend to attack
>   Must not be known;
>   If it is unknown,
>   The enemy will have to
>   Reinforce many places;
>   The enemy will
>   Reinforce many places,
>   But I shall attack
>   Few.

Giles: [General Philip Henry] Sheridan [1831–88] once explained the reason for General Grant's [1822–85] victories by saying that "while his opponents were kept fully employed wondering what he was going to do, *he* was thinking most of what he was going to do himself."

Zhang Yu: He will have no idea where my chariots will actually go out to, or where my cavalry will actually come from, or where my infantry will actually proceed to, and therefore he will disperse and divide, in order to defend himself everywhere against me. Consequently, his force will be scattered and weakened and his strength divided and dissipated, and wherever I engage him, I can use a large host against his isolated units.

> By reinforcing his vanguard,
>   He weakens his rear;
> By reinforcing his rear,
>   He weakens his vanguard.
> By reinforcing his right flank,
>   He weakens his left;
> By reinforcing his left,
>   He weakens his right.
> By reinforcing every part,
>   He weakens every part.

Translator: Giles quotes from Frederick the Great's (1712–86) *Instructions to His Generals:* "A defensive war is apt to betray us into frequent detachment. Those generals who have had but little experience attempt to protect every point, while those who are better acquainted with their profession, having only the capital object in view, guard against a decisive blow, and acquiesce in smaller misfortunes to avoid greater."

> Weakness
>> Stems from
>> Preparing against attack.
> Strength
>> Stems from
>> Obliging the enemy
>> To prepare against an attack.

Translator: Giles quotes Colonel Henderson (George Francis Robert Henderson [1854–1903], instructor in tactics, military law, and administration at the Royal Military College, Sandhurst, author of *The Science of War* [posthumous, 1905]): "The highest generalship is to compel the enemy to disperse his army, and then to concentrate superior force against each fraction in turn."

> If we know
>> The place and the day
>> Of the battle,
>> Then we can engage
>> Even after a march
>> Of hundreds of miles.

Du You: The Skillful Warrior must know where and when a battle will be fought. He must measure the roads [to be traveled] and fix the date [of the encounter]. He must divide his army and march in separate columns. Those who are distant start first; those who are closer start later. Thus, troops setting out from distances of several hundreds of miles converge at the same time, like a throng converging on a city market.

Du Mu: Emperor Wu of the Liu-Song dynasty [Liu Yu, founding Emperor of the short-lived dynasty, who disposed of the last Emperor of the previous Jin dynasty and reigned for two years until his own death in 422] sent Zhu Lingshi to attack Qiao Zong in Shu [the western region nowadays known as Sichuan]. "Last year," said the Emperor, "Liu Jingxuan set out from within the Yangtze toward Huangwu. He returned having failed in his mission. The rebels would normally expect me to come from outside the Yangtze but will imagine that this time I will try to take them by surprise, by attacking from within the river again. In which case they will certainly defend the city of Fucheng with a strong force and guard the roads in the interior. So if I proceed toward Huangwu, I will fall straight into their trap. Instead, I will take the main force outside the Yangtze and take the city of Chengdu, thus distracting their troops toward the region within the river. This is my indirect tactic for controlling the enemy." But the Emperor was concerned that this plan of his would become known to the enemy and that the rebels would thereby know his weakness and strength, where his empty and full points were. So he gave General Zhu a sealed letter, with instructions to open it only when he had reached White Emperor City [along the Yangtze]. Thus, when it set off, the army did not know where or how it was going to be divided. When General Zhu reached White Emperor City, he opened the letter, and read, "The main force is to take the city of Chengdu from outside the river; Zang Xi and Zhu Lin will take Guanghan from the central river road; the weakest troops will be dispatched from within the river on ten tall boats toward Huangwu." Sure enough, Qiao Zong was defending the region within the river with a strong force, and General Zhu destroyed him.

Giles: What Master Sun evidently has in mind is that nice calculation of distances and that masterly employment of strategy which enable a general to divide his army for the purpose of a long and rapid march, and afterwards to effect a junction at precisely the right spot and the right hour in order to confront the enemy in overwhelming strength. Among many such successful junctions which military history records, one of the most dramatic and decisive was the appearance of Blücher just at the critical moment on the field of Waterloo.

> But if neither day
>   Nor place
>   Is known,

Then left cannot
Help right,
Right cannot
Help left,
Vanguard cannot
Help rear,
Rear cannot
Help vanguard.
It is still worse
If the troops
Are separated
By a dozen miles
Or even by a mile or two.

Zhang Yu: If we do not know the place where our enemy plans to assemble his forces or the day on which they will join battle, our unity will be dissipated through our preparations for defense, and the positions we hold will be insecure. Then, if we suddenly encounter a powerful enemy, we shall engage battle in a flurried condition, and no mutual support will be possible among wings, vanguard, or rear, especially if there is any great distance between the front and rear divisions of the army.

Giles: The mental picture we are required to draw is probably that of an army advancing towards a given rendezvous in separate columns, each of which has orders to be there on a fixed date. If the general allows the various detachments to proceed at haphazard, without precise instructions as to the time and place of meeting, the enemy will be able to annihilate the army in detail.

Translator: More than one modern commentator has observed that one of the best recent examples of this (letting "neither day nor place be known") was the Normandy landings, whose success was due in no small part to the fact that the Germans knew neither the day nor the place.

According to my assessment,
    The troops of Yue
    Are many,

But that will avail them little
In the struggle.
So I say
Victory
Is still possible.

Giles: Master Sun was in the service of [the ancient state of] Wu. [The state of] Yue coincided roughly with the present province of Zhejiang. Alas for these brave words! The long feud between the two states ended in 473 B.C. with the total defeat of Wu by Gou Jian, and its incorporation into Gou's kingdom of Yue.

The enemy may be many,
But we can prevent
An engagement.

Jia Lin: The enemy may be many in number, but if he does not know our military circumstances, we can always keep him busy with his own preparations, so that he has no time to plan for an engagement.

Zhang Yu: Divide them and dissipate their strength, so that they cannot assemble their force and advance. Then how can they possibly engage us?

Scrutinize him,
Know the flaws
In his plans.

Rouse him,
Discover the springs
Of his actions.

Zhang Yu: Eventually, by noting the enemy's joy or anger, we can conclude what his policy is. Zhuge Liang did this by sending the insulting present of a woman's headdress to the enemy general Sima Yi. But Sima [despite his anger] still refused to engage battle [because his Emperor commanded him to stand firm]. [See *The Three Kingdoms*, Chapters 103–4.]

Make his form visible,
    Discover his grounds
    Of death and life.

Probe him,
    Know his strengths
    And weaknesses.

The highest skill
    In forming dispositions
    Is to be without form;
    Formlessness
    Is proof against the prying
    Of the subtlest spy
    And the machinations
    Of the wisest brain.

The Book of Master Zhuang, Chapter 6, "The Great and Venerable Teacher": The Way has its reality and its signs, but has neither action nor form. You can hand it down, but you cannot receive it; you can get it, but you cannot see it. [Compare Watson, p. 81.]

Exploit the enemy's dispositions
    To attain victory;
    This the common man
    Cannot know.
    He understands
    The forms,
    The dispositions
    Of my victory;
    But not
    How I created the forms
    Of victory.

Giles: Everybody can see superficially how a battle is won; what they cannot see is the long series of plans and combinations which has preceded the battle.

Translator: Jean Lévi (p. 195) points out that the Taoist *Book of Master Huainan* (ca. 140 B.C.) returns again and again to this underlying paradox: that the supreme form of military forms or dispositions is to present no form.

> Victorious campaigns
>   Are unrepeatable.
>   They take form in response
>   To the infinite varieties
>   Of circumstance.

Wang Xi: There is only one basic principle underlying victory, but the forms and dispositions leading to it are infinite.

Translator: Compare Wang Xi's comment with Giles's quotation from Colonel Henderson's *The Science of War:* "The rules of strategy are few and simple. They may be learned in a week. But such knowledge will no more teach a man to lead an army like Napoleon than a knowledge of grammar will teach him to write like Gibbon."

> Military dispositions
>   Take form like water.
>   Water shuns the high
>   And hastens to the low.

The Way and Its Power, **Chapter 8:** The highest excellence is like water. Water profits the whole of creation, but it never contends.

The Way and Its Power, **Chapter 78:** Nothing in the world is as soft and yielding as water, but when it attacks something hard, nothing can surpass it.

Translator: Jean Lévi (p. 196) draws attention to the way in which Master Sun "defends a feminine conception of war, the strength inherent in weakness. He echoes *The Way and Its Power* in showing that war is not a matter of force and heroism, but of ruse and humility."

> War shuns the strong
> And attacks the weak.

Giles: Like water, it takes the line of least resistance.

Translator: It is frequently remarked that the secret of the Vietcong's success was their mastery of this maxim. And Mao and his forces had "an almost uncanny ability to determine points of Nationalist weakness, which permitted them to exploit these qualities and led inevitably to an accelerating disintegration of the Nationalist position" (Griffith, p. 55).

> Water shapes its current
>   From the lie of the land.
> The warrior shapes his victory
>   From the dynamic of the enemy.

Li Quan: How else but from the enemy's dynamic can I fashion victory?

Du Mu: From the enemy's "emptiness" [weakness].

> War has no
>   Constant dynamic;

Mei Yaochen: Its energy evolves in response to the enemy.

> Water has no
>   Constant form.

Mei Yaochen: Its form evolves from the land.

Translator: "Of itself, water has no form. It is constantly *con*forming, it evolves through adaptation. It is because it always adapts that it always progresses. In the same way, it is only by adapting to the enemy's situation that I can triumph. The enemy's situation is for me as the lie of land is for the water. I mold myself upon the enemy's situation; I espouse him rather than thwarting him. I never stiffen into any form, but instead I conform. As a result, victory is irresistible, irreversible, like water in its course, never going astray, always flowing downward, without a moment's hesitation!" (Translated from Jullien, p. 205, who is skillfully restating the Chinese commentators, as he so often does.)

Supreme military skill lies
    In deriving victory
    From the changing circumstances
    Of the enemy.

Du Mu: In war, the potential energy emerges from the enemy's circumstances. It does not depend on us, so it is not constant. It is like water, which takes its form from the land; the form does not lie in the water, it is not a constant. By responding to the downward slope of the land, water can carry boulders downstream; by responding to the enemy's circumstances, the warrior is able to change and adapt to a supreme degree.

Among the Five Elements
    There is no one
    Constant supremacy.

Translator: As Wu Jiulong (1990, p. 105) comments, "The ancient Chinese considered these five elements or phases [earth, water, fire, metal, and wood] to be the basis of the organization of all matter. According to the Five Element School of the Warring States period, they 'produce' one another and 'control' one another. What Master Sun is saying is that the permutations involved in this complex natural process are as subtle and unfathomable as those involved in the field of military strategy."

The Four Seasons
    Have no
    Fixed station;

Wang Xi: They revolve, one taking the place of the other.

There are long days
    And short;
    The moon
    Waxes
    And it
    Wanes.

Wang Xi: Like the changes [the perpetually shifting and flexible improvisations] of the Warrior Adept: there is no single, unchanging Way.

Chapter Seven

The Fray

Zhang Yu: The two armies fight it out face-to-face in the fray. Before entering the fray, we need to know the "empty and full," the enemy's and our own weaknesses and strengths. This section therefore follows on from the previous one.

Master Sun said:

In War,
The general
Receives orders
From his sovereign,
Assembles troops,
And forms an army.
He makes camp
Opposite the enemy.
The true difficulty
Begins with
The fray itself.

Chen Hao: There are old and well-established rules for the assembling of troops and the forming of an army, and for making camp. It is with the fray itself that the difficulty commences.

The difficulty of the fray
Lies in making
The crooked
Straight

Cao Cao: Make a show of being far away, then march with all speed and arrive before the enemy.

Du Mu: Fool the enemy, cause him to be remiss, while you press swiftly ahead.

***The Way and Its Power*, Chapter 22:**   Be twisted, and thus be complete; be crooked, and thus be straight.

Translator: As Giles says, "This is one of those highly condensed and somewhat enigmatical expressions of which Master Sun is so fond." Part of the problem lies in the ambiguity of the Chinese pair *yu/zhi*, which can mean both "crooked/straight" and "circuitous/direct."

> And in making
> An advantage
> Of misfortune.

He Yanxi: Suppose the country that you are attacking is a long way away, and the roads to it are twisting and mountainous. To gain the upper hand, divide your troops and send out surprise sorties. Follow the advice of local guides, take shortcuts, catch the enemy unawares, striking him when he is least prepared. Through the judicious use of speed, you will have made an advantage of misfortune.

Giles: Signal examples of this saying are afforded by the two famous passages across the Alps—that of Hannibal [247–183 B.C.], which laid Italy at his mercy, and that of Napoleon two thousand years later, which resulted in the great victory of Marengo [1800].

> Take a roundabout route,
>   And lure the enemy
>   With some gain;
> Set out after him,
>   But arrive before him;
>   This is to master
>   The crooked
>   And the straight.

Cao Cao: Take a roundabout [crooked] route, and make it seem to involve a great distance. You may start after the enemy, but if you calculate carefully and estimate distances correctly, you can still arrive before him.

Du Mu: Let the enemy think your route long and tortuous, and he will drop his guard; lure him with the prospect of some gain, and he will lose concentration. Then march with utmost speed, and take him by surprise, setting out after him, but arriving before him [at the place of battle], in time to seize the strategic positions.

When the troops of Qin attacked Han [270 B.C.], the king of Zhao [a Han ally] first consulted Lian Po, who advised him that the distance was too great and the intervening country too rugged and difficult [for them to intervene in Han]. The king then turned to Zhao She, who admitted the hazardous nature of the march, but said, "We shall be like two rats fighting in a hole—and the braver one will win!" So he set out from the Zhao capital of Handan, but when he had traveled no more than a dozen miles, ordered his men to pitch camp. For twenty-eight days they dug themselves firmly in. General Zhao deliberately gave the spies sent by Qin the impression that he and his men were loath to travel all the way to Han. Then, as soon as the spies had reported back to their masters on what they had seen, Zhao set off on a forced march, pressing on through two nights and a day. He took the Qin army by surprise, occupied the heights to their north, and won a resounding victory.

The fray can bring
   Gain;
   It can bring
   Danger.

Cao Cao: All depends on the skill of the warrior.

Throw your entire force
   Into the fray
   For some gain,
   And you may still
   Fail.

Cao Cao: You may arrive late.

Mei Yaochen: It is cumbersome and slow to commit the whole army to a maneuver.

Jia Lin: Better conceive a subtle plan, keep it secret, and deceive the enemy into thinking that you are taking a long, roundabout [crooked] route. Then take him by surprise.

> Abandon camp and
>> Enter the fray
>> For some gain,
>> And you may lose
>> Your equipment.

Du Mu: Attacking with the whole army [baggage train and all] is cumbersome and slow. But attacking with light troops can mean leaving the baggage train unattended and sacrificing it.

Du You: The enemy may take advantage of this "empty" [weak] spot and annihilate your rear while you are attacking with light troops.

> Order your men to
>> Carry their armor
>> And make forced march,
>> Day and night,
>> Without halting,
>> March thirty miles
>> At double speed
>> For some gain,
>> And you will lose
>> All your commanders.
>> The most vigorous men
>> Will be in the vanguard;
>> The weakest,
>> In the rear.

One in ten
Will arrive.

Cao Cao: Do not fight after marching thirty miles. Your commanders will all be taken.

Du Mu: An average day's march is ten miles, at the end of which soldiers normally pitch camp. They can make a forced march of thirty or forty miles, but if they engage in battle immediately afterward, they will be exhausted, and all their officers will be captured.

Li Quan: On one occasion, when pursuing Liu Bei, Cao Cao covered a hundred miles in twenty-four hours. . . . This led to his subsequent defeat at the famous Battle of Red Cliff [A.D. 208]. And when Pang Juan pursued Sun Bin [ca. 341 B.C.], he met his end at Maling.

March fifteen miles
    For some gain,
    And the commander
    Of the vanguard
    Will fall;
    Only half the men
    Will arrive.

March ten miles
    For some gain,
    And two in three men
    Will arrive.

Without its equipment,
    An army is lost;
Without provisions,
    An army is lost;
Without base stores,
    An army is lost.

Without knowing the plans
   Of the feudal lords,
   You cannot
   Form alliances.

Without knowing the lie
   Of hills and woods,
   Of cliffs and crags,
   Of marshes and fens,
   You cannot
   March.

Without using local guides,
   You cannot
   Exploit
   The lie of the land.

Du Mu: As Master Guan says, "In War, a general must study the maps of the region. He must know which are the difficult passages for wagons, which stretches of river are liable to flooding; he must be familiar with the mountain ranges and valleys, the rivers and the topography and relief in general, the variations in vegetation, the distances involved in the various routes, the relative size and importance of the various fortified towns and cities, the relative poverty of the different areas. All this he must know. Only when all of this is stored in his memory can he take proper advantage of the lie of the land."

And Duke Li Jing once said, "Cloak your attack in secrecy, as do the bands of local brigands. Choose brave men and intelligent commanders. With the help of local guides, penetrate deep into the mountains and forests, making no sound, leaving no trace. Sometimes such men wear upon their feet moccasins incised in imitation of the paws of animals, leaving nothing but animal imprints on the mountain trails; sometimes they hide themselves in the undergrowth, wearing headgear in imitation of the plumage of birds. In this way they can hear the most distant sounds, they can see the most remote sights. They can be all concentration and gauge the exact moment for action. They can be all attention and perceive the slightest sign. From the trace of some movement in the water, they know when the enemy is crossing a ford; from the trembling of a branch, they know of the approach of enemy reinforcements.

Translator: The last fourteen lines of Master Sun's text occur again in Chapter 11.

> War
>   Is founded
>   On deception;

Du Mu: Deceive the enemy, keep him ignorant of your true situation, and the victory is yours.

Wang Xi: This means making the crooked straight, making an advantage of misfortune.

Translator: It has been observed that General Schwarzkopf was following Master Sun to the letter in the Gulf War, when he fooled Saddam Hussein as to the true nature of his attack, threatening an amphibious assault in the east, but launching an "end run" in the west. Giles alludes to Turenne (Louis XIV's marshal of France, 1611–75), according to whose tactics deception of the enemy, especially as to the numerical strength of his troops, took a very prominent position.

> Movement is determined
>   By advantage;

Zhang Yu: Move only when you see an advantage; do not make futile attacks.

> Division and unity
>   Are its elements
>   Of Change.

Cao Cao: Dividing and uniting troops—these changes derive from [observation of] the enemy.

Du Mu: At times divide, at others unite; perplex the enemy. Observe his response to your dispositions, then improvise accordingly and emerge the victor.

Zhang Yu: At times divide and disperse your dispositions, at other times unite and concentrate your potential. These changes derive from the actions of the enemy.

Translator: As Brigadier General Sam Griffith points out (p. 51), Chairman Mao paraphrases this verse several times. For example, "A commander proves himself wise . . . by being able to disperse, concentrate or shift his forces in time according to specific circumstances. This wisdom in foreseeing changes and this sense of right timing are not easy to acquire. . . ."

Be rushing as a wind;

Cao Cao: Striking the void.

Mei Yaochen: Coming without trace.

Be stately as a forest;

Meng: When marching slowly, order and ranks must be preserved like [the rows of trees in] a forest, to guard against surprise attack.

Be ravaging as a fire;

Zhang Yu: As it says in *The Book of Songs*, "Fierce as a raging fire, which no man can check."

Be still as a mountain;

Zhang Yu: As Master Xun [Chapter 15, "Discussing Military Affairs"] says, "When it is drawn up in camp [i.e., still], it [the army of the Perfect Man] is like a solid rock; whoever butts against it will be broken, smashed to pieces."

Translator: According to Brigadier General Griffith (p. 106), these four phrases were used by the sixteenth-century Japanese warrior Takeda

Harunobu (the Zen monk "Archbishop Shingen," d. 1573) as slogans on his banners. This same general, while reputed to have been a studious and meditative scholar, was also a ruthless and ferocious commander, whose camp equipment apparently included three large kettles for boiling criminals.

Be inscrutable as night;

Zhang Yu: When dark clouds cover the sky and it is impossible to detect the first light of morning.

Be swift as thunder or lightning.

Zhang Yu: Strike suddenly, like a clap of thunder or a bolt of lightning, too quick to be repulsed. As the Ancient Duke says, "A clap of thunder leaves no time to cover the ears; a flash of lightning strikes before the eyes can blink." [Compare Chen Hao's comment in Chapter 2.]

Plunder the countryside,
And divide the spoil;

Cao Cao: Let the enemy create your victory.

Zhang Yu: This is simply a matter of enforcing the earlier advice of Master Sun, that "a wise general should feed his army off the enemy." The enemy will be reluctant to share their modest possessions.

Extend territory,
And distribute the profits.

Chen Hao: Quarter your soldiers on the land, and let them sow and plant it.

Giles: It is by acting on this principle, and harvesting the lands they invaded, that the Chinese have succeeded in carrying out some of their most memorable and triumphant expeditions, such as that of Ban Chao [A.D. 32–102] who penetrated the Caspian, and in more recent times of [the Manchu general] Fukangan [d. 1796] and Zuo Zongtang [1812–85].

Translator: Fukangan commanded several expeditions into Central Asia and Tibet; Zuo Zongtang was largely responsible for the creation of the province of Xinjiang (formerly referred to as Chinese Turkestan) in 1884. It must be remembered that Giles was writing during the last days of imperialism, when China's ambitions in Central Asia seemed only reasonable.

> Weigh the situation carefully
> Before making a move.

> Victory belongs to the man
> Who can master
> The stratagem of
> The crooked
> And the straight.

> This is the
> Art of the Fray.

Giles: With these words the chapter would naturally come to an end. But there now follows a long appendix in the shape of an extract from an earlier book on War, now lost, but apparently extant at the time when Master Sun wrote.

> The Military Primer says:

Mei Yaochen/Wang Xi: An ancient military classic.

Giles: Considering the enormous amount of fighting that had gone on for centuries before Master Sun's time between the various kingdoms and principalities of China, it is not in itself improbable that a collection of military maxims should have been made and written down at some earlier period.

> When ears do not hear,
> Use gongs and drums.
> When eyes do not see,
> Use banners and flags.

Gongs and drums,
  Banners and flags
  Are the
  Ears and eyes
  Of the army.

Zhang Yu: If sight and hearing are focused simultaneously on the same object, the maneuvers of a million soldiers will be like those of a single man. Hence Master Sun's earlier statement: "Fighting with many is the same as fighting with few; it is a matter of marshaling men with gongs, identifying them with flags."

With the army focused,
  The brave will not
  Advance alone,
  Nor will the fearful
  Retreat alone.

Du Mu: When Master Wu fought against the state of Qin, there was an officer who, before the battle commenced, was unable to control his ardor. He advanced, and returned with a pair of heads. Master Wu ordered him to be beheaded. The army commissioner protested, "He is a talented officer. He should not be beheaded." To which Master Wu replied, "I do not question the fact. But he acted without orders." The man was beheaded.

Zhang Yu: As the saying goes, those who advance against orders and those who retreat against orders are equally to blame.

This is the Art of
  Managing Many.

In night fighting,
  Use torches and drums;
In daylight,
  Use banners and flags;
  So as to transform

The ears and eyes
Of the troops.

Chen Hao: At the end of the Tian-bao era [A.D. 742–56], Li Guangbi hastened with five hundred cavalry to Heyang, with a great display of torches. [The rebel leader] Shi Siming, at the head of his large force, did not dare obstruct their passage.

A whole fighting force
Can be robbed
Of its spirit;

Li Quan: Robbed of its zeal and courage. The state of Qi attacked the state of Lu at Changshao. The Qi drums sounded, and the duke of Lu was about to join battle, when his counselor Cao Gui advised him that the time was not yet come. When the Qi drums had sounded three times, Cao said the time was right. They joined battle, and the Qi army was utterly defeated. The duke of Lu asked Cao what his reasoning had been. "Battle," replied the counselor, "is a matter of courage and spirit. After one drum roll, their spirits were up; after two, they had begun to droop; after three, they were disheartened. They were disheartened, we were full of spirit. That was why we won."

Zhang Yu: In War, by instilling a sense of anger in all ranks of the army, we can make them irresistible. The enemy will be at their keenest when they first arrive, and at this time we should not engage them but wear them down, wait for their zeal and courage to weaken, and then attack. In this way, we can rob them of their spirit.

Master Wu's Art of War, **Chapter 4, "On Generalship":**   In War, there are four keys: spirit, terrain, situation, strength.

A general
Can be robbed
Of his presence of mind.

Zhang Yu: The mind is the general's chief asset. It enables him to create order out of disorder, to replace fear with courage. The Skillful Warrior disturbs and disorders the enemy, harasses and perplexes him, harries him and fills him with fear. He robs him of his presence of mind, his ability to think strategically. . . . Duke Li said, "Attack is not restricted to attacking cities and military formations. We master the art of attacking the mind." Attacking the mind involves nurturing our own mind, our own sense of ease and order, and then robbing the enemy of his.

Mei Yaochen: If the army has lost its spirit, the general will lose his presence of mind.

The soldier's spirit
   Is keenest
   In the morning;

Translator: I cannot resist giving Giles's characteristically Edwardian comment (complete with references to Livy): "Always provided, I suppose, that he has had breakfast. At the battle of the Trebia [218 B.C.], the Romans were foolishly allowed to fight fasting, whereas Hannibal's men had breakfasted at their leisure."

By noon
   It has dulled;
   By evening
   He has begun
   To think of home.

The Skillful Warrior
   Avoids the keen spirit,
   Attacks the dull
   And the homesick;

Translator: Chairman Mao makes use of this maxim of Master Sun's: "During the Jiangxi opposition to the Third Extermination campaign of Chiang Kai-shek, the Red Army carried out an extreme retreat. . . . But this was essential to our ultimate victory, because at the time of the Third Extermination, the enemy forces were more than ten times more numerous than those of the Red Army. When Master Sun talks of 'avoiding the keen spirit, and attacking the dull and the homesick,' he means allowing the enemy to become exhausted and demoralized, in order to overcome its superior forces" (*Selected Works*, p. 192).

This is
Mastery of Spirit.

Zhang Yu: Nurturing one's own spirit and robbing the enemy's.

He confronts chaos
  With discipline;
He treats tumult
  With calm.
This is
Mastery of Mind.

Du Mu: As *The Marshal's Treatise* says, "His own mind is firm." He lets the enemy fashion his victory. His mind is already firm, but he regulates it, makes it peaceful and strong, so that he is not disturbed by events, not deluded by thoughts of gain. He waits for the enemy to become chaotic, he waits for the enemy to become tumultuous, and then he launches his attack.

He Yanxi: The general must use the subtlety of his one mind, and with it he must confront the myriad host of the enemy and oppose the ravening wolves; he must contemplate wisely the vagaries of circumstances, the ups and downs of victory and defeat; he must remain calm, or how can he continue to respond to events with infinite resource, how can he remain unconfused? He must remain unmoved in the face of great adversity; he must be undeluded by the infinite complexities of the world. His discipline must be sufficient to confront the enemy's chaos; his calm must be sufficient to confront the enemy's tumult; then he can view the enemy as if he were some petty thief.

He meets distance
  With closeness;
He meets exhaustion
  With ease;

He meets hunger
    With plenty;
This is
    Mastery of Strength.

Zhang Yu: The skillful mastery of one's own strength and exhaustion of
the enemy's.

He does not intercept
    Well-ordered banners;
He does not attack
    A perfect formation.
This is
    Mastery of Change.

Zhang Yu: It is essential to know and understand changing circumstances. This Way of Change, the skillful mastery of change, consists in responding to the enemy's circumstances.

These are axioms
    Of the Art of War:
    Do not advance uphill.
    Do not oppose an enemy
    With his back to a hill.

Cao Cao: This concerns the potential energy of the terrain.

Zhang Yu: Zhuge Liang said, "When fighting on hilly terrain, do not face
uphill. When an enemy comes downhill, do not confront him. The potential
of the situation is not favorable. Draw him away to level ground, and fight
him there."

Do not pursue an enemy
    Feigning flight.

Du Mu/Li Quan: For fear of an ambush.

Do not attack
Keen troops.
Do not swallow
A bait.

Mei Yaochen: The fish that is greedy for bait gets caught; the army that is greedy for bait is defeated. When enemy troops fish for us, we must never take the bait.

Zhang Yu: *The Three Stratagems* says, Beneath every morsel of succulent bait lies a hooked fish.

Do not thwart
A returning army.

Meng: When men are thinking of going home, they will fight to the death, and no one will be able to stand in their way.

Zhang Yu/Du Mu/Giles: When troops are abroad, they all have their thoughts set on the return home. Whoever stands in their way they will fight to the death. As the [great general] Han Xin [d. 196 B.C.] said, "Who can hope to defeat soldiers that are thinking of going home?" [In A.D. 198] Cao Cao was trapped between two of his enemies, who controlled each outlet of a narrow pass. He knew he was in a desperate situation. He bored a hole in the mountainside and laid an ambush in it. Then he marched on with his baggage train. When it grew light, Zhang Xiu, the opposing general, seeing that Cao Cao had retreated, pressed after him in hot pursuit. As soon as their whole army had passed by, Cao Cao's hidden troops fell on its rear, while Cao himself turned and met his pursuers in front, so that they were thrown into confusion and annihilated. Cao Cao said afterward, "The brigands tried to thwart my army as it was returning and brought me to battle in a desperate position [on death ground]: hence I knew the way to victory." [Compare *The Three Kingdoms,* Chapter 18.]

Leave a passage
For a besieged army.

Du Mu: Let the enemy believe that there is a road to safety. This belief will prevent him from fighting with the courage of despair. Then attack him.

He Yanxi: Cao Cao besieged the city of Huguan and issued an order: "When the city falls, every resident is to be buried [alive]." Months went by, and still the city did not fall. Cao Ren said to his lord, "When besieging a city, one should always leave open a passage to safety [a gate to life]. But you, my lord, have let it be known that they will all be put to death, so they are fighting for their lives. Besides, the city is well fortified, and they have plenty of provisions. If we attack, a large number of officers and men will be wounded. . . . To protract this siege of a strong city, to fight against men determined to fight to the death, is not a good plan." Cao Cao followed his advice, and the city surrendered.

Do not press
An enemy at bay.

Chen Hao: Birds and beasts when brought to bay will scratch and bite.

Zhang Yu: If your adversary has burned his boats and destroyed his cooking pots and is prepared to stake all on a battle, he must not be pressed too hard.

He Yanxi/Giles: The Chinese general Fu Yanqing of the [short-lived] Later Jin dynasty, during the period of the Five Dynasties, together with his colleague Du Zhongwei, was surrounded by a vastly superior army of Khitans [in the year A.D. 945]. The country was bare and desertlike, and the little Chinese force was soon in dire straits for want of water. . . . Men and horses were dying of thirst in large numbers. At last Fu Yanqing said, "We are desperate men at bay! Far better to die for our country than to go with fettered hands into captivity!" A strong gale happened to be blowing from the northeast and darkening the air with dense clouds of sandy dust. Du Zhongwei was for waiting until this had abated before deciding on a final attack. But luckily another officer, Li Shouzhen by name, was quicker to see an opportunity and said, "They are many, and we are few, but in the midst of this sandstorm our numbers will not be discernible. Victory will go to the strenuous fighter, and the wind will be our best ally." Accordingly, Fu Yanqing made a sudden and wholly unexpected onslaught with his cavalry, routed the barbarians, and succeeded in breaking through to safety.

Du Mu: King Fu Chai [of Wu, son of Master Sun's patron He Lü] once said, "Wild beasts when at bay will fight desperately. How much more true is this of men?" Under the reign of Emperor Xuan of the Han dynasty [74–49 B.C.], General Zhao Chong'guo went to suppress the Qiang tribesmen [in the southwest]. When the Qiang saw his great army, they abandoned their own baggage train and set out to cross the river. The way was through a narrow gorge, and Zhao followed them at a leisurely pace. One of his officers said to him, "Why are we moving so slowly, when such a prize lies within our grasp?" Zhao replied, "One should never press an enemy at bay. If I go after them in a leisurely fashion, they will not turn around. If I press them, they will turn and fight to the death." His officers praised his skill. In the event, the Qiang drowned in large numbers and were utterly defeated.

This is
The Art of War.

Chapter Eight

The Nine Changes

Wang Xi: Nine simply stands for a large number. In war, there are infinite variations.

Zhang Yu: Change here refers to the sort of improvisation that ignores precedents and rules, the flexibility that discovers an expedient for every situation.

Translator: The Nine Changes are probably the nine injunctions, from "On intractable terrain, do not encamp" down to "There are terrains not to contest." The final (tenth) injunction, "There are ruler's orders not to obey," can be applied to all nine.

Master Sun said:

In War,
The general
Receives orders
From his sovereign,
Then assembles troops
And forms an army.

Zhang Yu: This echoes the previous chapter.

Translator: As Giles remarks, this is "repeated from Chapter 7, where it is certainly more in place. It may have been interpolated here merely in order to supply a beginning to the chapter." Ames comments that "the uncharacteristic brevity of this chapter would suggest some substantial textual problem."

On intractable terrain,
   Do not encamp;

Zhang Yu: Mountains and forests, cliffs, crags, marshes, fens—any terrain that is hard to navigate is classified as intractable. It provides nothing to depend on, so the army cannot camp there.

Translator: These types of terrain occur again with certain variations in Chapter 11 (as does Zhang Yu's description of "intractable terrain," word for word).

On crossroad terrain,
   Join forces with allies;

Zhang Yu: Terrain connecting on all four sides, where it is appropriate to approach one's neighbors and form alliances.

On dire terrain,
   Do not linger;

Zhang Yu: Terrain situated across the frontier, in hostile territory.

Li Quan: Country in which there are no springs or wells, no flocks or herds, vegetables or firewood.

Jia Lin: Gorges, chasms, and precipices, with no through roads.

On enclosed terrain,
   Make strategic plans;

Jia Lin: When we are enclosed on all sides by precipices, when the enemy can come and go but we are unable to move freely, on terrain such as this there is indeed need of ingenious and strategic thinking, if we are to prevent the enemy from injuring us and save ourselves.

On death terrain,
   Do battle.

Li Quan:　Place troops in a position where they face certain death, and they will identify with the conflict. Such was the case when Han Xin defeated the army of Zhao [leading his men out of Well Ravine, by means of a subtle stratagem].

Mei Yaochen:　There are obstacles before and behind. A decision is taken to fight to the death.

> There are roads
>　Not to take.

Li Quan:　Especially those leading through narrow defiles, where an ambush is to be feared.

Silver Sparrow Mountain Bamboo Strips:　Where shallow penetration prevents our vanguard from properly functioning or deep penetration cuts us off from our own rearguard. In such a situation, a move brings no gain, and staying still leads to capture.

Translator:　This and the four following passages from the Bamboo Strips are taken from the text reconstructed as "The Four Changes." See Li Ling (1997, p. 176).

> There are armies
>　Not to attack.

Silver Sparrow Mountain Bamboo Strips:　As when two armies are encamped facing each other. We calculate that we have the strength to defeat the enemy and take their commander captive. But in the longer term, they may have some cunning stratagem up their sleeve. . . . In a situation such as this, we choose not to attack.

Cao Cao:　It may be possible to attack an army, but the terrain may be precipitous and inhospitable. By staying there, one would risk losing a former gain; and any gain brought by holding it would be trifling. The enemy troops, on the other hand, being hard-pressed, would fight to the death.

Wang Xi:　In my opinion, troops proffered as bait, crack troops, troops with well-ordered banners and in perfect formation should not be attacked.

Chen Hao: When you see some trivial gain but cannot defeat the enemy, do not attack, for fear of exhausting your men's strength.

Du Mu: Armies not to attack include: keen troops, a returning army, a desperate army, an army on death terrain.

> There are towns
>   Not to besiege.

Silver Sparrow Mountain Bamboo Strips: We may calculate that we have the strength to take a town, but if taking it confers no advantage, and if, having taken it, we would have trouble holding on to it . . . then we would choose not to besiege it.

Cao Cao: If a town is small and well fortified and has ample provisions, it should not be besieged. I myself decided to pass by Huabi and press on into the heart of Xuzhou, and as a result I took fourteen important district cities.

Du Mu: This probably refers to an enemy in a strategic position, behind walls and deep moats, with a good supply of grain and food. Their purpose is to detain our army. Even if we were to attack such a city and take it, there would be no particular advantage; and if we were to attack it and not to take it, the assault would certainly wear down our own military power. So we should not besiege it at all.

Zhang Yu: No town should be besieged that, if taken, cannot be held or, if left alone, will not cause any trouble. Xun Ying, when urged to attack Biyang, replied, "The city is small and well fortified; even if I were to succeed in taking it, it would be no great feat of arms; whereas if I were to fail, I should make myself a laughingstock."

Giles: In the seventeenth century, sieges still formed a large proportion of war [in Europe]. It was Turenne who directed attention to the importance of marches, countermarches and manoeuvres. He said: "It is a great mistake to waste men in taking a town when the same expenditure of soldiers will gain a province."

> There are terrains
>   Not to contest.

Silver Sparrow Mountain Bamboo Strips (fragmentary): Mountains and valleys that offer no sustenance . . . empty. . . . Do not contest these.

Du Mu: Wu Zixu advised Fu Chai [king of Wu], saying, "If we were to attack the state of Qi, even if we were to win it, it would be like [possessing] a field of stones."

> There are ruler's orders
>> Not to obey.

Silver Sparrow Mountain Bamboo Strips: When his orders go against the . . . changes just described, do not obey them.

Cao Cao: If they are inappropriate to circumstances, do not be restrained by the ruler's orders.

Du Mu: Master Weiliao said, "War is an instrument of ill omen. Combat is contrary to virtue. Generals are officers of death. They know neither Heaven nor Earth, they respect neither enemy nor their own lord."

Zhang Yu: King Fu Chai said, "If it is right, do it; do not wait for orders."

Translator: This is not a tenth injunction, but a general observation applicable to all of the previous nine.

> The general
>> Who knows the gains
>> Of the Nine Changes
>> Understands War.

Jia Lin: He relies on the dynamic of opportunity, he adapts to changing circumstances, he follows the prospect of gain and lets gain decide, he is not a stickler for precedent. In this way he can enjoy the fruits [gains] of total flexibility.

> The general
>> Ignorant of the gains

Of the Nine Changes
May know the lie of the land,
But he will never reap
The gain
Of that knowledge.

Jia Lin: He may know the lie of the land, but if in his mind he is not at-
tuned to change, this will not only prevent him from reaping the gain, it will
expose him to harm. A general should prize adapting to change.

Zhang Yu: Every kind of ground or land has certain fixed natural features (the lie of the land) and also contains a certain dynamic for change. A
knowledge of the topographical features will avail little on its own, unless it
is supplemented by an understanding of the [sometimes unpredictable] dynamic for change.

The warrior
    Ignorant of the Art
    Of the Nine Changes,
May know
The Five Gains,
But will not get the most
From his men.

Jia Lin: If he can adapt to change when face-to-face with the potential
of the situation, then the gain will remain unchanged and the harm will stay
with the enemy. There is no constant model. If he can grasp the principle
of this, he will be able to get the most out of his men.
    A road may be [topographically speaking] short, but it may also abound
in natural obstacles and be a potential site [dynamic] for an ambush; it
should therefore not be taken. An army may be [topographically] open to attack, but if it is desperate and likely to fight to the death [the dynamic], it
should not be attacked. A city may be isolated and therefore topographically
open to siege, but if it is well stocked, if the morale of its troops is high, if
their commander is intelligent and his ministers loyal, an [unpredictable,
dynamic] element of change creeps in, and the place should not be besieged. Ground may be contestable, but if we know that, once taken, it will

be difficult to hold and that it will bring no gain but will probably lead to counterattack and casualties, again an element of change must be allowed for, and that ground should not be contested. Under normal circumstances, it is right to obey the sovereign's orders, but there are some circumstances in which interference from the court is harmful, and in that case the orders should be disobeyed. Such changes as these have to be grasped [flexibly] in the light of circumstances; they cannot be determined beforehand. An in-flexible approach will only lead to defeat.

Giles: We see the uselessness of having an eye for weaknesses in the enemy's armour without being clever enough to recast one's plans on the spur of the moment.

> The wise leader
>> In his deliberations
>> Always blends consideration
>> Of gain
>> And harm.

Cao Cao: In an advantageous [gain] situation, he ponders disadvantage [harm]; in a disadvantageous situation, he ponders advantage.

> By tempering thoughts of
>> Gain,
>> He can accomplish
>> His goal;

Du Mu: If we want to win an advantage [gain] from the enemy, we must not fix our minds exclusively on that advantage, but must also consider the threat [of harm] posed by the enemy and take this into consideration in our calculations.

Mei Yaochen: If we temper thought of gain with consideration of harm, then our goal becomes feasible.

> By tempering thoughts of
>> Harm,

He can extricate himself
From calamity.

He Yanxi: Gain and harm give rise to each other. The enlightened constantly reflect on this.

Du Mu: If we wish to extricate ourselves from a calamity inflicted by the enemy, we must do more than consider the power of the enemy to harm us. We must never lose sight of our own ability to gain an advantage over the enemy. This thought must temper our perception of calamity and enter into our planning. Then it will be possible to avert the calamity. That is why Master Sun has just said, "The wise leader in his deliberations always blends consideration of gain and harm." For example, if the enemy is surrounding us and all we think of is the [negative] idea of breaking out and escaping, our troops' morale will sag and the enemy will be sure to pursue us and attack. We should urge our men on to fight and counterattack, and let the [positive] prospect of victory, the thought of gain, motivate them to break the encirclement.

He reduces the feudal lords
   To submission
   By causing them
   Harm;

Jia Lin: There are many ways of doing this. He can entice away the enemy's best and wisest men, so that he is left without ministers. He can introduce traitors into the enemy's ranks and render his government ineffectual. He can sow dissension between ruler and ministers, by means of intrigue and deceit. He can cause exhaustion among the enemy's men and squandering of his treasure, through subtle scheming. He can corrupt the enemy's morals with sensual pleasure. He can unsettle his mind with lovely women. All of these methods, if carried out with subtlety and secrecy, can harm the enemy and reduce him to submission.

Zhang Yu: Get the enemy into a position where he must inevitably suffer harm, and he will submit of his own accord.

Translator: Giles comments, "Some of the ways of inflicting this injury enumerated by Jia Lin would only occur to the Oriental mind."

He wears them down
  By keeping them
  Constantly occupied;

Du You: He prevents them from having any rest, as the state of Han did to the state of Qin, by advising them to dig a canal.

He precipitates them
  With thoughts of
  Gain.

Meng: We cause them to forget the Changes (Giles: the reasons for acting otherwise than on their first impulse) and hasten in our direction. We, meanwhile, work the Changes and have the upper hand. We get the best out of our men.

The Skillful Warrior
  Does not rely on the enemy's
  Not coming,
  But on his own
  Preparedness.

Giles: Lord Roberts [British general in India, Afghanistan, and the Boer War, born in 1832], to whom the sheets of the present work were submitted previous to publication, wrote: "Many of [Master] Sun Wu's maxims are perfectly applicable to the present day, and this one is one that the people of this country would do well to take to heart.

He does not rely on the enemy's
  Not attacking,
  But on his own
  Impregnability.

Zhang Yu: He must always think of calamity and take precautions.

There are Five Pitfalls
For a general:

Recklessness,
    Leading to
    Destruction;

Translator: Recklessness: literally, the sense that one is doomed to die.

Cao Cao: Bravery without forethought.

Zhang Yu: The reckless warrior, willing to fight to the death, may not succumb to brute force, but can still be lured into an ambush and put to death. Hence *The Marshal's Treatise* says, "Courting death does not win the victory." If a general has no strategy, he will send his vanguard to their deaths and still come out the loser.

Du Mu: A foolish general who is also brave is a calamity. Lord Yellow Stone said, "The brave are set on achieving their goal; the foolish are impervious to death." Master Wu said, "People always look for courage in a general. But courage is only a part of the picture. A courageous man is liable to fight recklessly and to ignore thoughts of [long-term] gain. Such a man is not a Skillful General."

Cowardice,
    Leading to
    Capture;

Translator: Cowardice: literally, the desire to get out alive.

Cao Cao: He who sees an advantage but is too afraid to advance.

Du Mu: During the Eastern Jin dynasty [A.D. 317–420], Liu Yu crossed the Yangtze in pursuit of the rebel Huan Xuan and fought him at Zhengrong Island. Liu's troops were only a few thousand and were hugely outnumbered by the rebel troops. But Huan, fearing the consequences of defeat, had a light getaway skiff constantly moored at the ready beside his warship, which greatly undermined the morale of his men. As a result, when the imperial troops attacked downwind with fireships, they utterly routed Huan's forces.

Meng: The cowardly general, set on getting home alive and reluctant to fight, undermines the morale of his men and makes them vulnerable to attack. As the Ancient Duke said, "By letting slip [an opportunity for] gain, he faces disaster."

He Yanxi: *The Marshal's Treatise* says, "He who values survival above all else will be prone to hesitate." Hesitation is a great calamity.

A hot temper,
    Prone to
    Provocation;

Du Mu: An enemy of this temperament is easily insulted and provoked into making a rash move that will lead him into defeat. [In A.D. 357], when the Tibetan prince Yao Xiang was attacked by a force led by Deng Qiang, Fu Huangmei, and others, he shut himself behind his walls and refused to fight. Deng Qiang said to Huangmei, "Yao Xiang has a headstrong temperament and is easily provoked. We should keep up the pressure, and eventually he will lose his temper and come out, in which case we will take him in one battle." Huangmei followed this advice; Yao Xiang came out to fight in a fury and was duly cut down.

Du You: An angry, impulsive man is easily provoked and sent to his death. His anger prevents him from seeing the difficulties.

Wang Xi: The great quality in a general is steadiness.

A delicacy of honor,
    Tending to
    Shame;

Giles: This need not be taken to mean that a sense of honour is really a defect in a general. What Master Sun condemns is rather an exaggerated sensitiveness to slanderous reports, the thin-skinned man who is [unnecessarily] stung by opprobrium, however undeserved.

A concern for his men,
    Leading to
    Trouble.

Du Mu: A general who is [overly] compassionate and filled with concern for his men will be prevented by his fear of casualties from giving up a short-term gain for a long-term one.

Giles: Here again, Master Sun does not mean that the general is to be careless of the welfare of his troops. All he wishes to emphasise is the danger of sacrificing any important military advantage to the immediate comfort of his men. This is a short-sighted policy, because in the long run the troops will suffer more from the defeat, or, at best, the prolongation of the war, which will be the consequence. A mistaken feeling of pity will often induce a general to relieve a beleaguered city, or to reinforce a hard-pressed detachment, contrary to his military instincts. It is now generally admitted that our repeated efforts to relieve the town of Ladysmith in the South African War [of 1899–1902] were so many strategic blunders which defeated their own purpose. And in the end, relief came through the very man who started out with the distinct resolve no longer to subordinate the interest of the whole to sentiment in favour of a part. An old soldier of one of our generals who failed most conspicuously in this war, tried once, I remember, to defend him to me on the ground that he was always "so good to his men." By this plea, had he but known it, he was only condemning him out of Master Sun's mouth.

These Five Excesses
    In a general
    Are the
    Bane of war.

If an army is defeated
    And its general slain,
    It will surely be because of
    These Five Perils.
They demand the most
    Careful consideration.

Chapter Nine

On the March

Zhang Yu: Once one knows the Nine Changes, one can choose one's goal and march.

Master Sun said:

In taking up position
And confronting the enemy:

Zhang Yu: The section below, from "Cross mountains" to "These are places of ambush, lairs for spies," concerns taking up position; the subsequent section, from "When the enemy is close at hand and makes no move" to "must be regarded with great vigilance," concerns confronting the enemy.

Giles: The rest of the chapter [after the two sections already identified by Zhang Yu] consists of a few desultory remarks, chiefly on the subject of discipline.

Cross mountains,
Stay close to valleys;

Du Mu: Once the army has crossed the mountains, it should stay close to the valleys, which have the advantage of water and grass. As Master Wu said, "Do not stay in Heaven's Ovens—the mouths of large valleys." In other words, stay *close* to the valleys but not *in* them.

Zhang Yu: Stay close to the valleys because of the supply of water and grass, but also because it is safer there. In the Later Han, Ma Yuan was sent to exterminate the Qiang tribesmen of Wudu. The Qiang brigands were up in the hills, and Ma occupied a favorable position, not offering battle but seizing all the supplies of water and grass. The Qiang were eventually forced to surrender out of sheer hunger and exhaustion. They clearly had not grasped the advantage of staying close to the valleys.

> Camp high,

Giles: Not on high hills, but on knolls or hillocks elevated above the surrounding country.

> And face the open;

Cao Cao: The Yang, or sunny, side.

> Fight downhill,
> Not up.

Cao Cao: Do not confront the enemy from a lower position.

> These are positions in
>   Mountain warfare.

> Cross rivers,
>   Then keep a distance
>   From them.

Cao Cao: In order to tempt the enemy to cross after you.

Zhang Yu: In order not to be impeded in your movements.

> If the enemy crosses a river
> Toward you,
> Do not confront him
> In midstream.
> Let half his troops cross
> Before you strike.

Master Wu's Art of War, **Chapter 2:**   When the enemy is crossing a river and only half his force is across, then you can attack.

Zhang Yu: Wait until he is halfway across the river. Then his ranks will be disorderly, his vanguard out of contact with his rear, and an attack will be sure to bring victory.

He Yanxi: In the Spring and Autumn period, the duke of Song came to the state of Chu to do battle at Hong. Before the Chu army had crossed the river, the Song troops were already drawn up in battle array. The Song marshal said. "The enemy are many, and we are few. I request permission to attack before they cross." The duke would not grant him permission. The Chu forces crossed, and before they had time to draw up their ranks, the marshal asked again. Again the duke refused. The Chu army drew up their battle array, and the Song army finally attacked and was roundly defeated. The duke himself was wounded in the thigh, and his vanguard totally destroyed. It was because the duke of Song went against this maxim that he was defeated.

Translator: As Brigadier General Griffith points out, this story is the source of Chairman Mao's remark: "We are not like the duke of Song!"

Li Quan: As in the great victory won by Han Xin over Long Ju [the Chu general] at the Wei River.

Translator: Giles bases his description of this famous battle between Han and Long on the account in the *History of the Former Han:* "The two armies [Han and Chu] were drawn up on opposite sides of the river. In the night, Han Xin ordered his men to take some ten thousand sacks filled with sand and construct a dam a little higher up. Then, leading half his army over, he attacked Long Ju; but after a time, pretending to have failed in his attempt, he hastily withdrew to the other bank. Long Ju was much elated by this unlooked-for success. Exclaiming, 'I felt sure that Han Xin was a coward!,' he pursued him and began crossing the river in his turn. Han Xin now sent a party to cut open the sandbags, thus releasing a great volume of water, which swept down and prevented the greater portion of Long Ju's army from getting across. He then turned upon the force which had been cut off, and annihilated it, Long Ju himself being amongst the slain. The rest of the army, on the further bank, scattered and fled in all directions."

If you wish to do battle,
Do not confront the enemy
Close to the river.

Du Mu: Or he will have misgivings and not cross.

Du You: If you wait for the enemy too close to the river, he will not cross [and will thereby deny you the opportunity to attack].

Occupy high ground,
And face the open.

Zhang Yu: Either draw up your troops on the riverbank or anchor your boats in the river itself; in either case, it is essential to be above the enemy and to face open, sunny ground.

Do not advance
Against the flow.

Du Mu: Do not take up position downstream, in case the enemy opens the sluice gates and floods you out.

Zhang Yu: [The state of Wu attacked the state of Chu.] Chu ordered its minister to consult the oracle [about the outcome of a battle]. The response was not favorable. Marshal Sima said, "We are upstream, how can it be un-favorable?" So they attacked Wu and were victorious.

Translator: This is the seventh stratagem in *The Hundred Ingenious Stratagems,* a work probably dating from the early Ming dynasty, which takes as its point of departure maxims from Master Sun and several other military treatises. The historical illustration is the same as that given by Zhang Yu.

These are positions in
River warfare.

Cross salt marshes
   Rapidly;
   Never linger.

Wang Xi: Salty, low-lying terrain offers no sustenance.

Zhang Yu: Such damp, unhealthy terrain, with scant vegetation, should be passed through quickly.

   If you must do battle
   In a salt marsh,
   Keep water plants
   Close by
   And trees
   Behind you.

Li Quan: If you are obliged to linger and do battle, this position will be less dangerous and vulnerable.

   These are positions in
   Salt marshes.

   On level ground,
     Occupy easy terrain.

Cao Cao: Terrain suited to chariots and cavalry.

Translator: This is Cao Cao's idea. The use of cavalry became commonplace in the fourth century B.C. largely inspired by the nomadic barbarians (the Xiongnu). But in Master Sun's own time, if we place that in the first half of the fifth century B.C., there were chariots and mounted archers, but not cavalry proper.

Du Mu: Easy ground is smooth and firm.

Zhang Yu: Level ground, free from depressions and hollows, suitable for rapid, sudden attacks.

> Keep high land
> To the right and rear:

Du Mu: The Grand Duke said, "An army should have a stream or marsh on its left and a hill or tumulus on its right."

Translator: Note how similar this kind of advice is to the advice given by geomantic experts on the situating of a dwelling place. In both cases, the "client" is being advised how to derive the most benefit from the "dynamic" of the situation and its topographical features.

> Keep death in front,
> And life to the rear.

Du Mu: Death means low; life means high.

Zhang Yu: Although Master Sun calls it "level" ground, there are slight elevations, and these must be to the right and rear, if we are to exploit the lie of the land; low land must be in front and high land behind, if we are to launch a swift attack.

> These are positions on
> Level ground.

> Observation of
> These four types of positions

Zhang Yu: Mountain, river, salt marsh, and level ground.

> Enabled the Yellow Emperor
> To defeat
> The Four Emperors.

Li Quan: The Yellow Emperor received his military treatise from his minister Feng Hou.

Translator: Strategic military knowledge, like sexual knowledge, medical knowledge, geomantic knowledge, and other branches of occult knowledge, was often said to have been revealed to the great mythical ancestor of Chinese civilization, the Yellow Emperor, in a mysterious fashion, usually by a woman (guardian of the arcana). According to one (probably quite late) version of the legend, the Yellow Emperor lay for three nights in a mist on the sacred peak of Mount Tai and was there instructed in the secrets of a military treatise, not by his minister but by the Dark Girl, a creature half human and half bird. Similarly, Zhang Liang was said to have received his military treatise (*The Treatise of the Grand Duke*) from a strange old gentleman, whom he met again thirteen years later in the form of a yellow stone; and Sun Bin received his instruction from the mysterious Master of Spirit Valley.

The excavated Bamboo Strip text contains a lengthy expansion of this reference to the Yellow Emperor, listing the four other Emperors that he defeated (the Red, Green, Black, and White).

> Armies prize high ground,
>   Shun low;

Mei Yaochen: High ground is not only more agreeable and salubrious, it is strategically superior; low ground is not only damp and unhealthy, it is also disadvantageous for fighting.

> They esteem Yang,
>   Avoid Yin.

Zhang Yu: Yang is east and south; Yin is west and north.

Mei Yaochen: Yang ground is clear and easy; Yin ground is dark and contrary.

Translator: For Yang and Yin in this passage, the French translator Jean Lévi, like Marcel Granet before him, uses the southern dialectal expressions *adret* and *ubac,* the sunny and shady side of the mountain, following the traditional interpretation of the Chinese commentators, which seems perfectly natural in this context. But he correctly points out that the Chinese words have a much wider and more abstract range of meanings. In the very first sentences of Chapter 1, Master Sun has already referred to Yin and Yang as an aspect of Heaven, one of the Five Fundamentals in all military planning. This sets the Chinese commentators off on lengthy speculations. But it should never be forgotten that even the earliest commentators date from several centuries after Master Sun, who was himself far less involved in the intricacies of the Yin-Yang polarity. The treatise of his descendant Sun Bin is far more pervaded by the terms and by the Yin-Yang way of thinking.

> Nurture life,
>> Occupy solid ground.
>> Your troops will thrive,
>> Victory will be sure.

Du Mu: The life force is Yang; solid ground is high. Nurture the life force of your troops on high ground, and you will not suffer from dampness and other Yin ailments. You will be healthy and victorious.

> On mound,
>> Hill,
>> Bank,
>> Or dike,
>> Occupy the Yang,
>> With high ground
>> To right and rear.

Du Mu/Mei Yaochen: Occupy the eastern and southern flanks, not necessarily the heights, but a position with an open clear aspect in front of it, and the high "solid" ground to the right and behind you.

Zhang Yu: A Yang aspect means clarity; high ground behind you means security.

> Use the lie of the land
>> To the troops' benefit.

Mei Yaochen: The strategic dynamic of the land is working for you.

> When rains upstream
> Have swollen the river,
> Let the water subside
> Before crossing.

> If you come to
> Heaven's Torrents,

Cao Cao/Mei Yaochen: Great waters in precipitous ravines.

Translator: I am following Wang Xi's textual emendation here, as proposed by Wu Jiulong.

> Heaven's Wells,

Cao Cao/Mei Yaochen: Places enclosed on every side by steep slopes, with pools of water at the bottom collecting the water of the torrents.

> Heaven's Prisons,

Mei Yaochen: Places surrounded by precipices on three sides—easy to get into, but hard to get out of.

> Heaven's Nets,

Mei Yaochen: Thickets choked with such dense undergrowth that spears cannot be used.

> Heaven's Traps,

Mei Yaochen: Low-lying muddy morasses, impassable for chariots and horsemen.

> Heaven's Cracks:

Mei Yaochen: Narrow passages between beetling cliffs.

Translator: In a fragment cited from a later source, these Heaven's Cracks are listed together with "grave tumuli and old walls" as places to be avoided in war. See Li Ling (1997, p. 181).

> Quit such places
> With all speed.
> Do not go near them.
> Keep well away,
> Let the enemy
> Go near them.
> Keep them in front;
> Let him have them
> At his rear.

Sun Bin's Art of War, **Chapter 8:**   The five deadly terrains are: Heaven's Wells, Heaven's Prisons, Heaven's Nets, Heaven's Cracks, and Heaven's Pits. These Five Tombs are death [traps]. Do not stay in them.

> If you march by
> Ravine,
> Swamp,
> Reedy marshland,
> Mountain forest,
> Thick undergrowth:
> Beware,
> Explore them diligently.
> These are places
> Of ambush,
> Lairs for spies.

Zhang Yu: We must also be on our guard against traitors who may lie hidden, spying out our weaknesses and eavesdropping on our commands.

When the enemy is
   Close at hand
   And makes no move,
   He is counting on
   A strong position;

Wang Xi: His position is strong, so he is unafraid.

Giles: Here begin Master Sun's remarks on the reading of signs, much of which is so good it could almost be included in a modern manual like General Baden-Powell's *Aids to Scouting*.

If he is
   At a distance
   And provokes battle,
   He wants his opponent
   To advance.

Giles: Probably because we are in a strong position from which he wishes to dislodge us.

Du Mu: If he were to come close to us and try to force a battle, he would seem to despise us and we would be less likely to respond to the challenge. So he keeps a distance.

Chen Hao: Having once lured us into advancing, he will seize the opportunity to attack.

If he is
   On easy ground,
   He is luring us.

Zhang Yu: If the enemy has quit the strong ground and taken up position on exposed terrain, it must be either because there is some hidden advantage or because he wants to lure us into battle.

If trees move,
   He is coming.

Cao Cao: They are felling trees to clear a passage.

Zhang Yu: Every army sends out scouts to climb high places and observe the enemy. If a scout sees that the trees of a forest are moving and shaking, he can deduce that they are being cut down to clear a passage for the enemy's march. Another interpretation takes it to mean that they are cutting wood for weapons.

If there are many screens
   In the grass,
   He wants
   To perplex us.

Du You: The presence of screens or sheds in the midst of thick vegetation is a sure sign that the enemy has fled and, fearing pursuit, has constructed these hiding places in order to make us suspect an ambush.

Giles: It appears that these "screens" were hastily knotted together out of any long grass which the retreating enemy happened to come across.

Birds rising in flight
   Are a sign
   Of ambush;

Zhang Yu: If birds that are flying along in a straight line suddenly soar upward into the sky, it means that soldiers are setting an ambush below.

Beasts startled
   Are a sign
   Of surprise attack.

Zhang Yu: Surprise attacks are usually launched from some precipitous height or out of dense undergrowth, and this startles the creatures lying hidden there into sudden movement.

Dust high and peaking
  Is a sign
  Of chariots approaching;

Mei Yaochen: Horses and chariots are heavier than men and raise a higher cloud of dust.

Zhang Yu: They also stay in the same track, and so the dust rises higher in columns. Every army on the march sends scouts ahead who, on sighting dust raised by the enemy, gallop back and report it to the commander in chief.

Translator: Giles offers us a quotation from Baden-Powell's *Aids to Scouting*: "As you move along, say, in a hostile country, your eyes should be looking afar for the enemy or any signs of him: figures, dust rising, birds getting up, glitter of arms, etc."

Dust low and spreading
  Is a sign
  Of infantry approaching;

Du Mu: Foot soldiers move more slowly, abreast, so the dust stays lower and is more widespread.

Dust in scattered strands
  Is a sign
  Of firewood's being collected;

Zhang Yu: Men are sent off in parties to gather firewood in various places, so the dust rises in scattered strands.

Dust in drifting pockets
  Is a sign
  Of an army encamping.

Zhang Yu: In planning the defenses for a camp, small detachments of light cavalry will be sent out in all directions to survey the position and determine the weak and strong points. Hence the small drifting pockets of dust.

Humble words, coupled with
   Increased preparations,
   Are a sign
   Of impending attack;

Du Mu: The enemy's envoys come to us with words of appeasement. Meanwhile, they are busy fortifying their position. They appear afraid of us, but their real aim is to make us contemptuous and slack, after which they will attack us.

Zhang Yu/*Records of the Grand Historian*/Giles: The Qi general Tian Dan was defending the city of Jimo, besieged by the Yan forces under the general Qi Jie [parts of this famous story have already been alluded to by the commentators in Chapter 2, where it illustrates the importance of motivating troops with anger, and also in Chapter 3, where it is an example of how to win a victory out of a situation of weakness, by lying low and waiting for an opening]. [When he knew his men were ready to fight], General Tian [to everyone's surprise] took a mattock and began working along with his troops, while he enrolled the men's wives and concubines in the ranks. He distributed the last rations of food. Regular soldiers were told to keep out of sight, and the women were sent up onto the city walls. Envoys were sent to the enemy camp to surrender. The Yan commander was over-joyed. Then General Tian collected a large quantity of silver from the citizens and ordered the wealthy inhabitants of Jimo to deliver it to the Yan commander, and to plead with him, saying, "When our town surrenders, we beg you not to plunder our homes and take our wives and concubines prisoner." Qi Jie, in excellent humor, granted their prayer; but as a result, his men in the Yan camp became slacker and more complacent than ever. Meanwhile, Tian Dan got together a thousand oxen, decked them with pieces of red silk, painted their bodies, dragonlike, with colored stripes, and fastened sharp blades on their horns and well-greased rushes on their tails. When night came on, he lit the ends of the rushes and drove the oxen through a number of holes which he had pierced in the walls, backing them up with a force of five thousand picked troops. The animals, maddened with pain, dashed furiously into the enemy camp, where they caused the ut-most confusion and dismay; for their tails acted as torches, showing up the hideous pattern on their bodies, and the weapons on their horns killed or wounded any with whom they came into contact. In the meantime the band of five thousand had crept up with gags in their mouths and now threw themselves on the enemy. At the same moment a frightful din arose in the city itself, all those that remained behind making as much noise as possible by banging drums and hammering on bronze vessels, until heaven and earth were convulsed by the uproar. Terror-stricken, the Yan army fled in disorder, hotly pursued by the men of Qi, who succeeded in slaying their general Qi Jie. The result of the battle was the ultimate recovery of some seventy cities that had belonged to the Qi state.

> Strong words, coupled with
> An aggressive advance,
> Are a sign
> Of impending retreat.

Cao Cao: Deception.

> Light chariots
> Emerging first
> On the wings
> Are a sign
> Of battle formation.

Cao Cao: They want to fight.

> Words of peace,
> But no treaty,
> Are a sign
> Of a plot.

Li Quan: If there is talk of peace, but no proper treaty, there is a plot going on. This is what Tian Dan did at Jimo.

Chen Hao: If for no apparent reason the enemy asks for peace, it must be that his country is in trouble and he is looking for a respite. Or else he knows of some way that we can be undermined and wants to forestall our suspicions by talking of peace. Then he will pounce.

> Much running about

Giles: Every man hastening to his proper place under his own regimental banner.

> And soldiers parading
> Are a sign
> Of expectation.

Li Quan: They are about to join battle.

Giles: The critical moment has come.

> Some men advancing
> And some retreating
> Are a sign
> Of a decoy.

Du Mu: Feigned confusion, designed to lure us into advancing.

> Soldiers standing
> Bent on their spears
> Indicate great
> Hunger.

Li Quan: They are too weak even to stand upright.

> Bearers of water
> Drinking first
> Indicate great
> Thirst.

Zhang Yu: If the bearers drink before they return to camp with the water, the thirst of the entire army can be imagined.

> An advantage perceived,
> But not acted on,

Indicates utter
Exhaustion.

Zhang Yu: They know they are too worn out to fight, so even though they can see an opportunity, they do not dare take it.

Birds gather
On empty ground.

Chen Hao: If the enemy has gone and left the camp empty, birds will no longer be afraid and will gather on his camp ground. . . . Master Sun is telling us how to distinguish between the true and the false in the enemy's situation.

Shouting at night
Is a sign
Of fear.

Du Mu: Fear makes men restless. They shout at night, to keep up their courage.

Confusion among troops
Is a sign
That the general
Is not respected.

Chen Hao: When the general's orders are not strict and his behavior undignified, the officers will be confused.

Banners and flags moving
Are a sign
Of disorder.

Du Mu: When Duke Zhuang of Lu defeated Qi at Changzhuo, Cao Gui begged to pursue the Qi army. The duke asked him why, to which he replied, "I have seen how disorderly their chariot ruts are and how their flags droop. That is why I wish to pursue them." [See *The Zuo Commentary*, Legge's translation, pp. 85–86.]

> If officers
>> Are prone to anger,
>> The men become weary.

Chen Hao: When a general embarks impetuously on unnecessary projects, he exhausts his men.

> If they feed
>> Grain to their horses
>> And meat to their men;

Giles: In the ordinary course of things, the men would be fed on grain and the horses would chiefly eat grass.

Translator: The commentators are not sure if this refers to horse meat or slaughtered cattle. Either way, these are desperate measures.

> If they fail to
>> Hang up their pots
>> And do not
>> Return to their quarters;
> Then they are
>> At bay.

Mei Yaochen: They abandon their cooking pots, to cook no more; they sleep out in the open and do not return to their quarters; this means they wish to fight a decisive battle, that they have set their hearts on victory.

Translator: The last word of Master Sun's text, *qiongkou* (literally, "hard-pressed") seems to have originated with Master Sun. He also uses it in Chapter 7. Lévi uses the expressive French term *aux abois*, which conjures up the image of a stag "at bay" and the pack of dogs howling, in other words, of an enemy "with his back against the wall." As Master Sun says several times, such men are dangerous.

Men whispering together,
Huddled in small groups,

Du Mu: Muttering under their breath.

Are a sign
Of disaffection.

Excessive rewards
Are a sign
Of desperation.

Du Mu/Giles: When an army is hard-pressed, there is always a fear of mutiny, and lavish rewards are given to humor the men.

Excessive punishments
Are a sign
Of exhaustion.

Giles: Because in such a case discipline has become relaxed and unwonted severity is necessary to keep the men to their duty.

If a general is by turns
    Tyrannical
    And in terror
    Of his own men,
    It is a sign of
    Supreme incompetence.

He Yanxi: The competent general should seek a balance of tolerance and severity.

Envoys
    With words of conciliation
    Desire cessation.

Du Mu: Either they are desperate or they desire cessation for some other reason.

> Protracted, fierce
>> Confrontation,
>> With neither engagement
>> Nor retreat,
>> Must be regarded
>> With great vigilance.

Cao Cao/Giles: A maneuver of this sort may be simply a ruse to gain time for some unexpected flank attack or the laying of an ambush.

> In War,
>> Numbers
>> Are not the issue.
> It is a question of
>> Not attacking
>> Too aggressively.

Wang Xi: Do not rely just on military force. Use planning, strategic wisdom, and accurate assessment of the enemy before acting.

Translator: As Giles comments, this marks the beginning of the last section of the chapter, consisting of a "few desultory remarks, chiefly on the subject of discipline." Modern commentators have drawn the parallel with the American effort in Vietnam, where vastly superior resources were powerless against guerrilla warfare.

> Concentrate your strength,
> Assess your enemy,
> And win the confidence of your men:
> That is enough.

Rashly underestimate your enemy,
    And you will surely be
    Taken captive.

Chen Hao/Giles: It is said in *The Zuo Commentary*, "Bees and scorpions carry poison; how much more so will a hostile state!" Even a puny opponent should never be underestimated.

Discipline troops
    Before they are loyal,
    And they will be
    Refractory
    And hard to put to good use;
    Let loyal troops
    Go undisciplined,
    And they will be altogether
    Useless.

Cao Cao: Even if a cordial trust and empathy already exist, discipline is needed, or they will become arrogant and slack and hard to put to any good use.

Command them
    With civility,
    Rally them
    With martial discipline,

Wang Xi/Giles: In the words of Master Wu, "The ideal commander unites culture *[wen]* with a martial temper *[wu]*; the profession of arms requires a combination of hardness and tenderness."

    And you will win their
    Confidence.

Consistent and effective orders
    Inspire obedience;

Inconsistent and ineffective orders
Provoke disobedience.

When orders are consistent
And effective,
General and troops
Enjoy mutual trust.

Du Mu: In time of peace, a general ought to show sympathy and confidence toward his men and also make his authority respected, so that when they come face-to-face with the enemy, orders may be executed and discipline maintained, because they all trust and look up to him.

Zhang Yu/Giles: The general has confidence in the men under his command, and the men have confidence in obeying him. Thus the trust is mutual. Master Weiliao said, "The art of giving orders is not to rectify minor blunders and not to be swayed by petty doubts. . . ."

Giles: Vacillation and fussiness are the surest means of sapping the confidence of an army.

Chapter Ten

Forms of Terrain

Zhang Yu: Once an army is on the march and crosses the border, it must examine the forms of terrain and [on this basis] create its path to victory. Hence this chapter follows "On the March."

Translator: The word *xing*, "form," works very much in counterpoint with the word *shi*, which is used as the title for Chapter 5 and which I have often (but not always) translated as "potential (or dynamic) energy." *Xing* itself has already been used as the title of Chapter 4 and recurs frequently in that chapter and in Chapter 6, referring to the outward forms, or dispositions, of an army, from which one can learn much as to that army's underlying strength or weakness. Here the word is being used in conjunction with earth or terrain. The latent energy of the earth finds manifestation in recognizable, that is, visible, forms, patterns, or configurations (in *fengshui*, certain shapes of mountains and water courses). In the military context, the forms or configurations of terrain and the ways in which they are put to use by opposing armies are essential elements in strategic planning. This goes right back to Chapter 1, where Earth is the third fundamental, after the Tao and Heaven. Master Sun has already begun the discussion of terrain in the previous chapter (with his treatment of the maneuvers appropriate to mountains, rivers, salt marshes, and level ground). He develops it at greater length in this and the following chapter. But in addition to discussing matters of terrain, he also addresses a number of detailed and practical issues of generalship.

Master Sun said:

There are different forms of terrain:

Accessible terrain,

Mei Yaochen/Giles: Terrain plentifully provided with roads and other means of communication.

Entangling terrain,

Mei Yaochen/Giles: Like a net, in which one can easily become entangled.

Translator: Wu (1990, p. 170) quotes the Qing-dynasty commentator Zhao Benxue: "The terrain before you slopes downward and is easy going, but on the way back, the slope is against you." Lévi just calls it *scabreux,* meaning "rugged" or "rough." Griffith has "entrapping."

Deadlock terrain,

Mei Yaochen: Terrain where both sides procrastinate.

Translator: Lévi: *neutralisant.* Griffith: "indecisive." Ames: "standoff."

Enclosed terrain,

Mei Yaochen: Two mountains enclosing a valley.

Precipitous terrain,

Mei Yaochen: Mountains and rivers, foothills and ridges.

Distant terrain.

Mei Yaochen: Flat country [on which two armies or camps are widely separated].

Translator: About this sixfold classification, Giles is rather scornful: "It is hardly necessary to point out the faultiness of this classification. A strange lack of logical perception is shown in the Chinaman's unquestioning acceptance of glaring cross-divisions such as the above." Later he writes, "Of the foregoing six forms of terrain, it will be noticed that the third [deadlock] and sixth [distant] have really no reference to the configuration of the country, and that only the fourth [enclosed] and fifth [precipitous] can be said to convey any definite geographic idea." Lévi occasionally uses the term *théâtre* instead of *terrain, terre,* or *lieu.*

> "Accessible" means that
>   Both sides
>   Can come and go freely.
>   On accessible terrain,
>   He who occupies
>   High Yang ground
>   And ensures
>   His line of supplies
>   Will fight
>   To advantage.

Jia Lin/Du You: Do not allow the enemy to cut your line of supplies [and communications].

Giles: Du Mu, who was not a soldier and can hardly have had any practical experience of fighting, goes into more detail and speaks of protecting the line of communications by a wall, or enclosing it by embankments on each side! In view of Napoleon's dictum, "the secret of war lies in the communications" (*Pensées de Napoléon Ier,* no. 47), we could wish that Master Sun had done more than skirt the edge of this important subject here and in Chapters 1 and 7. Colonel Henderson says: "The line of supply may be said to be as vital to the existence of an army as the heart to the life of a human being. Just as the duellist who finds his adversary's point menacing him with certain death, and his own guard astray, is compelled to conform to his adversary's movements, and to content himself with warding off his thrusts, so the commander whose communications are suddenly threatened finds himself in a false position, and he will be fortunate if he has not to change all his plans, to split up his force into more or less isolated detachments, and to fight with inferior numbers on ground which he has not had time to prepare, and where defeat will not be an ordinary failure, but will entail the ruin or the surrender of his whole army" (*The Science of War,* Chapter 2).

Translator: High Yang ground and the Yang heights both refer to elevated, south-facing, sunny positions.

"Entangling" means that
    Advance is possible,
    Withdrawal hard.
    On entangling terrain,
    If the enemy is unprepared,
    Go out and defeat him.
    But if he is prepared,
    And our move fails,
    It will be hard to retreat.
    The outcome will not be
    To our advantage.

Zhang Yu: If you examine the enemy's situation carefully and ascertain that he is unprepared, then you can make a single move and defeat him. But if he is at all prepared and you make a move that fails, you will be unable to take a stand and fight, and at the same time you will have no escape route.

"Deadlock" means that
    Neither side finds it
    Advantageous
    To make a move.

Du You: Neither side finds it advantageous to move, and the situation remains deadlocked.

    On deadlock terrain,
    Even if our enemy
    Offers a bait,
    We do not make a move;
    We lure him out;
    We retreat.
    And when half his troops
    Are out,
    That is our moment
    To strike.

Wang Xi: The enemy refuses to make a move; set up some cunning ambush, and pretend to retreat. Play a trick on him, and oblige him to advance toward you.

Zhang Yu: The *Art of War* of Li Jing [571–649] says, "On terrain that is advantageous to neither side, we should lure the enemy out by feigning retreat, wait until half his troops are out, and intercept him."

> On enclosed terrain,
>   If we occupy it first,
>   We must block it
>   And wait for the enemy.
>   If he occupies it first
>   And blocks it,
>   Do not go after him;
>   If he does not block it,
>   Then go after him.

Zhang Yu: There are high mountains on either side and a level valley in between. We are obliged to block the entrances to the valley with troops, in order to prevent the enemy from advancing into the valley. Then we can mount surprise attacks, and he cannot harry us. But if the enemy occupies this position first, if he succeeds in blocking the entrances to the valley, we should not go after him. If he does not dispose of sufficient troops to hold the entrances to the valley, then we may attack him and win the victory. This is the type of terrain Master Wu refers to as Heaven's Stove, "not to be entered."

Translator: Compare Heaven's Stove (already referred to by Du Mu in the previous chapter) with the list given later in the same chapter (Heaven's Torrents, Wells, Prisons, Nets, Traps, and Cracks).

> On precipitous terrain,
>   If we occupy it first,
>   We should hold the Yang heights
>   And wait for the enemy.
>   If the enemy occupies it first,

Do not go after him,
But entice him out
By retreating.

Cao Cao/Giles: The advantage of holding heights and defiles is that you cannot then be dictated to by the enemy.

Zhang Yu/Giles: If one should be first to occupy level ground, how much more so difficult and dangerous terrain? Here the initiative must never be ceded to the enemy. Occupy the Yang heights and wait for the enemy to tire—this will bring victory. If the enemy already holds the heights, then retreat with all speed, do not engage. Pei Xingjian [A.D. 619–82] was sent on an expedition against the Turkic tribes, and in the evening he pitched camp. Wall and ditch had already been built and dug when he gave orders to shift to a nearby hilltop. His officers were not happy with this and complained that they did not wish to tire the men. Pei insisted and gave orders for the move to be accomplished as rapidly as possible. That night there was a violent storm, and their earlier encampment was flooded to a depth of twelve feet. His officers were astonished. From this it can be seen that not only are the heights advantageous for the winning of victory, they also guard against the danger of flooding.

On distant terrain,
When strengths are matched,
It is hard to provoke battle,
And an engagement
Will not be advantageous.

Zhang Yu: When the two encampments are a distance apart and the two armies evenly matched, we should remain where we are, we should let the enemy make the move and not seek a battle.

Mei Yaochen: If strengths are evenly matched [and the two armies are distant from each other], it would be exhausting for us to make a long march in order to challenge a fresh enemy.

Translator: The word Master Sun uses here (which I have translated as "strength") is *shi*, elsewhere translated as "potential energy" or "dynamic."

Commentators differ as to whether this refers to the *shi* of the terrain or the *shi* of the opposing armies. The main point is, as Giles says, "that we must not think of undertaking a long and wearisome march at the end of which we should be exhausted and our adversary fresh and keen."

> These six constitute
> The Way of Terrain.
> It is the general's duty
> To study them diligently.

Mei Yaochen: The forms of terrain are a fundamental factor in aiding an army to achieve victory and must be carefully looked into.

> In War,
> The following are not
> Natural calamities,
> But the fault
> Of the general:

Zhang Yu: These are the six forms of defeat attributable to human causes.

> Flight,

Translator: The thirty-sixth and last of *The Thirty-six Stratagems* (the sixth of the final cluster of strategies reserved for defeat) is simply entitled "Flight Is Best." Nowadays, in colloquial speech, reference is often made to "taking the thirty-sixth option"—that is, flight, or getting out while one still can.

> Impotence,

Translator: The Chinese word means literally the unstringing of a bow, hence slack, lax, weak, undisciplined, perhaps insubordinate. As the commentators observe, this is the result of poor leadership from the commanding officers.

> Decay,

Translator: The Chinese word *xian* means a sinking or miring in such things as a bog or quicksands, or decadence, or vice. Here it refers to the decay or collapse of morale among the lower ranks.

> Collapse,
> Chaos,
> Rout.

If relative strengths are matched,

Mei Yaochen: Other than in numbers.

Zhang Yu: This strength refers to the bravery and intelligence of the commanders and the keenness of their weapons.

Translator: Again, strength here is *shi,* the underlying potential strength or dynamic.

> But one army faces another
> Ten times its size,
> The outcome is
> Flight.

Cao Cao: The general has incorrectly assessed troop strengths.

Li Quan: Nonetheless, with the advantage of terrain and with the help of a stratagem such as a surprise attack or an ambush, it may still be possible [to avoid flight].

Wang Xi: Flee before engaging battle.

> When troops are strong
> But officers weak,
> The result is
> Impotence.

Du Mu: When the rank and file are haughty and their commanding officers ineffectual and incapable of leadership, the result is a general state of decay and impotence. At the beginning of the Chang-qing era of our present [i.e., Tang] dynasty [A.D. 821], Tian Bu was sent to lead an army against Wang Tingcou. But his soldiers treated him with total contempt and gallivanted about the campgrounds, riding on donkeys, in the thousands. Tian Bu could not control them. Several months later, when he finally wished to engage battle, his troops simply turned and fled. Tian Bu ended up committing suicide.

> When officers are strong
>   But troops weak,
>   The result is
>   Decay.

Cao Cao: The officers are strong and want to advance, but the rank and file are weak and disintegrate. The end result is defeat.

Du Mu: If the rank and file are fearful and weak and an incorrect assessment is made of their strength, they will be sent into a death trap.

> When superior officers are angry
>   And insubordinate
>   And charge into battle
>   Out of resentment,
>   Before their general can judge
>   The likelihood of victory,

Chen Hao: They fight without caring whether they can win or not. So they are defeated.

> Then the outcome is
>   Collapse.

Giles: Du Mu gives a long extract from *The Zuo Commentary* (Duke Xuan, XII, 3), showing how the great battle of Bi [597 B.C.] was lost for the Jin state through the rashness of Xian Gu and through the resentful spite of

Wei Yi and Zhao Zhan. [Compare Watson, *Tso Chuan*, p. 89: "The rash action of Xian Gu in crossing the Yellow River with the troops under his command in defiance of the orders of the supreme commander of the expedition brought about the crossing of the remainder of the Jin troops and in time precipitated the costly battle of Bi." On page 94, Watson refers to Wei Yi and Zhao Zhan as "two malcontents" from Jin, who succeed by their provocative behavior in angering the state of Chu.]

Translator: Lévi emphasizes the lack of discipline and impetuousness of the "lieutenants." Such was the case with the French officers at the Battle of Agincourt (1415), he comments: "Brave soldiers, but no discipline whatsoever."

> When the general is weak
>   And lacking in severity,
>   When his orders
>   Are not clear,

The Book of Master Weiliao, **Chapter 4/Giles:**   If the officer gives his orders without hesitation, the men will not need to hear them a second time; if he acts without hesitation, the men will never lose their will to fight.

Master Wu's Art of War, **Chapter 3/Giles:**   The greatest fault in war is hesitation; the worst calamities for an army arise from indecision.

Translator: Giles quotes Baden-Powell, *Aids to Scouting,* p. xii: "The secret of getting successful work out of your trained men lies in one nutshell—in the clearness of the instructions they receive."

> When neither officers nor men
>   Have fixed rules

Du Mu: No regular routine.

> And troops
>   Are slovenly,

The outcome is
Chaos.

When a general
    Misjudges his enemy
    And sends a lesser force
    Against a larger one,
    A weaker contingent
    Against a stronger one;
    When he fails to pick
    A good vanguard,
    The outcome is
    Rout.

Cao Cao: In this situation, his troops are certain to flee.

Zhang Yu/Giles: If the bravest men are not selected for the vanguard, defeat is inevitable. Whenever there is fighting to be done, the keenest spirits should be appointed to serve in the front ranks, in order both to strengthen the resolution of our own men and to demoralize the enemy.

These six constitute
    The Way of Defeat.
    It is the general's duty
    To study them diligently.

Chen Hao: The six are [to recapitulate]: a failure to estimate the enemy's strength [leading to flight], a lack of authority [leading to impotence], poor training [leading to decay], unthinking anger [leading to collapse], ineffectual discipline [leading to chaos], failure to use crack troops [leading to rout].

The form of the terrain
    Is the soldier's ally;

Chen Hao/Giles: The advantages of weather and season are not equal to those connected with terrain.

> Assessment
>   Of the enemy
>   And mastery of victory;
>   Calculating the difficulty,
>   The danger,
>   And the distance
>   Of the terrain;
>   These constitute the Way
>   Of the Superior General.

Zhang Yu: Assessing enemy strengths and weaknesses, calculating the difficulty, danger, and distance of the terrain are the beginning and ending of the Art of the General.

> He who knows this
>   And practices it in battle
>   Will surely be
>   Victorious.
>   He who does not know it
>   And does not practice it
>   Will surely be
>   Defeated.

> If an engagement is sure
>   To bring victory,
>   And yet the ruler
>   Forbids it,
>   Fight;
>   If an engagement is sure
>   To bring defeat,

And yet the ruler
Orders it,
Do not fight.

Du Mu/Giles: Lord Yellow Stone once said, "When an army is on the march, authority must rest with the general; if the court gives the order to advance and retreat, success will be hard to achieve. That is why the sage ruler, the enlightened monarch, 'kneels and pushes the chariot wheel' [Giles's paraphrase: 'is content to play a humble part in furthering the country's cause'], acknowledging that affairs beyond the confines of the court are the absolute responsibility of the general."

Zhang Yu: Hence the saying "The decrees of the Son of Heaven are not heard in the military camp."

Translator: Giles quotes Napoleon, *Maximes de Guerre*, no. 72: "A general is not absolved from his responsibilities by an order emanating from his sovereign or minister, when the latter is far removed from the field of operations, and knows little, or nothing, of the most recent state of affairs."

He who advances
    Without seeking
    Fame,
    Who retreats
    Without escaping
    Blame,
    He whose one aim is
    To protect his people
    And serve his lord,
    This man is
    A Jewel of the Realm.

Li Quan: His decisions are made for the protection of others, not for his own interest.

Du Mu: Jewels of this kind are rare.

Translator: Giles remarks, "It was Wellington, I think, who said that the hardest thing of all for a soldier is to retreat." As Lévi points out, the expression "Jewel of the Realm" has a mystic resonance and is also used to refer to physical treasures, such as the venerable Nine Tripods that since earliest times mysteriously embodied the "vertu" or "mana" of the imperial dynasty.

> He regards his troops
> > As his children,
> > And they will go with him
> > Into the deepest ravine.
> He regards them
> > As his loved ones,
> > And they will stand by him
> > Unto death.

Du Mu/Giles: During the Warring States period, Wu Qi [this is the Master Wu several times referred to, who died in 381 B.C., and was author of his own treatise on the Art of War], when he was a general, wore the same clothes as his men and ate the same food as they did. He had no special mat to sleep on, he had no special horse to ride. He carried his own rations wrapped in a bundle and shared the soldiers' every hardship. Once, when one of his men had an infected abscess, he sucked out the pus. The man's mother, when she heard of this, burst into tears. "Your son is a humble soldier," protested a bystander. "And the general is sucking his wound clean for him! What are you crying for?" To which she replied, "Years ago, Lord Wu did the same thing for my husband, this boy's father, and he became Lord Wu's devoted follower from that day forward, till one day he met his death at the enemy's hands. Now I have only to wait for my son's death, in some unknown field of battle!"

Li Quan: If he cherishes his men like this, they will give him their last drop of strength. The viscount of Chu comforted his troops with a single word, and they felt as though they were wrapped in silk-lined garments. [Giles adds, "The Viscount of Chu invaded the small state of Xiao during the winter. The Duke of Shen said to him: 'Many of the soldiers are suffering severely from the cold.' So he made a round of the whole army, comforting and encouraging the men; and straightaway they felt as if they were clothed in garments lined with floss silk" (*The Zuo Commentary*, Duke Xuan, XII, 5).]

Zhang Yu: Another *Art of War* says, "The general must himself share in the toils of his men. In summer he does not open his sunshade; in winter he does not wear extra clothing. In dangerous places he dismounts and walks. He waits until the men have dug their own well before drinking. He waits until their food is cooked before eating. He waits until their encampment is finished before seeing to his own quarters."

If he is generous
  But cannot command,
If he is affectionate
  But cannot give orders,
If he is chaotic
  And cannot keep order,
Then his men
  Will be like
  Spoiled children,
  And useless.

Du Mu/Giles: It is written in the *Classic of the Yin Talisman,* "Harm comes from kindness." Duke Li wrote, "Those who fear me will not fear the enemy. Those who fear the enemy do not fear me."

Zhang Yu: The Skillful General is both loved and feared. That is all.

Giles: Du Mu recalls an instance [recorded at full length in *The Chronicle of the Three Kingdoms,* Chapter 54] of stern military discipline which occurred in A.D. 219, when Lü Meng was occupying the town of Jiangling. He had given stringent orders to his army not to molest the inhabitants nor to take anything from them by force. Nevertheless, a certain officer serving under his banner, who happened to be a fellow-townsman, ventured to appropriate a bamboo hat belonging to one of the people, in order to wear it over his regulation helmet as a protection against the rain. Lü Meng considered that the fact of his being also a native of Runan should not be allowed to palliate a clear breach of discipline, and accordingly he ordered his summary execution, the tears rolling down his face, however, as he did so. This act of severity filled the army with wholesome awe, and from that time forth even articles dropped in the highway were not picked up.

> If we know that our own troops
> Are capable of attacking
> But fail to see
> That the enemy
> Is not vulnerable,
> We have only
> Half of victory.

Mei Yaochen: We know self, but not other. Victory is possible, but by no means sure.

> If we know that the enemy
> Is vulnerable
> But fail to see
> That our own troops
> Are incapable of attacking,
> We have only
> Half of victory.

Mei Yaochen: We know other, but not self. Victory is possible, but by no means sure.

> If we know that the enemy
> Is vulnerable
> And know that our own troops
> Are capable of attacking,
> But fail to see
> That the terrain
> Is unfit for attack,

We still have only
Half of victory.

Mei Yaochen: We know self and other, but not terrain. Defeat is still possible.

The Wise Warrior,
    When he moves,
    Is never confused;
    When he acts,
    Is never at a loss.

Du Mu: Before any movement or action, victory and defeat are already determined. So he cannot be confused or at a loss.

Zhang Yu: He never makes a move recklessly, and so when he does move, he makes no mistakes. He never acts lightly, and so when he does act, he is never at a loss.

So it is said:
    "Know the enemy,
    Know yourself,
    And victory
    Is never in doubt,
    Not in a hundred battles."

Translator: The identical saying has already occurred in Chapter 3.

Know Heaven,
    Know Earth,
    And your victory
    Is complete.

Li Quan/Giles: Know these three things—the affairs of man, the seasons of Heaven, and the advantages of Earth—and victory will always be yours.

Chapter Eleven

The Nine Kinds of Ground

Wang Xi: These are the nine types of military ground, with their advantages and disadvantages.

Zhang Yu: There are nine essential dynamics [or potential energies, *shi*] of ground or terrain in war. Here the underlying dynamics of ground are discussed, which follows naturally from the previous chapter on its forms.

Giles: One would like to distinguish the Nine Kinds of Ground from the Six Forms of Terrain of Chapter 10 by saying that the Six Forms refer to the natural formation or geographical features of the country, while the Nine Kinds have more to do with the condition of the army, being "situations" as opposed to "grounds." But it is soon found impossible to carry out the distinction. Both are cross-divisions, for in Chapter 10 we have "deadlock" terrain [a situational category] side by side with "enclosed" terrain [a geographical category], while in the present chapter there is even greater confusion.

Translator: Perhaps the writer wanted there to be Nine Kinds of Ground just as there were nine Astrological Mansions in the sky. But nothing is very well worked out. Father Amiot remarks (p. 117), "It is a general fault of Chinese authors that they repeat the same principle, the same argumentation, the same words, several times." As other commentators and translators have pointed out, this particular chapter is long, disorganized and repetitive, and it shows signs of having been put together from disparate fragments, possibly jumbled bamboo strips (as indeed does much of *The Art of War*). Despite this, I have stayed with the accepted text.

Master Sun said:

In War,
    There are
    Nine Kinds of Ground:

    Scattering ground,
    Light ground,
    Strategic ground,
    Open ground,
    Crossroad ground,
    Heavy ground,
    Intractable ground,
    Enclosed ground,
    Death ground.

When the feudal lords
    Fight on home territory,
    That is
    Scattering ground.

Cao Cao: Officers and men long for home, and home is close at hand. They scatter easily.

Giles: So called because the soldiers, being near to their homes and anxious to see their wives and children, are likely to seize the opportunity afforded by a battle and scatter in every direction.

Du Mu: Being close to home, they lack the desperate resolve necessary to press forward, and find an all too easy place of refuge.

He Yanxi: The king of Wu asked for Master Sun's advice: "On scattering ground, troops think of home and refuse to fight. In this case, we must secure our position and lie low. But suppose the enemy attacks some of our small towns, plunders our countryside, prevents us from gathering firewood, cuts our lines of communication, and waits for a moment of weakness to attack us. What should we do then?" Master Sun replied, "The enemy has penetrated our territory deeply, he already has many of our towns behind his lines, his officers and men think of their army as their family, they are resolved to fight; whereas our own men are stationed at home, they are [too] close to home comforts and to their kin. If they form ranks, they do so without conviction, if they fight, they fight without the will to win. We must gather men together in large numbers; stock grain, fodder, and silk; fortify towns and control strategic positions; and meanwhile send out parties of light troops to cut off the enemy's supply lines. When the enemy fails to provoke us, when their supplies fail to arrive, when there is nothing left for them to plunder in the countryside and their men begin to grow weary and hungry, then we can lure them out and defeat them. If we are to engage them in the open, then we must have a favorable dynamic working for us, we must hold some strategic pass and lay an ambush. Otherwise, we must hide in the mists and darkness and take them unawares, catch them in a slack moment. There lies the path to victory."

Translator: This passage is one of nine extracts from "The Questions and Answers of King He Lü of Wu and Master Sun," quoted at length by the Song-dynasty commentator He Yanxi (and also present in the earlier encyclopedic work *Tongdian* by the Tang scholar Du You), under each of the nine categories of "ground" (see Li Ling, 1997, pp. 182–87, and Ames, 1993, pp. 199–223). Fragments of such questions and answers have also been found among the excavated Bamboo Strips, and they seem to be an interesting example of an early Warring States *Art of War* accretion, an illuminating (and relatively simple) expansion of the often gnomic sentences of the core text. Similar explanatory accretions (Commentaries and "Wings") became attached at an early stage to other Chinese classics, including that other great gnomic text, *The Book of Changes*.

When an army enters
   Enemy territory,
   But not deeply,
   That is
   Light ground.

Li Quan: It is easy [light] to retreat from.

Du Mu/Giles: When an army crosses a border, boats and bridges must be burned to demonstrate to the men that no one is hankering after home.

He Yanxi: The king of Wu asked for Master Sun's advice: "We have arrived on light ground. We have just entered enemy territory, and our officers and men still hanker after home. It is hard to advance and easy to retreat. We have no strong terrain behind us, such as a pass or other commanding height, and our men are easily afraid. The commanding general wants to press on, but his officers and men want to retreat. Thus upper and lower ranks are not of one mind. The enemy meanwhile has fortified his cities, has arrayed his troops in good order, and either confronts us or attacks our rear. What should we do?" Master Sun replied, "When troops first arrive in enemy territory, the officers and men are not yet focused on penetrating the terrain, they are not primed for battle. We must not go too close to the enemy's main cities, we must not use his main thoroughfares. Instead, we must present an air of trepidation and hesitation, give the impression of being about to retreat. Meanwhile, select a crack cavalry detachment, send them on ahead secretly, and make off with the enemy's horses and livestock. The rank and file, seeing the success of this advance, will lose their fear. We must then select some of our best foot soldiers and set them in a secret ambush. If the enemy comes, we must attack them without hesitation. If they do not come, they can withdraw without doing battle." Master Sun added, "On light ground such as you have described, we should select some of our bravest men and set an ambush on an important thoroughfare; then, when we retreat, the enemy will pursue us, and we can attack them."

> When the ground
>   Offers advantage
>   To either side,
>   That is
>   Strategic ground.

Translator: Literally, ground worth struggling for (*zheng*).

Cao Cao/Giles: Ground on which the few and the weak can defeat the many and the strong.

Li Quan: A key position, such as the neck of a pass. Whoever occupies it first will have the victory.

Du Mu/Giles: Contestable or strategically important ground. Failure to occupy such a strategic position can lead to disaster, as in the case of the army of Lü Guang, when it returned from its triumphant western expedition to Turkestan [A.D. 385]. It was the failure of his would-be opponents to seize control of either one of two strategic passes that enabled Lü to defeat them.

Giles: Thermopylae was strategic ground, because the possession of it, even for a few days only, meant holding the entire invading army in check and thus gaining invaluable time. Cf. *Master Wu's Art of War,* Chapter 5: "For those who have to fight in the ratio of one to ten, there is nothing better than a narrow pass."

He Yanxi: The king of Wu asked for Master Sun's advice: "Suppose the enemy arrives first and holds and defends key positions; suppose he deploys lightly armed and well-trained troops both offensively and defensively and is prepared for any surprise maneuver from our side. What should we do?" Master Sun replied, "With strategic ground, it is of paramount advantage to be the first to occupy it. If the enemy has indeed already done this, be cautious. Avoid attacking him. Lure him out by feigning retreat. Raise the standards, sound the drums, and make as if toward some place that he greatly cherishes. Drag firewood along the ground and create a cloud of dust, confuse his eyes and ears. Select some of your best men and lay a secret ambush, and he will be obliged to come to the rescue. Whatever he desires, give him; whatever he abandons, take. This is how to deal with an enemy who has occupied a strategic position first. If, on the other hand, we are there first and he uses this same strategy against us, then we should select some of our finest troops to defend the position; and simultaneously pursue the enemy with light troops and lay ambushes in defiles and on precipitous terrain. When the enemy engages with us in combat, the ambush will arise on both sides, and we will have total victory."

> When each side
>   Can come and go freely,
>   That is
>   Open ground.

Cao Cao: Ground covered with a network of roads [Giles: like a chessboard].

Du Mu: Level, extensive, well-watered ground in which one can come and go, suitable for battle and for building fortifications.

He Yanxi: The king of Wu asked for Master Sun's advice: "[I know that] on open ground, we should cut off the enemy's lines and make it impossible for him to move. We should complete our frontier fortifications, destroy his lines of communication, and secure passes and strategic heights. But supposing we do not plan this in advance and he has made preparations; then he will be able to move, but we will be powerless to do so. In such a situation, if the forces on either side are evenly matched in numbers, what should we do?" Master Sun replied, "If we are unable to move and he can move freely, we should select troops and lay an ambush. Then we maintain our defensive position, and make a show of being slack and helpless. Then the enemy will come out and will be taken unawares in our ambush."

When the ground
Borders
Three states
And the first to take it
Has mastery
Of the empire,
That is
Crossroad ground.

Meng: An example of this was the [small] state of Zheng, which was surrounded by the [large] states of Qi, Chu, and Jin.

Giles: Empire (*tianxia*) of course stands for the loose confederacy of states into which China was divided under the Zhou dynasty. The belligerent who holds this dominating position can constrain most of them to become his allies.

He Yanxi: The king of Wu asked Master Sun, "[I know that] on crossroad ground, one must arrive first. But suppose we are distant from the place and set off later than the enemy; suppose we cannot arrive there first, however hard we drive our horses and chariots; what should we do then?" Master Sun replied, "What is meant by crossroad ground is a place where we face the enemy and at the same time there are other states on each side—like a crossroads. The 'first to take it' is in fact the first party to send envoys with heavy bribes, to negotiate alliances with the neighboring states, to establish a friendly relationship. If we have achieved this, then, even if our troops arrive later than the enemy's, we will have solid support and our enemy will be without allies. Our allies will beat the drum and attack him, and he will take fright and be at his wits' end."

When an army enters
    Enemy territory deeply
    And holds
    Several fortified towns
    In its rear,
    That is
    Heavy ground.

Cao Cao: Ground that is difficult to retreat from.

Wang Xi: When an invading army has reached such a point, its situation is serious [heavy].

Li Quan: In such a situation, the resolve is firm. As when the great Qin general Bo Qi [d. 257 B.C.] invaded Chu [278 B.C.], and when Yue Yi [minister of the state of Wei] invaded Qi [284 B.C.]. These were both cases of being on "heavy" ground.

He Yanxi: The king of Wu asked for Master Sun's advice: "Suppose we have led our troops deep into enemy territory and our lines of supply have been broken. Even if we want to, our situation is such that we cannot retreat. What must we do to nourish ourselves on the enemy and not face defeat?" Master Sun replied, "On heavy ground, officers and men are courageous, and even if supplies are cut off, they can resort to pillage. Booty acquired by inferior ranks should be collected by the commanding officers. Those who have acquired most should be well rewarded. In this way, the men will not think of retreating. And if they do show signs of weakening, they must be forbidden to have such thoughts. Meanwhile, build deep moats and strong fortifications, demonstrate the intention of a long stay. If the enemy, under cover of opening up the roads, tries to destroy our lines of communication, send out fast, light chariots and bait him with the offer of cattle and horses. If he comes out, then beat the drums and follow him; meanwhile, lay an ambush and, at the time designated, fall on him from both sides. He will surely be defeated."

> When an army travels through
>> Mountains and forests,
>> Cliffs and crags,
>> Marshes and fens,
>> Hard roads,
>> These are
>> Intractable ground.

Cao Cao: [They contain] little that is solid.

Jia Lin: This is ground that has been ruined by the passage of water.

Mei Yaochen: Such ground is hard to traverse, let alone fight on.

He Yanxi: The king of Wu asked for Master Sun's advice: "Suppose we are on intractable ground, among mountains and rivers, cliffs and crags, on hard roads, our men exhausted after a long march; suppose the enemy is up ahead, has set ambushes behind us, is encamped to our left, and has taken up positions to our right. His finest chariots and cavalry hold the pass against us. What are we to do then?" Master Sun replied, "Send the light chariots three or four miles ahead of the main body of your troops. They are to lie in wait for the enemy, observe him in the pass, dividing into a left and a right detachment. Your commanding general meanwhile keeps a close eye on all directions and chooses an 'empty' moment [a moment of weakness on the part of the enemy] to strike. The various divisions then all come together and continue to harry the enemy until he is exhausted."

> Ground reached
>> Through narrow gorges,
>> Retreated from
>> By twisting paths,
>> Where a smaller force of theirs
>> Can strike our larger one,

That is
Enclosed ground.

Li Quan: Action and movement are hard.

Du Mu: Here both arrival and departure are difficult; but it is easy to lay ambushes, and one can be utterly defeated.

He Yanxi: The king of Wu asked for Master Sun's advice: "Suppose we are on enclosed ground, with a powerful foe ahead of us and dangerous passes behind. The enemy has cut our supply lines and is trying to provoke us into flight. Meanwhile, he beats his drums and makes a loud noise, without actually advancing, in order to observe our resources for battle. What should we do then?" Master Sun replied, "On enclosed ground, close the passes, to show that there is no way out. Then the army must become the family, all minds must be as one and all strengths united. For several days extinguish fires, so that there is no sign of smoke. This presents the outer 'form' of utter chaos and weakness. The enemy, seeing this, will scoff at us, will slacken and lower his state of preparedness. Then we boost our own troops' morale, we stir up their resolve, lay ambushes with our crack troops in the defiles and ravines on each side, and break out our main force with much beating of drums. If the enemy opposes us, we will attack with all our might, assaulting him from front, rear, and sides." The king asked again, "Suppose the enemy comes upon us on enclosed ground and himself lays ambushes and develops cunning schemes, lures us, perplexes us with much waving of flags and noise and confusion, so that we do not know which direction he is going in. What then?" Master Sun replied, "Let a thousand men wield banners, let them divide into parties and block the strategic roads, let light troops advance and challenge the enemy, let them draw up their ranks without actually attacking. If the enemy engages them, let them not retreat. This is the way to defeat their strategy."

Ground where mere survival
   Requires
   A desperate struggle,
   Where without
   A desperate struggle
   We perish,

That is
Death ground.

Cao Cao: A high mountain stands in front, a large river runs behind; advance is impossible, retreat is denied.

Li Quan: Blocked by mountains to the front and rivers to the rear, with supplies exhausted. In this situation, it is advantageous to act swiftly and dangerous to procrastinate.

Chen Hao/Giles: To be on death ground is like sitting in a leaking boat, like crouching in a burning house.

Du Mu: Duke Li had this to say about death ground: "Suppose our army invades enemy territory and fails to avail itself of local guides; it therefore falls into a deadly trap and is at the enemy's mercy. To the left plunges a ravine, to the right soars a mountain; the road is so precipitous that the horses have to be tied together and the chariots transported on ropes. There is no passage either in front or behind; there is no choice but to proceed in single file. Before our men can form ranks, the enemy suddenly appears in force. It is equally impossible to advance or to retreat. We seek battle but in vain; we adopt a defensive stance but are constantly hard-pressed. If we stay put, days and months will go by; if we make a move, we will be attacked front and rear. This wilderness offers neither water to drink nor grass for fodder; the troops are without supplies, the horses are worn out; we are exhausted and at the very end of our wits and strength. The pass is so narrow that a single man can hold it against ten thousand. The enemy holds every strategic advantage; we have lost every strategic initiative. Even suppose we had the finest soldiers and the sharpest weapons, how could we turn such a situation to our advantage?"

He Yanxi: The king of Wu asked for Master Sun's advice: "Suppose our troops have crossed the frontier and are on enemy territory. Now the enemy arrives in great numbers and surrounds us with a double cordon of troops. If we want to break out, we find every way blocked. We need to raise the men's morale and steel them for a last desperate stand, in order to break the net. What should we do?" Master Sun replied, "Dig deep the moats [of your camp] and build high its fortifications; make a show of being well dug in. Then stay put, do not make a move. Conceal your potential. Make a speech

to the men, invoking the desperate situation. Kill the oxen, burn the chariots, and hold a feast for the men. Burn your reserves of grain, fill your wells,
and level your ovens to the ground; cut the men's hair, shred their hats,
show that you have no other plan but to fight to the death. Thus you will fill
your men with the resolve of despair. Polish your armor, sharpen your
swords, and unite your men in a single surge of morale. Attack the enemy
from both sides at once, making a terrible din and beating the drums of
war. The enemy will take fright, incapable of withstanding this ferocious
assault. Meanwhile, your shock troops will attack separately from the
enemy's rear. This is called snatching salvation from despair. Hence the saying 'He who is in dire straits and can find no stratagem, is lost; he who is
lost and cannot fight to the death, is finished.'" The king of Wu went on to
ask, "Suppose our troops have surrounded the enemy, what then?" Master
Sun replied, "Steep mountains and valleys, hard to traverse, bring the
enemy to bay. Here is how he must be attacked. Hide your men in an ambush, and open a way for the enemy to retreat by. He will seek safety in retreat and will lose the will to fight. Attack him then, and despite his
superiority in numbers, he will be destroyed."

> On scattering ground,
>   Do not fight.

Li Quan: For fear that the men will scatter and flee.

> On light ground,
>   Do not halt.

Li Quan: For fear that they will flee.

> On strategic ground,
>   Do not attack.

Cao Cao: Do not attack, but concentrate on being the first to occupy the
advantage.

Li Quan: If the enemy has occupied the key position first, attack is out
of the question.

On open ground,
  Do not block.

Giles: Because the attempt would be futile, and would expose the blocking force itself to serious risks.

On crossroad ground,
  Form alliances.
On heavy ground,
  Plunder.

Du Mu: When an army occupies heavy ground, there is no gain to be had in advancing further, and retreat is impossible; one must therefore bring in grain for a protracted resistance and keep a close watch on the enemy.

Giles: On this, Li Quan has the following delicious note: "When an army penetrates far into the enemy's country, care must be taken not to alienate the people by unjust treatment. Follow the example of the Han Emperor Gaozu, whose march into Qin territory was marked by no violation of women or looting of valuables. (*Nota bene:* This was in 207 B.C. and may well cause us to blush for the Christian armies that entered Peking in A.D. 1900.) Thus he won the hearts of all. In the present passage, then, I think the true reading must be, not 'plunder,' but '*do not* plunder.'" Alas, I fear that in this instance, the worthy commentator's feelings outran his judgement. Du Mu has no such illusions.

Translator: The contemporary Chinese scholar Wu Jiulong (1990) makes the same observation as Giles: "Li's explanation, which is directly contrary to that of all the other commentators, expresses a worthy point of view, but is not, I fear, in line with Master Sun's own thinking."

On intractable ground,
  Keep marching.
On enclosed ground,
  Devise stratagems.

Cao Cao: Try out some indirect [unusual] stratagem.

Du You/Giles: In such a position, some cunning scheme must be devised to fit the circumstances, and if we can succeed in deceiving the enemy, the danger may be averted.

Giles: This is exactly what happened on the famous occasion when Hannibal was hemmed in among the mountains on the road to Casilinum, and to all appearances entrapped by the Dictator Fabius. The stratagem which Hannibal devised to baffle his foes was remarkably like that which Tian Dan had also employed with success exactly 62 years before [see Chapter 9]. When night came on, bundles of twigs were fastened to the horns of some 2,000 oxen and set on fire, the terrified animals being then quickly driven along the mountainside towards the passes which were beset by the enemy. The strange spectacle of these rapidly moving lights so alarmed and discomfited the Romans that they withdrew from their position, and Hannibal's army passed safely through the defile.

> On death ground,
>   Fight.

Jia Lin/Giles: Fight with all your might, and you may live; cling to your corner, and you will die.

> The Skillful Warrior of old
>   Could prevent
>   The enemy's vanguard
>   From linking with his rear,
>   Large and small divisions
>   From working together,
>   Crack troops
>   From helping poor troops,
>   Officers and men
>   From supporting one another.
>   The enemy,
>   Once separated,
>   Could not
>   Reassemble;

> Once united,
> Could not
> Act in concert.

Meng: He [the Skillful Warrior] launched several deceptive maneuvers. He was seen in the west and appeared out of the east; he lured his enemy in the north and attacked him in the south. He made him crazy and confused him so that his forces dispersed in disarray and could not be reassembled.

Zhang Yu: He took his enemy unawares, launching surprise attacks. He struck him suddenly with shock troops. The enemy came to the rescue of its vanguard and left its rear exposed; he responded on the left and created an opening on the right. The result was general panic and confusion, disorder and disintegration.

Mei Yaochen: If already separated, they were unable to reunite; if already united, they were unable to act together.

> When there was some gain
>> To be had,
>> He made a move;
>> When there was none,
>> He halted.

> To the question
>> "How should we confront
>> An enemy,
>> Numerous and well arrayed,
>> Poised to attack?"
> My reply is
>> "Seize something
>> He cherishes,
>> And he will do your will."

Cao Cao: Seize some strategic advantage he depends on.

Chen Hao: This refers not just to strategic advantages but to any person or thing of importance to the enemy.

Giles: By boldly seizing the initiative in this way, you at once throw the other side on the defensive.

Translator: Jullien puts this well (p. 166): "Instead of accepting a direct engagment with the enemy, which would be dangerous [in these circumstances], one must begin by 'destructuring' him—disconcerting him, destabilizing him."

> Speed
> > Is the essence of War.
> > Exploit the enemy's unpreparedness;
> > Attack him unawares;
> > Take an unexpected route.

Du Mu: This is the essence of War, to exploit the enemy's weakness. To attack the enemy unawares, taking an unexpected route, is a profound truth of War and the secret of the general's art.

He Yanxi: When the Wei general Meng Da was plotting to betray his state and go over to the House of Shu [in A.D. 227], the Wei general Sima Yi got wind of his intended treachery and made a forced march to Xincheng, where Meng was governor, covering the four hundred–odd miles in eight days. In taking this decision, he ignored the advice of his officers, who thought it more prudent to investigate the matter carefully first. "Meng is a man of no principles," said Sima, "and we should deal with him at once, while he is still hesitating." Meng had indeed reckoned that it would be at least a month before anything happened. He was caught unawares; Xincheng was taken and Meng himself executed. A second example of the efficacy of speed is that of [the great Tang general] Duke Li Jing, when he put down the rebel Xiao Xian in Hubei. He set off from Sichuan and sailed down the Yangtze gorges, taking Xiao completely by surprise. "In War," said Duke Li, in his own *Art of War,* "speed is of the essence."

> The Way of Invasion is this:
> > Deep penetration
> > Brings cohesion;

Your enemy
Will not prevail.

Plunder fertile country
To nourish your men.
Cherish your troops,

Wang Xi/Giles: Fuss over them, humor them, give them plenty of food
and drink, and look after them generally.

Do not wear them out.
Nurture your energy;
Concentrate it.

Du Mu: If your energy is whole and your strength abundant, victory will
be yours from the very outset. Exploit changing circumstances, and keep
your plans dark and inscrutable.

Chen Hao/Giles: In 224 B.C., Wang Jian, the famous general whose
military genius contributed largely to the success of the First Emperor [of
Qin], had invaded the state of Chu, where a universal levy was made to oppose him. But, being doubtful of the temper of his troops, he declined all
invitations to fight and remained strictly on the defensive. Day after day,
Wang kept inside his walls and would not come out, but devoted all his
time and energy to winning the affection and confidence of his men. He
took care that they should be well fed, sharing his own meals with them; he
provided facilities for bathing and employed every method of judicious in-
dulgence to weld them into a loyal and homogeneous body. After some time
had elapsed, he told certain persons to find out how the men were amusing
themselves. The answer was that they were contending with one another in
putting the weight and long-jumping. When Wang Jian heard that they were
engaged in these athletic pursuits, he knew that their spirits had been raised
to the required pitch and that they were now ready for fighting. By this
time, the Chu army, after repeating their challenge again and again, had
marched away eastwards in disgust. The Qin general immediately struck
camp and followed them, and in the battle that ensued, they were routed
with great slaughter. Shortly afterward, the whole of Chu was conquered
by Qin, and the Chu king was led into captivity.

Move your men about;

Giles: In order that the enemy may never know exactly where you are.

> Devise stratagems
> That cannot be fathomed.
> Throw your men
> Where there is no escape,
> And they will die
> Rather than flee.
> Men who have
> Faced death
> Can achieve anything;

Zhang Yu/Giles: Master Weiliao said, "Supposing one man were to run amok with a sword in the marketplace, and everybody else tried to get out of his way, it would not be that this man alone had courage and that all the rest were cowards. The truth is, a desperado [literally, "a man who must die"] will always defeat a man who still sets some value on his life [literally, "a man who must live"].

> They will give
> Their last drop of strength,
> Officers and men alike.

> Troops in desperate straits
> Know no fear.
> Where there is no escape,
> They stand firm;
> When they have entered deep,
> They persist;
> When they see no hope,
> They fight.

Li Quan: To the death.

They are alert
　Without needing
　Discipline;
　They act
　Without needing
　Instructions;
　They are devoted
　Without needing
　A compact;
　They are loyal
　Without needing
　Orders.

Forbid the consulting of omens,
　Cast out doubts,
　And they will go on
　To the death.

Du Mu/Giles: Lord Yellow Stone said, "Spells and incantations should be strictly forbidden and no officer allowed to inquire by divination into the fortunes of an army, for fear the soldiers' minds should be seriously perturbed." The meaning is that if all doubts and scruples are thus cast aside, your men will never falter in their resolution until they die.

Our men have no excess
　Of worldly goods,
　And yet they do not
　Disdain wealth;
　They do not expect
　To live long,
　And yet they do not
　Disdain long life.

Wang Xi: They have what they need and no more. If officers and men cared too much for worldly riches, they would cherish life at all costs. As it is, they fight to the death. If they had too much thought for self-preservation, they would have no will to fight.

Zhang Yu: Wealth and long life are things that all men cherish. So if they burn or throw away valuable possessions and sacrifice their own lives, it is not that they dislike them, but simply that they see no choice in the matter.

> On the day
>> They are ordered into battle,
>> They sit up and weep,
>> Wetting their clothes with their tears;
>> They lie down and weep,
>> Wetting their cheeks.

Cao Cao: Because they are all resolved to die.

Du Mu: They have all made a compact with death. Before the day of battle, the order is issued: "Today's affair depends upon this one act. If you do not put your lives at stake, your bodies will fertilize the fields and be carrion for the birds and beasts."

Zhang Yu/Giles: Such is their emotion. As at the mournful parting at the river Yi between Jing Ke and his friends, when the former was sent to attempt the life of the king of Qin (afterward the First Emperor) in 227 B.C. The tears of all flowed down like rain as he bade them farewell and uttered the following lines:

> *The shrill blast is blowing,*
> *Chilly the burn.*
> *Your champion is going*
> *—Not to return.*

Giles: We may remember that the heroes of the *Iliad* were equally child-like in showing their emotion.

But throw them
  Where there is no escape,
  And they will fight
  With the courage
  Of the heroes
  Zhu and Gui.

Giles/*Records of the Grand Historian*:   Zhuan Zhu was a native of
the state of Wu, and a contemporary of Master Sun himself. He was employed by Gongzi Guang [later to become King He Lü], to assassinate his
sovereign, Wang Liao, with a dagger that he secreted in the belly of a fish
served up at a banquet. He succeeded in his attempt but was himself immediately hacked to pieces by the king's bodyguard. This was in 515 B.C.
The other hero referred to, Cao Gui, performed the exploit which has made
his name famous 166 years earlier, in 681 B.C. The state of Lu had been
thrice defeated by Qi and was just about to conclude a treaty surrendering a
large slice of territory, when Cao Gui suddenly seized Lord Huan, the duke
of Qi, as he stood on the altar steps, and held a dagger against his chest.
None of the duke's retainers dared to move a muscle, and Cao Gui proceeded to demand full restitution, declaring that Lu was being unjustly
treated because she was a smaller and weaker state. Lord Huan, in peril of
his life, was obliged to consent, whereupon Cao Gui flung away his dagger
and quietly resumed his place amid the terrified assemblage without having
so much as changed color.

The Skillful Warrior
  Deploys his troops
  Like the *shuairan* snake,
  Found on Mount Heng.

Mei Yaochen: Swift reactions and responses.

Zhang Yu: *Shuai* means "swift." Strike it, and it retaliates swiftly. This is
a figure of battle formation. In the *Diagram of the Eight Formations* we
read, "Front is rear, rear is front. In every direction, each extremity is the
head. Strike the belly, and head and tail both come to the rescue."

Translator: The Eight Formations, although not mentioned by Master Sun himself, made up the classic repertoire of battle formations. Their invention was attributed to various ancient figures, from the legendary Yellow Emperor to Zhuge Liang (the Sleeping Dragon). According to the description in the *Taibo Yinjing* (written by Li Quan, the Tang commentator on *The Art of War*), the formations were divided among the Eight Trigrams. Four fell under the Yin catgegory and four under Yang. Their names were Heaven, Earth, Wind, Clouds, Flying Dragon, Winged Tiger, Soaring Bird, Curling Snake.

> Strike its head,
> And the tail lashes back;
> Strike its tail,
> And the head fights back;
> Strike its belly,
> And both head and tail
> Will attack you.
> To the question
> "Can an army be
> Like the *shuairan* snake?"

Mei Yaochen: In other words, is it possible to make the front and rear of an army react swiftly *[shuairan]* to an attack on the other, as though they were parts of a single [snakelike] body?

> I reply,
> "Yes, it can."
> Take the men of Wu
> And the men of Yue.
> They are enemies,
> But if they cross a river
> In the same boat
> And encounter a wind,
> They will help each other,
> Like right hand and left.

Mei Yaochen: This is the underlying dynamic of the situation.

Giles: The meaning is: if two enemies will help each other in a time of common peril, how much more should two parts of the same army, bound together as they are by every tie of interest and fellow-feeling. Yet it is notorious that many a campaign has been ruined through lack of cooperation, especially in the case of allied armies.

> It is not enough
> To tether horses
> And to bury
> Chariot wheels.

Giles: These quaint devices to prevent one's army from running away recall the Athenian hero Sophanes, who carried an anchor with him at the battle of Plataea, by means of which he fastened himself firmly to one spot. (See Herodotus, IX, 74.) It is not enough, says Master Sun, to render flight impossible by such mechanical means. You will not succeed unless your men have tenacity and unity of purpose, and, above all, a spirit of sympathetic cooperation. This is the lesson which can be learned from the *shuairan*.

Translator: Brigadier General Griffith makes a more modern comparison: "Such 'Maginot Line' expedients are not in themselves sufficient to prevent troops from fleeing."

> There must be a single courage
> Throughout:
> This is the Way
> To manage an army.

> Strong and weak,
> Both can serve,
> Thanks to the principle
> Of ground.

Mei Yaochen: Both strong and weak can be used, thanks to the underlying dynamic of the ground [or terrain].

Translator: Or, as Brigadier General Griffith puts it in his paraphrase of Zhang Yu: "The difference in quality of troops can be balanced by careful sector assignment. Weak troops can hold strong ground, but might break if put in a position less strong." Other commentators take this to mean that one can make use of both strong (or hard) and weak (or soft) features of the terrain. According to this interpretation, hard is Yang, soft is Yin.

> The Skillful Warrior
> Directs his army
> As if it were
> A single man.
> He leaves it no choice
> But to obey.

Niu and Wang (1990): The reason they are so united and so easy to command is that they find themselves in a situation, or on a terrain, where they have no option other than to fight.

> It is the business of the general
> To be still
> And inscrutable,
> To be upright
> And impartial.

> He must be able
> To keep his own troops
> In ignorance,
> To deceive their eyes
> And their ears.

Cao Cao: The troops can share in the joy of completion, but not in the travail of conception.

Zhang Yu: As the Hermit of the Evening Star put it: "In war, deception is to be prized; and it is not just the enemy that must be deceived, but one's own men, too. They must be enabled to follow, but not to understand."

The Way and Its Power, **Chapter 65:**   In the days of old, those who practiced Tao with success did not thereby enlighten the people but on the contrary sought to make them ignorant.

Translator: Giles quotes Colonel Henderson: "The infinite pains with which Stonewall Jackson [American Confederate general, 1824–63] sought to conceal, even from his most trusted field officers, his movements, his intentions, and his thoughts, a commander less thorough would have pronounced useless."

Giles/*History of the Later Han:***   In the year A.D. 88, Ban Chao took to the field with twenty-five thousand men from Khotan and other Central Asian states with the object of crushing Yarkand. . . . [His victory in this campaign was due to the fact that] he not only kept his own officers in ignorance of his real plans, but actually took the bold step of dividing his army in order to deceive the enemy.

> He changes his ways
>> And alters his plans
>> To keep the enemy
>> In ignorance.

> He shifts camp
>> And takes roundabout routes
>> To keep the enemy
>> In the dark.

> He leads his men into battle
>> Like a man
>> Climbing a height
>> And kicking away the ladder;

He leads them
Deep into the territory
Of the feudal lords
And releases the trigger.

Zhang Yu: Kicking away the ladder makes advance possible and retreat impossible; releasing the trigger means one can go forward and not backward. This was what Xiang Yu did when he sank his ships after crossing the river.

He burns his boats,
He breaks his pots.
He is like a shepherd
Driving his sheep
This way and that;
No one knows
Where he is going.

Du Mu: The men are aware of their orders to advance and retreat, but they know nothing of the goal of the offensive.

Translator: He keeps them in the dark so that he can exploit to the full the "potential of the situation" (Jullien, p. 177). This same idea was applied in the political domain, where it formed part of the classical tradition of despotism misnamed Legalism, of which twentieth-century Chinese totalitarianism is the direct heir. Citizens were to be treated like so many automata.

He assembles his troops
And throws them
Into danger;
This is the business
Of the commander.

Giles: Master Sun means that after mobilisation there should be no delay in aiming a blow at the enemy's heart. Compare with his earlier statement [in this chapter], "Throw your men where there is no escape, and they will die rather than flee." Note how he returns again and again to this point. Among the warring states of ancient China, desertion was no doubt a much more present fear and serious evil than it is in the armies of today.

These things must be studied:
The Variations
Of the Nine Kinds of Ground;

Zhang Yu: One must not be hidebound in interpreting the rules for the Nine Kinds of Ground [and how to respond to them].

The Advantages
Of Flexible Maneuver;

Giles: The saying "retreat in order to advance" almost exactly corresponds to the French *il faut reculer pour mieux sauter.*

The Principles
Of Human Nature.

Cao Cao: It is [for example] human nature to advance toward gain and to retreat from harm.

The Way of Invasion is this:
Deep penetration
Brings cohesion;
Shallow penetration
Brings scattering.

Translator: If these recurring references to deep penetration are beginning to sound like one of the Taoist or pseudo-Taoist sex handbooks, we should not be surprised. The two genres (Art of War, Art of Love) share a lot of vocabulary and ideas. See the Introduction for a brief discussion of this. Robert van Gulik (*Erotic Colour Prints of the Ming Period,* p. 113) gives a telling example from the *Jiji zhenjing* (*The True Classic of the Complete*

Union), a late-Ming sex handbook. The penultimate paragraph of the main text (describing the climax of the "sexual battle") reads, "I am in no hurry, but the enemy [the female partner] is hard pressed for time [one is almost tempted to translate "at bay"] and throws 'his' entire force into the battle. The arms clash as I advance and withdraw at will, using the enemy's food and exhausting 'his' supplies. Then I practise the tactics of the turtle, the dragon, the serpent and the tiger. The enemy surrenders 'his' arms and I gather the fruits of victory. This is called *jiji* [After Completion, the name of the penultimate hexagram in *The Book of Changes*], ensuring peace for one generation. I withdraw from the battlefield and dismiss my soldiers. I rest quietly to regain my strength. I convey the booty to the storeroom thereby increasing my power to the height of strength." The Commentary explains "throws 'his' entire force into the battle" as meaning that the woman's passion reaches its apex. "After Completion (i.e., after orgasm), I continue pushing my member in and out, alternating deep and shallow strokes according to the prescribed method. . . ." The commentator continues, "Using the enemy's food means sucking her tongue; exhausting 'his' supplies means pressing her breasts. Then the woman sheds her true essence completely and I have obtained the True Yang. . . . Withdrawing from the battlefield means descending from the horse."

When you leave your own territory
   And lead your men
   Across the border,
   You enter dire terrain.

Mei Yaochen: This is somewhere between light and scattering ground. Less far forward than light, but farther than scattering.

Wang Xi/Giles: This is terrain separated from home by a third state, whose territory we have had to cross in order to reach it. We must complete our business there quickly.

When there are lines of communication
   On all four sides,
   You are on
   Crossroad terrain.

When you penetrate deeply,
>
> You are on
>
> Heavy terrain.

When you penetrate superficially,
>
> You are on
>
> Light terrain.

When there are strongholds to your rear
>
> And narrow passes in front,
>
> You are on
>
> Enclosed terrain.

When there is no way out,
>
> You are on
>
> Death terrain.

Zhang Yu: There is nowhere to escape to, on the left or right, in front or behind.

> On scattering ground,
>
> We unite the will of our men.

Du Mu: Remain on the defensive, and their will is united; engage battle, and they scatter easily.

> On light ground,
>
> We keep them connected.

Du Mu/Giles: First, to guard against the desertion of our own troops, and second, against a sudden attack by the enemy.

> On strategic ground,
>
> We bring up our rear.

Zhang Yu/Giles: We must quickly bring up our rear, so that head and tail may both reach the goal.

Giles: That is, they must not be allowed to straggle a long way apart.

> On open ground,
>> We see to our defenses.

Wang Xi/Giles: Fearing a surprise attack.

> On crossroad ground,
>> We strengthen our alliances.

> On heavy ground,
>> We ensure continuity of supplies.

Giles: The commentators take this as referring to forage and plunder, not, as one might expect, to an unbroken communication with home base.

> On intractable ground,
>> We keep on the move.

Cao Cao: Move along swiftly.

> On enclosed ground,
>> We block the passes.

Meng/Giles: To make it seem that we are defending the position, when in fact we are planning to burst suddenly through enemy lines.

Mei Yaochen: We close off escape routes, in order to make our soldiers fight with [the fierceness of] desperation.

Wang Xi: We are afraid that our men will be tempted to run away.

Du Mu/Giles/*History of the Northern Qi Dynasty*:   In A.D. 532, Gao Huan, afterward Emperor of the Northern Qi dynasty, was surrounded by a great army under Erzhu Zhao and others. His own force was comparatively small, consisting only of two thousand horse and something under thirty thousand foot. There were gaps in the lines of the surrounding army. But Gao Huan, instead of trying to escape, actually blocked all the gaps with oxen and donkeys tied together. As a result, his men fought with the courage of despair and carried the day.

> On death ground,
> > We demonstrate
> > The desperateness
> > Of the situation.

Du You: Burn your baggage, throw away your provisions, fill your wells, level your stoves, and make it plain to your men that they cannot survive but must fight to the death.

Mei Yaochen: Survival arises from looking death in the face.

> It is in the soldier's nature that
> > When surrounded,
> > He resists;
> > When all seems lost,
> > He struggles on;
> > When in danger,
> > He obeys orders.

Zhang Yu/Giles/*History of the Later Han*:   In a perilous position, he obeys every order. Ban Chao [A.D. 31–101; his brother, the historian Ban Gu, wrote the *History of the Former Han*] arrived at Shanshan [a non-Chinese Central Asian kingdom, an oasis state situated between Dunhuang and Khotan] in A.D. 73. Guang, the king of the country, received him at first with great politeness and respect; but shortly afterward his behavior underwent a sudden change, and he became remiss and negligent. Ban Chao spoke about this to the officers of his suite: "Have you noticed that Guang's polite intentions are on the wane? This must signify that envoys have come from the northern barbarians, and that consequently he is in a state of indecision, not knowing with which side to throw in his lot. That surely is the reason. The truly wise man, we are told, can perceive things before they have come to pass; how much more, then, can he perceive those that are already manifest!" Thereupon he called one of the natives who had been assigned to his service, and set a trap for him, saying, "Where are those envoys from the Xiongnu who arrived some days ago?" The man was so taken aback with surprise and fear that he presently blurted out the whole truth. Ban Chao, keeping his informant carefully under lock and key, then summoned a gathering of his officers, thirty-six in all, and began drinking with them. When the wine had gone to their heads a little, he tried to rouse their spirits still further by addressing them thus: "Gentlemen, here we are in the heart of an isolated region, anxious to receive riches and honor by some great exploit. Now, it happens that an ambassador from the Xiongnu arrived in this kingdom only a few days ago, and the result is that the respectful courtesy extended toward us by our royal host has disappeared. Should this envoy prevail upon him to seize our party and hand us over to the Xiongnu, our bones will become food for the wolves of the desert. What are we to do?" With one accord, the officers replied, "Standing as we do in peril of our lives, we will follow our commander to the death!" [For the sequel of this adventure, see the beginning of Chapter 12.]

Without knowing the plans
  Of the feudal lords,
  You cannot
  Form alliances.

Without knowing the lie
  Of hills and woods,
  Of cliffs and crags,
  Of marshes and fens,
  You cannot
  March.

Without using local guides,
  You cannot
  Exploit
  The lie of the land.

Giles: With regard to local guides, Master Sun might have added that there is always the risk of going wrong, either through their treachery or some misunderstanding, such as Livy records (XXII, 13): Hannibal, we are told, ordered a guide to lead him into the neighbourhood of Casinum, where there was an important pass to be occupied; but his Carthaginian accent, unsuited to the pronunciation of Latin names, caused the guide to understand Casilinum instead of Casinum, and turning from his proper route, he took the army in that direction, the mistake not being discovered until they had almost arrived.

> Ignorance of any one
>   Of these points

Cao Cao: The advantages and disadvantages attendant on the Nine Kinds of Ground.

> Is not characteristic
>   Of the army of a great king.

Giles: *Bawang,* "one who rules by force" [or "hegemon"], was a term specially used for those princes who established their hegemony over other feudal states [during the Spring and Autumn period]. The famous Five Great Kings of the seventh century were Duke Huan of Qi, Duke Wen of Jin, Duke Xiang of Song, Prince Zhuang of Chu, and Duke Mu of Qin.

> When the army of a great king
>   Attacks a powerful state,
>   He does not allow the enemy
>   To concentrate his forces.
>   He overawes the enemy
>   And undermines his alliances.

> He does not strive
>   To ally himself
>   With all the other states;

He does not foster
  Their power;
He pursues
  His own secret designs,
  Overawing his enemies.

Li Quan/Giles: He can afford to reject entangling alliances and simply pursue his own secret designs, his prestige enabling him to dispense with external friendships.

Thus he can capture
  The enemy's cities
And destroy
  The enemy's state.

Giles: This paragraph, though written many years before the Qin state became a serious menace, is not a bad summary of the policy by which the famous Six Chancellors gradually paved the way for the final triumph under Shihuangdi [the First Emperor of Qin, who died in 210 B.C.]

Distribute rewards
  Without undue respect for rules;
Publish orders
  Without undue regard for precedent;

Wang Xi/Giles: In order to prevent treachery.

Cao Cao/Giles: *The Marshal's Treatise* says: "Give instructions only on sighting the enemy; give rewards only for deserving deeds." Your final instructions should not correspond with those previously posted up.

Zhang Yu: Your arrangements should not be divulged beforehand.

Jia Lin: Your rules and arrangements should not be fixed.

Translator: As Brigadier General Griffith summarizes (observing that the "verse" is obviously out of place), the general in the field need not follow "prescribed procedures" or "customary law" in respect to administration of his army.

> Deal with a whole army
>> As if it were a single man.
>> Apply them to their task
>> Without words of explanation.

Giles: Lord Mansfield once told a junior colleague to "give no reasons" for his decisions, and the maxim is even more applicable to a general than to a judge.

> Confront them with the advantage,
> But do not explain the danger.

> Throw them into
>> Perilous ground,
>> And they will survive;
> Plunge them into
>> Death ground,
>> And they will live.

He Yanxi/Giles/*History of the Former Han*:   In 204 B.C., the Han general Han Xin was sent against the army of Zhao and halted ten miles from the mouth of the Jingxing pass, where the enemy had mustered in full force. Here, at midnight, he detached a body of two thousand light cavalry, every man of which was furnished with a red flag. Their instructions were to make their way through narrow defiles and keep a secret watch on the enemy. "When the men of Zhao see me in full flight," Han Xin said, "they will abandon their fortifications and give chase. This must be the sign for you to rush in, pluck down the Zhao standards, and set up the red banners of Han in their stead." Turning then to his other officers, he remarked, "Our adversary holds a strong position and is not likely to come out and attack us until he sees the banner and drums of the commander in chief, for fear I should turn back and escape through the mountains." So saying, he first of all sent out a division consisting of ten thousand men, and ordered them to form in line of battle with their backs to the river Di. Seeing this maneuver, the whole army of Zhao broke into loud laughter. By this time it was broad daylight, and Han Xin, displaying the generalissimo's flag, marched out of the pass with drums beating and was immediately engaged by the enemy. A great battle followed, lasting for some time; until at length Han Xin and his colleague Zhang Ni, leaving drums and banner on the field, fled to the division on the riverbank, where another fierce battle was raging. The enemy rushed out to pursue them and to secure the trophies, thus denuding their ramparts of men; but the two generals succeeded in joining the other army, which was fighting with the utmost desperation. The time had now come for the two thousand horsemen to play their part. As soon as they saw the men of Zhao following up their advantage, they galloped behind the deserted walls, tore up the enemy's flags, and replaced them with those of Han. When the Zhao army turned back from the pursuit, the sight of these red flags struck them with terror. Convinced that the Hans had got in and overpowered their king, they broke up in wild disorder, every effort of their leader to stay the panic being in vain. Then the Han army fell on them from both sides and completed the rout, killing a great number and capturing the rest, among whom was King Ya himself. . . . After the battle, some of Han Xin's officers came to him and said, "In *The Art of War* we are told to have a hill or tumulus on the right rear, and a river or marsh on the left front. [This appears to be a blend of Master Sun, Chapter 9, and the Grand Duke.] You, on the contrary, ordered us to draw up our troops with the river at our back. Under these conditions, how did we manage to gain the victory?" The general replied, "I fear you gentlemen have not studied *The Art of War* with sufficient care. Is it not written there, 'Plunge your men into death ground, and they will live; throw them into perilous ground, and they will survive'? Had I taken the usual course, I should never have been able to bring my colleagues around. What says the *Military Classic*? 'Swoop down on the market-place and drive the men off to fight.' [This passage does not occur in the present text of Master Sun.] If I had not placed my troops in a position where they were obliged to fight for their lives, but had allowed each man to follow his own discretion, there would have been a general *débandade* [rout], and it would have been impossible to do anything with them." The officers admitted the force of his argument, and said, "These are higher tactics than we should have been capable of."

Translator: This story has already been told in brief in Chapter 4, where Li Quan uses it to illustrate Han Xin's "uncommon" skill as a general.

> When a force
>> Has fallen into danger,
>> It can
>> Snatch victory
>> From defeat.

Mei Yaochen: Until it has fallen into danger, its will is not sufficiently concentrated.

Translator: Giles has another characteristically Edwardian comment here: "Danger has a bracing effect."

> Success in war
>> Lies in
>> Scrutinizing
>> Enemy intentions
>> And going with them.

Cao Cao: If he shows an inclination to advance, lay an ambush for him and retreat; if he seems anxious to retreat, then set out and attack him.

Zhang Yu/Giles: If the enemy shows an inclination to advance, lure him on to do so; if he seems anxious to retreat, delay so that he can do so.

Translator: Another interpretation reads this as: "And in *feigning* to go along with them."

> Focus on the enemy,
>> And from hundreds of miles
>> You can kill their general.
>> This is

Success
Through cunning.

On the day
    You decide to attack,
    Close the passes,
    Destroy the tallies,

Giles: The special kind used at city-gates and on the frontier. Tablets of bamboo or wood, one half of which was issued as a permit or passport by the official in charge of a gate. When this half was returned to him, within a fixed period, he was authorised to open the gate and let the traveller through.

Break off intercourse
With envoys;
Be firm in the temple council
For the execution of
Your plans.

Translator: See Chapter 1.

If the enemy opens a door,
    Rush in.
    Seize what he holds dear,
    And secretly contrive
    An encounter.

Chen Hao: If we manage to seize a favorable position, but the enemy does not come, the advantage cannot be exploited. He who wishes to take a position that the enemy holds dear must begin by contriving a secret encounter with the enemy and inveigle him into going there.

Mei Yaochen: This subtly contrived "encounter" is achieved through the enemy's own spies, who will carry back certain information. We must then succeed in arriving before the enemy, even though we may have set off after him. We must set off after him in order to ensure that he arrives. We must arrive first in order to seize what he holds dear.

Discard rules,

Cao Cao: As defined by rule and compass.

Jia Lin: Victory is all that matters, and this cannot be achieved by following set rules.

Giles: Napoleon, as we know, according to the veterans of the old school whom he defeated, won his battles by violating every accepted canon of warfare.

Translator: As all previous translators concur, this passage is hopelessly corrupt. I have followed Jia Lin's emendation.

> Follow the enemy,
> To fight
> The decisive battle.

Du Mu: Fall in with the enemy's disposition, and when the dynamic of the situation offers a favorable opportunity, come out for the decisive battle.

> At first,
> Be like a maiden;

Amiot: Avant que la campagne commence, soyez comme une jeune fille qui ne sort pas de la maison; elle s'occupe des affaires du ménage, elle a soin de tout préparer, elle voit tout, elle entend tout, elle sait tout, elle ne se mêle d'aucune affaire en apparence. ["Before the campaign begins, be like a young girl who never leaves the house; she looks after the household, she takes care to prepare everything, she sees everything, hears everything, knows everything, but to outward appearance she is utterly uninvolved."]

> When the enemy opens the door,
> Be swift as a hare;

Amiot: La campagne une fois commencée, vous devez avoir la promptitude d'un lièvre qui, se trouvant poursuivi par des chasseurs, tâcherait, par mille détours, de trouver enfin son gîte, pour s'y réfugier en sureté. ["When the campaign has begun, you must react as swiftly as a hare, who, finding himself pursued by hunters, strives by a thousand twists and turns to find his way back to the refuge of his dwelling."]

> Your enemy will not
> Withstand you.

Chapter Twelve

Attack by Fire

Master Sun said:

There are Five Ways to
Attack by Fire.

The first is to burn
Men;

He Yanxi/Giles/*History of the Later Han*: Ban Chao was sent on a mission to the king of Shanshan [see previous chapter, where the first part of the story is used to illustrate obedience in the face of extreme danger]. Relations between the Chinese government and these border states in the Far West were often difficult. Ban found himself placed in great peril by the unexpected arrival of an envoy from the Xiongnu barbarians [the mortal enemies of the Chinese]. In consultation with his officers, he exclaimed, "Nothing ventured, nothing gained! [Literally, "Unless you enter the tiger's lair, you cannot seize the tiger's cubs."] The only course open to us now is to make an assault by fire on the barbarians under cover of night, when they will not be able to discern our numbers. Profiting by their panic, we shall exterminate them completely; this will dampen the king's courage and shower us in glory, besides ensuring the success of our mission." The officers all replied that it would be necessary to discuss the matter first with the Intendant. Ban Chao then fell into a passion: "It is today," he cried, "that our fortunes must be decided! The Intendant is only a run-of-the-mill civilian, who on hearing of our project will certainly be afraid and will bring everything out into the open. An inglorious death is no worthy fate for valiant warriors." All then agreed to do as he wished. Accordingly, as soon as night came on, he and his little band quickly made their way to the barbarian camp. A strong gale was blowing at the time. Ban Chao ordered ten of the party to take drums and hide behind the enemy's barracks, it being arranged that when they saw flames shoot up, they should begin drumming and yelling with all their might. The rest of his men, armed with bows and crossbows, he posted in ambuscade at the gate of the camp. He then set fire to the place from the windward side, whereupon a deafening noise of drums and shouting arose to the front and rear of the Xiongnu, who rushed out pell-mell in frantic disorder. Ban Chao slew three of them with his own hand, while his companions cut off the heads of the envoy and thirty of his suite. The remainder, more than a hundred in all, perished in the flames. . . . The following day Ban Chao sent for Guang, the king of Shan-shan, and showed him the head of the envoy. The whole kingdom was seized with fear and trembling, which Ban Chao took steps to allay by issuing a public proclamation. Then, taking the king's son as a hostage, he returned to make his report.

> The second is to burn
> Supplies;

Du Mu/Giles/*History of the Sui Dynasty*:   This refers to all kinds of grain and fodder. In order to subdue the rebellious population of southern China, Gao Geng recommended to Emperor Wen of the Sui dynasty (r. A.D. 589–605) to make periodic raids and burn their supplies of grain, a policy that in the long run proved entirely successful.

> The third is to burn
> Equipment;

Du Mu/Giles: An example of this is the destruction of Yuan Shao's wagons and impedimenta by Cao Cao in A.D. 200.

> The fourth is to burn
> Warehouses;

> The fifth is to burn
> Lines of communication.

Translator: The commentators have widely diverging theories as to the meaning of this last target. I follow Niu and Wang (p. 142) and take it to refer to the various means of communication (roads, bridges, boats, mountain passages) that enable an army to keep itself informed and supplied.

> Attack by fire
>   Requires means;
>   The material
>   Must be ready.

Jia Lin: It requires wind and dry weather.

Du Mu: We need dry plant matter, reeds, brushwood, straw, grease, oil, etc.

> There is a season
>   For making a fire;
>   There are days
>   For lighting a flame.

Mei Yaochen: A fire should never be started recklessly.

> The proper season is
>   When the weather is
>   Hot and dry;

Zhang Yu: Because the fire will catch more easily.

Translator: This is one of those (not altogether rare) occasions when the Chinese commentator seems to be stating the obvious.

> The proper days are
>   When the moon is in
>   Sagittarius,
>   Pegasus,
>   Crater,
>   Corvus.
>   These are the

Four Constellations
Of Rising Wind.

Translator: These are Giles's approximations, and Father Amiot more or less agrees (like several other early Jesuits in China, Amiot was a formidable astronomer). In Chinese, these four constellations are called the Basket, the Wall, the Wings, and the Chariot.

When attacking with fire,
    Adapt to
    These Five Changes of Fire:

If fire breaks out
    Within the enemy camp,
    Respond at once
    From without.

Cao Cao: Respond by sending troops.

Li Quan: Respond by exploiting the dynamic potential of the outbreak of fire.

Du You: Use spies to start a fire within the enemy camp, and then attack at once from without.

Du Mu: The prime object of fire is to throw the enemy into confusion and then to attack. Fire is not in itself the means for defeating the enemy. So attack as soon as you hear of the outbreak of fire. Once the fire has died down and order is reestablished, an attack will be futile.

If fire breaks out
    But the enemy remains calm,
    Wait,
    Do not attack.

Du Mu: If the effect of creating confusion is not produced, it means that the enemy is ready for us. A precipitate attack must be avoided. Wait for the ensuing changes.

> Let the fire reach
> Its height,
> And follow up
> If at all possible;
> If not,
> Wait.

Li Quan: If the fire has not thrown the enemy into confusion, do not attack.

Translator: I follow Niu and Wang (pp. 144–45) in taking these last two sections together.

> If fire attack is possible
>   From without,
>   Do not wait
>   For fire to be started
>   Within;
>   Light
>   When the time is right.

Du Mu/Zhang Yu/Giles/*History of the Later Han:* The previous passages refer to fire's being started within. But if the enemy is settled in a waste place littered with quantities of grass, or if he has pitched his camp in a position that can be burned out, we must carry our fire against him at any seasonable opportunity and not wait on in hopes of an outbreak occurring within, for fear our opponents should themselves burn up the surrounding vegetation and thus render our own attempts fruitless. The famous Li Ling [fl. 99 B.C.] once baffled the leader of the Xiongnu barbarians in this way. The latter, taking advantage of a favorable wind, tried to set fire to the Chinese general's camp but found that every scrap of combustible vegetation in the neighborhood had already been burned down. On the other hand, Bocai, a general of the Yellow Turban rebels, was badly defeated in A.D. 184 through his neglect of this simple precaution. At the head of a large army, he was besieging Changshe, which was held by Huangfu Song. The garrison was very small, and a feeling of nervousness pervaded the ranks. So Huangfu Song called his officers together and said, "In War, there are various indirect methods of attack, and numbers do not count for everything [see Master Sun, Chapter 5]. Now, the rebels have pitched their camp in the midst of thick grass, which will easily burn when the wind blows. If we set fire to it at night, they will be thrown into a panic, and we can make a sortie and attack them on all sides at once, thus emulating the achievement of Tian Dan" [see the commentary to Master Sun, Chapter 9]. That same evening, a strong breeze sprang up; so Huangfu Song instructed his soldiers to bind reeds together into torches and mount guard on the city walls, after which he sent out a band of daring men, who stealthily made their way through the lines and started the fire with loud shouts and yells. Simultaneously, a glare of light shot up from the city walls, and Huangfu Song, sounding his drums, led a charge, which threw the rebels into confusion and put them to headlong flight.

> When starting a fire,
>   Be upwind;
>   Never attack
>   From downwind.

> A wind that rises
>   During the day
>   Lasts long;
>   A night wind
>   Soon fails.

> In War,
>   Know these
>   Five Changes of Fire,
>   And be vigilant.

Zhang Yu: It is not enough to know how we should attack the enemy with fire; we must also be on guard against the enemy's fire attacks on us.

Keep a close eye on the positions of the stars, know the days when the wind will rise, and be prepared.

Translator: The ever-helpful Messrs. Niu and Wang recapitulate for us as follows: The ways in which the warrior should be responsive to the Five Changes of Fire are (1) by responding at once when a fire breaks out within the enemy camp; (2) by being cautious when a fire breaks out within but the enemy remains calm; (3) by lighting a fire from without if the time is right; (4) by always starting a fire upwind; (5) by not relying on a night wind.

> Fire
>> Assists an attack
>> Mightily.

> Water
>> Assists an attack
>> Powerfully.

Zhang Yu: Water can divide enemy troops. With the enemy's potential divided, our own potential is stronger.

> Water
>> Can isolate,
>> But it cannot
>> Take away.

Cao Cao: Fire can help to win victory. Water can only isolate and divide, it cannot deprive the enemy of his stores.

Zhang Yu: Water can only isolate an army, cut off its van from its rear, and bring a temporary victory. It cannot destroy the enemy's supplies and utterly annihilate him, as fire can. Han Xin used water to flood Long Ju [see Chapter 9] and thereby achieved a temporary victory; but when Cao Cao destroyed Yuan Shao's baggage train by fire [in A.D. 200], Yuan Shao was not only defeated, he was utterly annihilated.

To win victory,
   To complete an objective,
   But not to follow through
   Is a disastrous
   Waste.

Mei Yaochen: If one wishes to be sure of victory, one must seize the right moment and act, using means such as fire and water. One should never sit tight and hold on to existing gain. This is disastrous.

Translator: Giles comments that this is "one of the most perplexing passages" in *The Art of War*. My own translation is, I am afraid, no more than a rather wordy paraphrase based on Mei Yaochen's commentary (which in this instance differs from the others). With Niu and Wang, I take the passage to be referring to the need to follow through on an attack by fire.

Hence the saying
   "The enlightened ruler
   Considers deeply;
   The effective general
   Follows through."

Zhang Yu: The ruler must consider and ponder strategy; the general must follow through with victory.

Never move
   Except for gain;

Li Quan: The enlightened ruler and the effective general will not send troops into battle unless they can see a definite gain.

Never deploy
   Except for victory;
Never fight
   Except in a crisis.

Cao Cao: Fight only as a last resort.

> A ruler
>> Must never
>> Mobilize his men
>> Out of anger;
> A general
>> Must never
>> Engage battle
>> Out of spite.

Zhang Yu: A war arising out of anger usually leads to defeat.

> Move
>> If there is gain;
> Halt
>> If there is no gain.

Cao Cao/Zhang Yu: Do not embark on war out of personal emotion. Look to the objective gain or loss. As Master Weiliao said, "Do not make war out of anger. If you see victory, fight; if you do not, then hold back."

> Anger
>> Can turn to
>> Pleasure;
> Spite
>> Can turn to
>> Joy.

Zhang Yu: The senses bring pleasure; the mind experiences joy.

> But a nation destroyed
>> Cannot be
>> Put back together again;

A dead man
Cannot be
Brought back to life.

Mei Yaochen: The anger of a moment can turn to pleasure soon enough; the spite of a moment can soon turn to joy. But if you destroy a nation and take the lives of many men, these cannot be brought back so easily.

So the enlightened ruler
    Is prudent;
The effective general
    Is cautious.
This is the Way
    To keep a nation
    At peace,
    And an army
    Intact.

Translator: Niu and Wang go to great lengths to maintain a connection between the last part of this chapter and the title, "Attack by Fire." But it seems to me that, as is often the case, this short "chapter" is not an organic whole. These last few observations, which are surely of a general nature, may have been tacked on here by mistake, by a "copyist working with un-connected bamboo or wooden slips" (Yates, 1985, p. 219). As D. C. Lau warns us (p. 322), with texts such as this we must "guard against forcing a unified sense out of what does not in fact belong together."

Chapter Thirteen

Espionage

Zhang Yu: In order to have a true knowledge of the enemy, spies are indispensable. And the art of spying requires the utmost secrecy.

Translator: As the thirteenth-century Shiite *wazir* Nasir al-Din al-Tusi wrote: "The most effective weapon with which to fight an enemy is knowledge of his projects and intentions. . . . To achieve this, every scrap of information must be collected together concerning the decision-making process . . ."(quoted by Chaliand, p. 444).

Master Sun said:

Raising an army
    Of a hundred thousand men
    And marching them
    Three hundred miles
    Drains the pockets
    Of the common people
    And the public treasury
    To the daily sum of
    A thousand taels of silver.
    It causes commotion
    At home and abroad
    And sets countless men
    Tramping the highways
    Exhausted.

***The Way and Its Power,* Chapter 30:**   Where troops have been quartered, brambles and thorns spring up.

Mei Yaochen: They are exhausted by the need to transport supplies.

> It keeps seven hundred thousand families
> From their work.

Cao Cao: Of old, eight families made up a neighborhood; if one family sent a man to the war, the other seven families had to support them. So when a hundred thousand troops were mobilized, seven hundred thousand families were thereby prevented from tending their crops properly.

Du Mu: In olden times, land was divided into nine parts [as in the Chinese character for a well, *jing,* which resembles exactly the grid for the game of naughts and crosses, or ticktacktoe]. Each of these nine parts was approximately fifteen acres in extent. The central plot was held in common, and here the well was dug and the cottages were built where the eight families who farmed the eight surrounding parcels of land lived.

Mei Yaochen: There will be a shortage of men at the plow.

> Two armies may
>   Confront each other
>   For several years,
>   For a single
>   Decisive battle.

> It is callous
>   To begrudge the expense of
>   A hundred taels
>   Of silver
>   For knowledge
>   Of the enemy's situation.

Wang Xi: This refers to the cost of employing spies.

Translator: Giles's note here succeeds excellently in spelling out Master Sun's thinking: "The argument is certainly ingenious. Master Sun begins by drawing our attention to the frightful misery and vast expenditure of blood and treasure which war always brings in its train. Now, unless you are kept informed of the enemy's condition, and are ready to strike at the right moment, a war may drag on for years. The only way to get this information is to employ spies, and it is impossible to obtain trustworthy spies unless they are properly paid for their services. But it is surely false economy to grudge a comparatively trifling amount for this purpose, when every day that the war lasts eats up an incalculably greater sum. This grievous burden falls on the shoulders of the poor, and hence Master Sun concludes that to neglect the use of spies is nothing less than a crime against humanity."

> Such a miser is
>> No commander of men,
>> No support to his lord,
>> No master of victory.

Translator: Giles's comment, though not of strict relevance or even necessarily true, is challenging and of considerable intrinsic interest: "This idea, that the true object of war is peace, has its root in the national temperament of the Chinese. Even so far back as 597 B.C., these memorable words were uttered by Prince Zhuang of the Chu state: 'The character [i.e., word in the Chinese script] for [military] "prowess" is made up of [the graphic elements] "to stay" and "a spear" (cessation of hostilities). Military prowess is seen in the repression of cruelty, the calling in of weapons, the preservation of the appointment of Heaven, the firm establishment of merit, the bestowal of happiness on the people, putting harmony between the princes, the diffusion of wealth'" (*The Zuo Commentary*, XII, 3).

> Prior information

Li Quan: Through the use of spies.

> Enables wise rulers
> And worthy generals
> To move

And conquer,
Brings them success
Beyond that of the multitude.

This information
Cannot be obtained
From spirits;
It cannot be deduced
By analogy;

Cao Cao: It cannot be obtained by prayer; nor can it be obtained by deductive reasoning.

It cannot be calculated
By measurement.

Li Quan: Properties such as length and distance can be calculated and measured. Not so enemy dispositions.

Translator: The duke of Wellington (1769–1852) remarked, "All the business of war, and indeed all the business of life, is to endeavour to find out what you don't know by what you do; that's what I call 'guessing what was at the other side of the hill'" (*Croker Papers*, 1885).

It can be obtained only
From men,
From those who know
The enemy's dispositions.

Mei Yaochen: Information about spirits can be sought through divination; information about natural phenomena can be acquired through deductive reasoning; knowledge of the principles of the natural universe can be gained through measurement and calculation. But military intelligence can be obtained only through the use of spies.

There are Five Sorts of Spies:

Local,
Internal,
Double,
Dead, and
Live.

When these five sorts of espionage
Are in operation,
No one knows
The Way of it.
It is called
The Mysterious Skein,
The Lord's Treasure.

Du Mu: When spies operate, no one knows how the information is divulged. It is a mystery, a treasure.

Mei Yaochen: It is a mysterious skein of threads, to be prized by the ruler.

Translator: Giles quotes again from what seems to have been one of his favorite books, Baden-Powell's *Aids to Scouting*: "Cromwell, one of the greatest and most practical of all cavalry leaders, had officers styled 'scout masters,' whose business it was to collect all possible information regarding the enemy, through scouts and spies, etc., and much of his success in war was traceable to the previous knowledge of the enemy's moves thus gained."

Local spies
Come from among our enemy's
Fellow countrymen;

Du Mu: Treat the people of the enemy country kindly, and use them as spies.

Internal spies,
   From among our enemy's
   Officials;

Du Mu/Giles: Such officials include worthy men who have been de-graded from office, criminals who have undergone punishment; also, fa-vorite concubines who are greedy for gold, men who are aggrieved at being in subordinate positions or who have been passed over in the distribution of posts, others who are anxious that their side should be defeated in order that they may have a chance of displaying their ability and talents, fickle turncoats who always want to have a foot in each camp. Officials of these several kinds should be secretly approached and bound to one's interests by means of rich presents. In this way you will be able to find out the state of affairs in the enemy's country, ascertain the plans that are being formed against you, and moreover disturb the harmony and create a breach be-tween the sovereign and his ministers.

He Yanxi/Giles: In A.D. 303, Luo Shang, governor of Yizhou, sent his general Wei Bo to attack the rebel Li Xiong of Shu in his stronghold at Pi. After each side had experienced a number of victories and defeats, Li Xiong had recourse to the services of a certain Putai, a native of Wudu. He began by having him whipped until the blood came and then sent him off to Luo Shang, whom he was to delude by offering to cooperate with him from inside the city, agreeing to light a beacon at the right moment for making a general assault. Luo Shang, trusting these [his "internal spy's"] promises, marched out all his best troops, placing Wei Bo and others at their head, with orders to attack at Putai's bidding. Meanwhile, the rebel Li Xiong's general had pre-pared an ambuscade on the line of march. Putai raised long scaling-ladders against the city walls, and now lighted the beacon fire. Wei Bo's men raced up on seeing the signal and began climbing the ladders as fast as they could, while others were drawn up on ropes lowered from above. More than a hun-dred of Luo Shang's soldiers entered the city in this way, every one of whom was forthwith beheaded. Li Xiong then charged with all his forces, both in-side and outside the city, and routed the enemy completely. [This is presum-ably given as an example of "setting up" an internal spy to achieve one's own end, and illustrates, as Giles points out, the need for extreme caution in deal-ing with "internal spies." It seems rather curious that He Yanxi should offer it as his prime example, even though he himself ends with the significant sentence "This is an example of the potential effect of internal spies."]

Double spies,
    From among our enemy's
    Own spies.

Du You/Giles: We use generous bribes and liberal promises to win over
the enemy's spies to our service.

Dead spies
    Are those for whom
    We deliberately create
    False information;
    They then pass it on
    To the enemy.

Translator: The ultimate deception!

Du Mu/Giles: We ostentatiously do things calculated to deceive our
own spies, who must be led to believe that the intelligence has been unwit-
tingly disclosed. Then, when these spies are captured in the enemy's lines,
they will make an entirely false report and the enemy will take measures accordingly, only to find that we do something quite different. The spies will
thereupon be put to death.

Zhang Yu: An example of the "dead spy" was Li Yiqi, who was sent in
203 B.C. by the king of Han to open peaceful negotiations with Qi. The
king of Qi, being subsequently attacked without warning by Han Xin and
infuriated by what he considered the treachery of Li Yiqi, ordered the unfortunate envoy to be boiled alive.

Live spies
    Are those who return
    With information.

Du Mu/Giles: They move to and fro between the enemy camp and ours.
Such "live" spies must be men of keen intellect, though in outward appearance fools; of shabby exterior, but with a will of iron. They must be active,

robust, endowed with physical strength and courage; thoroughly accustomed to all sorts of dirty work, able to endure hunger and cold, and to put up with shame and ignominy.

> In the whole army,
>> None should be closer
>> To the commander
>> Than his spies,
>> None more highly rewarded,
>> None more confidentially treated.

Du Mu: Spies must be treated on a "mouth to ear" basis [i.e., no one else must share in the communication].

Translator: Giles quotes yet again from Turenne, who, as he says, made perhaps larger use of spies than any previous commander: "Spies are attached to those who give them most; he who pays them ill is never served. They should never be known to anybody; nor should they know one another. When they propose anything very material, secure their persons, or have in your possession their wives and children as hostages for their fidelity. Never communicate anything to them but what is absolutely necessary that they should know."

> Without wisdom,
>> It is impossible
>> To employ spies.

Mei Yaochen/Giles: In order to use them, one must know fact from falsehood and be able to discriminate between honesty and double-dealing.

> Without humanity and justice,
>> It is impossible
>> To employ spies.

Translator: Could anyone call the treatment accorded to dead spies either humane or just?

Zhang Yu: Treat them with generosity and trust. When once they have been attracted by generous pay, deal with them honestly, and they will work for you to their utmost.

> Without subtlety and ingenuity,
>> It is impossible
>> To ascertain
>> The truth of their reports.

Mei Yaochen/Giles: Be on your guard against the possibility of spies' going over to the service of the enemy.

> Subtlety of subtleties!
>> Spies have
>> Innumerable uses.

Mei Yaochen: There is nothing they cannot discover.

> If confidential information
>> Is prematurely divulged,
>> Both spy and recipient
>> Must be put to death.

Chen Hao: To punish the spy, and to close the other man's mouth, and thus prevent the enemy from acquiring the information.

> In striking an army,
>> In attacking a city,
>> In killing an individual,
>> It is necessary to know beforehand
>> The names of the general
>> And of his attendants,
>> His aides,
>> His doorkeepers,

His bodyguards.
Our spies must be instructed
To discover all of these
In detail.

Enemy spies,
   Come to spy on us,
   Must be sought out,
   Bribed,
   Won over,
   Well accommodated.
   Then they can be
   Employed as
   Double agents.

From the double agent
   We discover
   Local and internal spies.

Zhang Yu/Giles: We must tempt the double agent into our service, because it is he that knows which of the local inhabitants are greedy of gain and which of the officials are open to corruption.

From the double agent
   We learn how best
   To convey misinformation
   To the enemy.

Zhang Yu/Giles: Because the double agent knows how the enemy can best be deceived.

From the double agent
   We know how and when
   To use
   Live spies.

The ruler
> Must know all five of these
> Sorts of spies;
> This knowledge must come
> From the double agent;
> So the double agent
> Must be
> Treated generously.

Of old,
> The rise of the Yin dynasty
> Was due to Yi Zhi,
> Who had served under the Xia;

Translator: Yi Zhi was a minister under Cheng Tang, First Emperor of the Yin (or Shang) dynasty (ca. 1600–ca. 1076 B.C.), which replaced the Xia dynasty (ca. 2000–ca. 1600 B.C.). He helped to overthrow the infamous last tyrant of Xia, Jie Gui.

> And the rise of the Zhou dynasty
> Was due to Lü Ya,
> Who had served under the Yin.

Translator: Lü Ya (also known as Lü Shang) is the Ancient Duke occasionally referred to by the commentators and supposedly himself author of a famous treatise on war, entitled *The Six Quivers*. He served under the last tyrant of the Yin/Shang dynasty, Zhou Xin, and later helped to overthrow him and found the Zhou dynasty (ca. 1027–221 B.C.). As Giles comments, "We can hardly doubt that Master Sun is holding these two up as illustrious examples of the double agent, or something closely analogous." Mei Yaochen, for one, however, "appears to resent any such aspersion on these historic names."

Only the enlightened ruler,
> The worthy general,
> Can use
> The highest intelligence

For spying,
Thereby achieving
Great success.

Du Mu/Giles: Just as water, which carries a boat from bank to bank, may also be the means of sinking it, so reliance on spies, while productive of great results, is often the cause of utter destruction.

Spies
Are a key element
In warfare.
On them depends
An army's
Every move.

Jia Lin/Giles: An army without spies is like a man without ears or eyes.